THE YEARS WITH ROSS

james thurber

THE YEARS WITH ROSS

With Drawings by the Author

PERENNIAL ⬛ CLASSICS

First Perennial Classics edition published 2001.
Perennial Classics are published by Perennial, an imprint of HarperCollins Publishers.

Library of Congress Cataloging-in-Publication Data
Thurber, James
    The years with Ross / James Thurber.—1st Perennial classics ed.
      p. cm.
    Based on a series of articles published in the Atlantic monthly.
    Originally published: Boston, Little, Brown, [1957].
    ISBN 0-06-095971-1
    1. Ross, Harold Wallace, 1892–1951. 2. Journalists—United States—Biography. 3. New Yorker (New York, N.Y.: 1925). I. Title.
PN4874.R65 T5 2001
070.4'1'092—dc21
[B]   00-045290

15 16 17 18 19 ❖/RRD 16 15 14 13 12

To Frank Sullivan

Master of humor, newspaperman,
good companion, friend to Ross,
this book is dedicated with the
love and admiration I share with
everybody who knows him.

Contents

Contents

Foreword to the Perennial Classics Edition

James Thurber wrote *The Years with Ross* toward the end of his most productive and gifted period, and he managed to make both less and more of his subject than he quite intended. More, because he turned Ross, the creator and first editor of the *New Yorker,* into a legend: the Casey Stengel of American letters, the guy who wanted to know if *Moby-Dick* was the whale or the man and scribbled "Who he?" all over his writer's copy. And this, in turn, made less of Ross—in the eyes of many *New Yorker* veterans, painfully less—because it turned him from the great and far-seeing editor they knew into a kind of Thurber husband who lucked out by hiring Thurber. For those who think that Ross really *was* like Stengel, i.e., a superb manager of talents who skillfully hid his shrewd judgment behind an assumed mask of colorfulness, it is easy to see Thurber's Ross as a caricature, or even a betrayal.

This wasn't Thurber's intention, of course—his love for Ross shines from every page of his book—but if a competitive subtext emerges, it's no surprise. No writer really thinks he couldn't have done it all by himself. All writers pay extravagant compliments to their editors, while secretly thinking how lucky the editor is to have around a writer so magically adaptable and forbearing. In their hearts, writers think of editors as little as society ladies think of maître d's: one tips them heavily and listens wide-eyed to their advice on the menu, but the point is to keep that table. (And, in *their* hearts, all editors think of writers as maître d's do society ladies: spoiled, demanding children—if only, sigh, you could run a restaurant without them.) Thurber's Ross is a wonderful comic figure—too comic, perhaps, for the taste of those who revere him. But Thurber revered him too, and the special virtue of *The Years with Ross* is that he manages to make a completely comic creation into a convincingly heroic one. Thurber's Ross is half-beleaguered American white man, half-wide-eyed gee-whizzer; one part W. C. Fields on his sleeping porch, two parts the hero of *Tom Swift and His Amazing Magazine*; "an aw-shucks farm boy from Colorado trying to land a 1900 biplane in the middle of Fifth Avenue," as Thurber himself put it so memorably.

What might help make this book matter for new readers in a new century (who can be assumed not to care less about how writers got paid under a "drawing system" in 1942) would be to take it away from *New Yorker* lore-making (and the *New Yorker* generally, and wouldn't that be nice) and to concentrate on the thing that truly makes it matter: the story it tells about how writers and editors together, in the years between Pershing and Pearl Harbor, made a new kind of American music. Between what Thurber and his contemporaries were able to put in and what Ross and his contemporaries knew to take out, a style emerged that still strikes a downbeat for most good American writing today. Putting the *New Yorker* aside—and surely it is time we did; let the magazine speak for itself, as it must for as long as it lives—there is something permanent in *The Years with Ross* about how a writer learns to write, what an editor can teach him, and how the tone they shape together can be around for other writers when both of them are gone.

Thurber matters, still and first, because, even in his later, garrulous manner, his is one of the wonderful original voices of American writing. He is the most complicated, emotionally complex, touching, and original of all his generation of *New*

Yorker writers. A. J. Liebling is funnier and larger-souled and infinitely more worldly. E. B. White is a more natural stylist (and the creator of a lot of what's good in Thurber). Joe Mitchell is a more precise and self-conscious artist, with an artist's sense of the mystery in all simple things. But Thurber, though an eclectic writer, is the most volatile, difficult, and, in a good sense, moody of them all—the most emotionally direct and, therefore, the most memorable. The style of understatement he learned from White in particular involved imposing a certain amount of taciturn discretion and fastidiousness on a man who was neither indirect nor modest, and the marriage of the two things—the modest style and the boastful guy, the crazy man and the sane sentences—made him among the most moving and soulful, not to mention one of the funniest, twentieth-century American writers.

He was also probably the best and purest *tonal* writer we've ever had. Thurber is a tonal writer in the simple sense that his is a voice we know rather than a set of jokes we laugh at. Where almost every comic writer before him comes at us in aphorisms or epigrams—or else in the epigram's cousin from Milwaukee, the wisecrack—Thurber just makes sentences. (When he tried phrase-making, it always fell a little flat: "Let us not look before us in fear, or behind us in nostalgia, but around us in awareness," which Ted Sorenson could have written.) Thurber is memorable in paragraphs and pages rather than in lines. He doesn't "turn phrases"; he just turns the corner on to the next sentence. No one worked harder or went further to slim down the space between American speaking and writing voices, between the way we talk and the way we write. (Auden said somewhere that the one writer whom Max Beerbohm must have envied would have been Thurber, because he did with a natural sound what Beerbohm achieved with a lot of hard blowing.)

Though *The Years with Ross* is not Thurber's very best writing, the natural tone is still there, and rereading it recalls how hard it must have been to do every time he did it. Some of the difficulties arise for technical reasons. Though it is hard to write sentences that sound like talk, it is even harder to know how to put them together, since the conjunctions of natural speech are mostly pauses and "ahem's" and interjections. Insert "and's" in their place and pretty soon, if you're not careful, you're stuck with a pseudo-biblical Irish croon, à la late Hemingway, whether you want it or not.

There are tricks to getting around this, and Thurber knew them all. By the time he wrote *The Years with Ross* these tricks had become second nature to him so that his performance is a little like the late Luis Tiant's accumulated guile and instinct after the fastball has gone. There is the use of the right deflating words: "dogged," "jumpy," and "puzzled" make their usual Thurberian appearances. There is the trust that the reader can make the connections between sentences for himself so that all the "hence's" and "thus's" and "therefore's" and "of course's" that afflict an ordinary journalist's prose can drop right out. Look, for instance, at these simple sentences, chosen pretty much at random:

> He let an editor go in the early years because the man brought his wife into Ross's office to meet him. Ross looked up and there she stood, seeming to be closing in on him from all sides. Very few women even among those employed there, could enter the inner sanctum of old Surrounded. Of the privileged females my second wife, Helen, was one.

This gets you just where you're going (from a general idea to a new person), uses a funny image (of the encroaching woman) to get you there, and leaves out three-fourths of the stuff that most of us would have felt compelled to put in—all those apprehensive qualifications (who the editor was, when it happened, who Helen was, and what she's going to do in the story) that usually go hand in hand with memoir writing.

Yet, though the apprehensive qualifications are left out, an apprehensive nervousness is left in. It's funny that Thurber's literary hero was Henry James, who seems *all* apprehensive qualification, until one sees that the effect of nervous energy, of a mind working naturally, can be communicated on the page equally well by elaboration or by omission—either very long and legato or very short and staccato, as in Miles Davis's trumpet playing—just so long as you keep away from strict time.

Flat omission was one device Thurber loved. Another weirdly simple device that Thurber mastered is the unostentatious use of one- and two-syllable words. Take another passage plucked at random:

> Ross didn't like it at all when he found out, bumbling into what we called the Goings On room, that the girls there brewed both tea and coffee every afternoon, and he was appalled when he bumped into a Coca-Cola machine that had been installed when he was away. "If we have a candy counter, I don't want to know where it is," he bawled.

Here Thurber's writing and Ross's speaking voice really are made to run together, while the entire two pages that surround this little passage have exactly six three-syllable words—all obvious and easy ones (morosely, becoming, afternoon, understand, telegram, surrounded) with only one, "morosely," requiring even a microsecond's thought to recall what it means. The style makes space between word and thing so small that you forget you're reading and just think you're hearing, which is what a tonal writer is trying to make you think. It's an extraordinarily, almost ridiculously, simple device; nonetheless, the atmosphere of naturalness it creates is enormously effective—oh, sorry. Let's just say that when it works it works like a charm. (It also goes along with the elimination of semicolons, dashes, or any other punctuation aside from periods and commas. In the *five* pages on either side of the quote above there is one dash, and that's for effect within a quote, and one semicolon, which should actually be a colon.) It sounds easy to do when you say how he does it, but it's as hard as hell to do while still saying things worth getting said. (Though just doing it, if I did it at all right right there, gets the tone going.)

This is one of the things that make Thurber almost parody-proof. There isn't an affected, or a finely turned, or a purplish sentence in the book. This may be why the writers who claim to have been turned on to writing by him, and they include everyone from John Updike to Wilfrid Sheed, never sound like Thurber but always sound like *someone*. To write like Thurber you just write well.

One of the things that make *The Years with Ross* something more than a magazine memoir is the way one senses Thurber's need to put down his own story while also sensing the hard-won decorum which made him understand that writing down your own story was a little second-rate. He found (and partly invented) a figure, Ross, Thurber's Ross, through whom he could be reflected. What we have, then, is essentially an auto-biography with a deferred object at its center, like one of those Renaissance portraits whose ostensible subject is the Nativity but whose obvious preoccupation is the artist's own portrait, over there among the shepherds.

Still, it's Ross who's there in the manger, and the need, or readiness, to find an editor to canonize was hardly Thurber's alone. It spoke to a national need. Only Americans make their editors into saints, or even gods. English editors remain anonymous, occasionally popping up above the battlements to do something unexpected, like translating Proust. (English writers wouldn't take editing, anyway. Dr. Johnson was as much a miscellaneous journalist as Liebling, but you could no more imagine him listening to an editor than talking to a horse: "Sir, your queries are impertinent, unmeaning, and unhelpful.") French editors, though feared, are not quite *revered,* although

French publishers often are. There is no one more powerful than a French editor in power, and no one more kicked around once he's out. (In France, journalism is a direct form of politics, and no equivalent of the general interest magazine exists, despite valiant tries, because there is no general interest. The party line soon overwhelms everything else.)

The twentieth-century American need to have genius-editors is partly the result of the American need to have genius-*everythings*, which also gives us Irving Thalberg, Bill Walsh, and whichever media man helped win the last primary. It's also partly the result of the isolation of American writers, a condition of American writing, which gives them a very tenuous relation to their audience. The editor becomes the audience, and so the dependency relationship grows. Yet the more important reason that the cult of editors began in America back in the twenties is that at the time everybody, from Wolcott Gibbs to Gertrude Stein, really was climbing Mount Plain, trying to ascend to a pure American tone. The editors played the role of the Sherpas, while the writers got to plant the flag. (Truth be told, editors don't really mind this any more than Sherpas seem to, since they both get the incomparable pleasure of the insider's headshake: "You shoulda seen it when it came in / when he started up the mountain.")

Some future literary historian will be baffled by the idea of a distinct *New Yorker* style, but will immediately be able to see a common plain style running right through the American twenties, thirties, and forties. (That Thurber debuted in the magazine, as he reveals in this book, with parodies of Stein and Hemingway tells you something about the common background.) Editors who are, before anything else, taker-outers, lighteners of the overpacked sentence, played an essential role in getting up that mountain.

So in the annals of American mythologizing, the cult of Ross is the mirror image of the cult of Maxwell Perkins, with Ross wearing the comic, rumpled mask and Perkins the pen-

sive, thoughtful one. Perkins, the Scribner's editor who handled Hemingway, Fitzgerald, and Thomas Wolfe, plays the
role of the editor-as-pensive-sage. The key word with Perkins
is "quietly": "Perkins listened to Wolfe, nodding his head, then
quietly removed six pages." (If that sentence doesn't actually
exist in a memoir, it will.) The key word with Ross is "noisily":
"Ross noisily entered the room. Goddam it, Hamburger, he
cried." Yet shared by the soft-spoken man and the loud man
was a gift for getting naturally garrulous, boastful, and self-
involved people (i.e., writers) to make it sing by toning it
down.

You could climb Mount Plain with a map taken from a
high style—Joyce's *Dubliners,* say—or from a low one, and
Ross, crucially, grabbed it low. He got it from the small-town
newspaper, which was in good shape in his and Thurber's day.
A baptism in small-town newspapering was one of the things
they had in common. (Even the first-person plural "we," which
people for some reason persist in seeing as a *New Yorker* eccen-
tricity or innovation, was the weary signature style of every
American small-town editorial writer in the nineteenth century.) It was the old-time newspaperman's values—the love of
hard fact, the "Goddamnit there's a story in this swizzle stick!"
enthusiasm—that Ross brought to reporting, which turned it
into literature. Straight statement, the power of the weird
observation, unadorned observation, the love of facticity for its
own sake—all of these things, applied to ambitious writing,
kept it sane and funny. It is this cataloguing, empirical impulse,
whose origin point is the catalogue of riverboats in *Life on the
Mississippi,* which not only separates Ross's *New Yorker* from
other magazines but also sets Thurber's casual as far apart from
Beerbohm's as Fitzgerald's luxe is from Wilde. In reading
Ross's comment sheets, which Thurber includes in his book,
what's striking is not the scattershot digressions but how hard
Ross works to get Thurber to pay attention to how simply

turning a "dinner party" into a "buffet supper" might turn a gassy and talky casual into something credible.

Yet, though the house style was a subgenus of American Plain (just as Ross was one variety of the larger species, American Genius) there are as many plain styles as fancy ones, and what made Ross's version special was that it was fact-besotted, rather than just fact-based. Most journalists treat facts gingerly, out of fear ("What if I get it wrong?") rather than delight ("Isn't it fun to get it right!"). The facts Ross liked best took the form of flat statements, preferably impersonal, rather than personal observations. (Hemingway, for instance, whose style is in lots of ways very close to Thurber's, didn't write out of facts so much as sense-impressions, *his* facts.)

The style Ross midwifed also wasn't afraid of breezy generalizations—it thrived on them in fact—so long as they were funny, and Ross knew they got funny by being idiosyncratic. Joe Mitchell, for instance, depends a lot on what had already been done by Joyce and Hemingway, but what makes him different is that his particular flat, descriptive statements are usually universals, statements not about a scene but about a permanent situation, what this guy is *always* like. ("Commodore Dutch is a brassy little man who has made a living for the last forty years by giving an annual ball for the benefit of himself.")

In that vein, it is still striking to see how much juice Thurber, in *The Years with Ross,* gets out of impersonal universal statements: not how the weather was but how this guy or that thing typically *is*—the highly particularized generalization, a house specialty. "[Ross was] by far the most painstaking, meticulous, hairsplitting, detail-criticizer the world of editing has known" is every bit as much a Thurber sentence as its near neighbor "Ross sat on the edge of the chair several feet away from the table, leaning forward, the fingers of his left hand spread upon his chest, his right hand holding a white knitting needle which he used for a pointer."

Ross didn't just like highly particularized generalizations.

He *talked* in them. *The Years with Ross* is most alive in Thurber's memories of Ross's own vivid, bizarre universals: "Goddamn it, I hate the idea of going around with female hormones inside me" and "I thought babies were born early in the morning or late at night" and, best of all, refusing to go into the Sainte-Chapelle in Paris because "Stained glass is damned embarrassing." Not only did some of Ross's writing style, as we see it in his letters, get mixed into Thurber's, but some of his speaking voice got in there, too. This maybe helps us see the particular kind of talent that Ross could spot. He could spot a man or woman who could find the right balance of nice detail work and funny overview—who could get it down right *and* sum it up humorously. This is a lot harder to do than it sounds—and a lot harder to find than you'd think.

Which finally brings us back, as we were bound to be, to the Magazine. What's clear in Thurber's book is that for Ross the *New Yorker* was a cause and even a crusade, but never a church. The difference is that a crusade always has a goal, a destination, which lies someplace outside itself, whereas a church has only a dogma and a rite, endlessly repeated. If the *New Yorker* of Ross's, and then of William Shawn's, time had been simply a very clubby church—or, even worse, a very churchy club—it would hardly be worth remembering, much less remain an institution whose values you'd fight to keep. Like the man said, stained glass is damned embarrassing.

If, on the other hand, that tradition offers a set of values about writing and reading that are available for any writer or reader to embrace anywhere he wants to, then it does matter. I think it does offer those values, and Thurber's book helps define them. They were summed up best, perhaps, by Joseph Mitchell, one of the greatest of Ross's boys. A nipper once asked him the first, familiar, fatuous *New Yorker* question: Was there any continuous thread, any common element of style, among all the writers who had made the magazine so distinctive? "Well, tell you the truth, none of 'em could *spell*," he said in his strong, gentle Southern accent. And then he leaned forward and added, almost under his voice, "and really none of us, including Ross, really knew anything about grammar." He breathed again; it was good to get that fact out at last. "But each one of them . . . each one had a kind of wild exactitude of his own."

A wild exactitude! It was, and remains, a thrilling, a permanent, an almost undefaceable phrase. Neither mere exactitude—the dreary procession of facts—nor wildness itself—the kind of language-bending rhetorical overkill that many people mistake for originality—but the two together. Get it exactly right, and go a little crazy. Put it simply, and put it down with all your heart. Make lists of things, and make them come to life by the passion you put into the listing. Write with "and's" instead of "but's" or "therefore's," and let the "and's" imply all the other, fussier conjunctions to the reader's complicit mind.

That wild exactitude defines the tradition that Ross started and that Thurber memorializes here. It belongs to any writer who wants to take it up, and the years with Ross are his past to claim the moment that he does. Naturally, those of us who draw our paychecks at that particular window think it still goes on at the magazine itself, and we knock ourselves out trying to make sure it can. But it doesn't belong to us any more than it ever did. A lot of the best *New Yorker* writers—that is, the most accomplished masters of a natural American tone, from Randall Jarrell to Will Cuppy—never wrote for the *New Yorker,* or not enough. Mitchell's wild exactitude is not a corporate brand, but an ideal. I sometimes think of Thurber's late, lovely fable of the last flower, where the world continues because one man, one woman, and one flower are left after the Apocalypse to continue it. Ross's years, Thurber's tone, will go on, I believe, if there remains only one weird and moving fact, one writer to point at it, and one reader to take heart at its presence.

Adam Gopnik
New York City

These memos were discovered this summer as we sorted through cartons of Thurber files. They are a treasure, not only because of the authors and the content, but also because the Thurber "credo," written before his eyesight failed, gives us a rare example of his early handwriting and signature. We have no record of the drawing that brought about this exchange and with all the rest that does not seem important now. What we do have is a firsthand glimpse of a Thurber/Ross, cartoonist/editor interaction. This new edition of *The Years with Ross* gives us the perfect opportunity to share our find with you. We hope you enjoy it as much as we have.

Rosemary Thurber & family, August, 2000

Credo:

To me it is funnier for two men who have nothing at all in their heads to "have something in common" than for two men who have tomahawks in their heads to have a gag in common. I believe the best humor grows out of the ordinary, the every-day, and the possible, and not out of the tricky, the fantastic, and the impossible;

As long as a great deal of life revolves about a man and a woman in a room, I will draw pictures of men and women in a room.

Thurber

Thurber: (via Lobrano)

    To me there is glaring fallacy in this credo. I had no idea whatever that these men had nothing at all in their heads, therefore mistaking the idea entirely. I assumed it to be two men of identical appearance. (So, I will add, has everyone x else whom I have heard express an opinion about the pictures. Reasoning further, I would say that it is absolutely impossible for an artist to draw a picture of a man with nothing at all in his head--or to draw a picture of a man with genius in his head. It is impossible for an artist to show (except in a most limited way, by conventional characteri**a**tzations) what is in a man's head at all. Moreover, the chance of two men of identical appearance having nothing whatever in their heads is, probably, greater than infinity to one. The chance of two men being identical ~~proximately~~ in appearance, whatever is in their heads, ~~iroximatrx~~ is infinity to one.

    Yours sincerely,

    H. W. Ross.

Foreword

This book began as a series of a few pieces for the *Atlantic Monthly,* but it soon became clear to me that the restless force named Harold Wallace Ross could not be so easily confined and contained. What set out to be a summer task of reminiscence turned out to be an ordeal of love. I say ordeal, not only because of the considerable research that had to be done, over a period of a year and a half, but because the writing of the pieces necessitated my dealing with so many friends and colleagues, whom I had to bother continually. I need not have worried about this, for, without exception, everyone I turned to for opinion and guidance and help seemed to drop everything and come running to my assistance. There are far too many of them to list here, but their names and their contributions to this collection of memories sparkle on almost every page.

From the very beginning of the enterprise, I determined that it should not become a formal schematic biography, of the kind that begins: "There was joy in the home of George and Ida Ross that November day in 1892 when their son Harold was born, and emitted his first cries of discontent and helplessness," and then proceeds, step by step, and year by year, to trace the career of the subject up until the day of his death. This book, perversely perhaps, begins with the death of its subject. The pattern is not one of strict and familiar chronological order, and the unity I have striven for, whether I have achieved it or not, is one of effect. I have taken up various aspects of the life and career of H. W. Ross, and treated each one as an entity in itself. The separate pieces are not progressive chapters, and the reader may pick up Ross at any point, beginning with any of the installments. Each one runs a deliberately planned gamut of time, in which the scheme is one of flashbacks and flashforwards.

The chapter called "The First Years" contradicts the book's title by concerning itself with a brief history of the *New Yorker* before I became a member of its staff. This seemed essential in what is, in a way, a short informal history of Ross's weekly up to the time of his death. I have not tried to assess the literary and artistic merits of the *New Yorker* since then, or to trace the steady, now almost staggering, story of its material success. This was done, with great competence and thoroughness, in an article called "Urbanity, Inc.," written by Howard Rutledge and Peter Bart in the *Wall Street Journal* of June 30, 1958. Five months after that, one November issue of the magazine ran to 248 pages, which would have both pleased and appalled Harold Ross. He would also marvel at the financial behavior of his once frail weekly during the recession of 1958. While all other magazines were losing from eight to twenty-five per cent of paid advertising linage, the *New Yorker* actually gained three per cent. It annually rejects a quarter of a million dollars' worth of ads which it regards as distasteful or not up to *New Yorker* standards.

Several magazines, beginning about 1940, asked me to write about the editor of the *New Yorker,* but I kept turning them down. Then Charles Morton, of the *Atlantic,* began a barrage of letters, one of which reached me in Bermuda in May, 1957, on the very day I gave up writing a play I had been working on for several months. I said I would see what I could do, and the result is here finally between covers.

One of the minor problems that grew into a quandary as I went along was Ross's virtual inability to talk without a continuous flow of profanity. As in the case of many other Americans, it formed the skeleton of his speech, the very foundation of his manner and matter, and to cut it out would leave him unrecognizable to his intimates, or even to those who knew him casually. I intensely believe that Ross was never actually conscious of his profanity, or of the nature of blasphemy itself. He was simply using sounds that made communication possible for him, and without which he would have been almost tongued-tied. Ross's "goddam" referred to a god that had nothing to do with the Deity, and his "Geezus," as I have spelled it, belongs in the same category. For those appalled by even this sort of circumlocution, I have no apology or defense. In Ross's own letters, notes, and opinion sheets, I have not made any changes of spelling or anything else.

I was finishing the last six chapters of this book in London in the summer of 1958 when I got the news of the untimely death of Wolcott Gibbs, one of the most important figures in the career of Harold Ross and in the history of his magazine. I have no words that would adequately express my deep shock and my sense of personal loss. There have been many deaths of *New Yorker* people since I went to work there so many years ago, each of them a sad and grievous blow to the rest of us. I am partly consoled, in the case of Wolcott Gibbs, by the closeness and warmth of our relationship during the writing of this book. Even though he was in the hospital at the time, he took on the considerable task of editing the chapter called "Dishonest Abe and the Grand Marshal" and later of supervising the galley proofs of "The Last Years," since I was in Europe when they came from the printers. A fortnight before he died, he sent me a letter in answer to one of my many queries. It was a letter typical of Wolcott Gibbs at his best—sharp, ironic, funny, and, I am glad to say, cheerful. He had in his hands, before he died, that fine new collection of his best work over the years, *More in Sorrow*. In his Preface he said that he was pleased with the way I had written about his *New Yorker* career in this book. Wolcott was not a man easy to please, and no one's pleasure gratified me more than his, and no one's judgment meant more to me.

Everybody on the *New Yorker,* from William Shawn and Raoul Fleischmann on down, was friendly and helpful to me during the building of this memorial, and I especially want to thank Ebba Jonsson, *New Yorker* librarian, and her staff, Daise Terry and her girls, and Stewart Johnson, head of the Checking Department, and his assistants, for their kindness, patience, and continuous cooperation.

J.T.
West Cornwall
Connecticut

THE YEARS
WITH ROSS

1

A Dime a Dozen

Harold Ross died December 6, 1951, exactly one month after his fifty-ninth birthday. In November of the following year the *New Yorker* entertained the editors of *Punch* and some of its outstanding artists and writers. I was in Bermuda and missed the party, but weeks later met Rowland Emett for lunch at the Algonquin. "I'm sorry you didn't get to meet Ross," I began as we sat down. "Oh, but I did," he said. "He was all over the place. Nobody talked about anybody else."

Ross is still all over the place for many of us, vitally stalking the corridors of our lives, disturbed and disturbing, fretting, stimulating, more evident in death than the living presence of ordinary men. A photograph of him, full face, almost alive with a sense of contained restlessness, hangs on a wall outside his old office. I am sure he had just said to the photographer, "I haven't got time for this." That's what he said, impatiently, to anyone—doctor, lawyer, tax man—who interrupted, even momentarily, the stream of his dedicated energy. Unless a meeting, conference, or consultation touched somehow upon the working of his magazine, he began mentally pacing.

I first met Harold Ross in February, 1927, when his

weekly was just two years old. He was thirty-four and I was thirty-two. The *New Yorker* had printed a few small pieces of mine, and a brief note from Ross had asked me to stop in and see him some day when my job as a reporter for the New York *Evening Post* chanced to take me uptown. Since I was getting only forty dollars a week and wanted to work for the *New Yorker,* I showed up at his office the next day. Our meeting was to become for me the first of a thousand vibrant memories of this exhilarating and exasperating man.

You caught only glimpses of Ross, even if you spent a long evening with him. He was always in mid-flight, or on the edge of his chair, alighting or about to take off. He won't sit still in anybody's mind long enough for a full-length portrait. After six years of thinking about it, I realized that to do justice to Harold Ross I must write about him the way he talked and lived—leaping from peak to peak. What follows here is a monologue montage of that first day and of half a dozen swift and similar sessions. He was standing behind his desk, scowling at a manuscript lying on it, as if it were about to lash out at him. I had caught glimpses of him at the theater and at the Algonquin and, like everybody else, was familiar with the mobile face that constantly changed expression, the carrying voice, the eloquent large-fingered hands that were never in repose, but kept darting this way and that to emphasize his points or running through the thatch of hair that stood straight up until Ina Claire said she would like to take her shoes off and walk through it. That got into the gossip columns and Ross promptly had his barber flatten down the pompadour.

He wanted, first of all, to know how old I was, and when I told him it set him off on a lecture. "Men don't mature in this country, Thurber," he said. "They're children. I was editor of the *Stars and Stripes* when I was twenty-five. Most men in their twenties don't know their way around yet. I think it's the goddam system of women schoolteachers." He went to the window behind his desk and stared disconsolately down into the street, jingling coins in one of his pants pockets. I learned later that he made a point of keeping four or five dollars' worth of change in his pocket because he had once got stuck in a taxi, to his vast irritation, with nothing smaller than a ten-dollar bill. The driver couldn't change it and had to park and go into the store for coins and bills, and Ross didn't have time for that.

I told him that I wanted to write, and he snarled, "Writers are a dime a dozen, Thurber. What I want is an editor. I can't find editors. Nobody grows up. Do you know English?" I said I thought I knew English, and this started him off on a subject with which I was to become intensely familiar. "Everybody thinks he knows English," he said, "but nobody does. I think it's because of the goddam women schoolteachers." He turned away from the window and glared at me as if I were on the witness stand and he were the prosecuting attorney. "I want to make a business office out of this place, like any other business office," he said. "I'm surrounded by women and children. We have no manpower or ingenuity. I never know where anybody is, and I can't find out. Nobody tells me anything. They sit out there at their desks, getting me deeper and deeper into God knows what. Nobody has any self-discipline, nobody gets anything done. Nobody knows how to delegate anything. What I need is a man who can sit at a central desk and make this place operate like a business office, keep track of things, find out where people are. I am, by God, going to keep sex out of this office—sex is an incident. You've got to hold the artists' hands. Artists never go anywhere, they don't know anybody, they're antisocial."

Ross was never conscious of his dramatic gestures, or of his natural gift of theatrical speech. At times he seemed to be on stage, and you half expected the curtain to fall on such an agonized tagline as "God, how I pity me!" Anthony Ross played him in Wolcott Gibbs's comedy *Season in the Sun*, and an old friend of his, Lee Tracy, was Ross in a short-lived play called *Metropole*, written by a former secretary of the editor.

Ross sneaked in to see the Gibbs play one matinee, but he never saw the other one. I doubt if he recognized himself in the Anthony Ross part. I sometimes think he would have disowned a movie of himself, sound track and all.

He once found out that I had done an impersonation of him for a group of his friends at Dorothy Parker's apartment, and he called me into his office. "I hear you were imitating me last night, Thurber," he snarled. "I don't know what the hell there is to imitate—go ahead and show me." All this time his face was undergoing its familiar changes of expression and his fingers were flying. His flexible voice ran from a low register of growl to an upper register of what I can only call Western quacking. It was an instrument that could give special quality to such Rossisms as "Done and done!" and "You have me there!" and "Get it on paper!" and such a memorable tagline as his farewell to John McNulty on that writer's departure for Hollywood: "Well, God bless you, McNulty, goddam it."

Ross was, at first view, oddly disappointing. No one, I think, would have picked him out of a line-up as the editor of the *New Yorker*. Even in a dinner jacket he looked loosely informal, like a carelessly carried umbrella. He was meticulous to the point of obsession about the appearance of his magazine, but he gave no thought to himself. He was usually dressed in a dark suit, with a plain dark tie, as if for protective coloration. In the spring of 1927 he came to work in a black hat so unbecoming that his secretary, Elsie Dick, went out and bought him another one. "What became of my hat?" he demanded later. "I threw it away," said Miss Dick. "It was awful." He wore the new one without argument. Miss Dick, then in her early twenties, was a calm, quiet girl, never ruffled by Ross's moods. She was one of the few persons to whom he ever gave a photograph of himself. On it he wrote, "For Miss Dick, to whom I owe practically everything." She could spell, never sang, whistled, or hummed, knew how to fend off unwanted visitors, and had an intuitive sense of when the coast was clear so that he could go down in the elevator alone and not have to talk to anybody, and these things were practically everything.

In those early years the magazine occupied a floor in the same building as the *Saturday Review of Literature* on West 45th Street. Christopher Morley often rode in the elevator, a tweedy man, smelling of pipe tobacco and books, unmistakably a literary figure. I don't know that Ross ever met him. "I know too many people," he used to say. The editor of the *New Yorker*, wearing no mark of his trade, strove to be inconspicuous and liked to get to his office in the morning, if possible, without being recognized and greeted.

From the beginning Ross cherished his dream of a Central Desk at which an infallible omniscience would sit, a dedicated genius, out of Technology by Mysticism, effortlessly controlling and coördinating editorial personnel, contributors, office boys, cranks and other visitors, manuscripts, proofs, cartoons, captions, covers, fiction, poetry, and facts, and bringing forth each Thursday a magazine at once funny, journalistically sound, and flawless. This dehumanized figure, disguised as a man, was a goal only in the sense that the mechanical rabbit of a whippet track is a quarry. Ross's mind was always filled with dreams of precision and efficiency beyond attainment, but exciting to contemplate.

This conception of a Central Desk and its superhuman engineer was the largest of half a dozen intense preoccupations. You could see it smoldering in his eyes if you encountered him walking to work, oblivious of passers-by, his tongue edging reflectively out of the corner of his mouth, his round-shouldered torso seeming, as Lois Long once put it, to be pushing something invisible ahead of him. He had no Empire Urge, unlike Henry Luce and a dozen other founders of proliferating enterprises. He was a one-magazine, one-project man. (His financial interest in Dave Chasen's Hollywood restaurant was no more central to his ambition than his onetime investment in a paint-spraying machine—I don't know whatever became of that.) He dreamed of perfection, not of power or personal fortune. He was a visionary and a practicalist, imperfect at both, a dreamer and a hard worker, a genius and a plodder, obstinate and reasonable, cosmopolitan and provincial, wide-eyed and world-weary. There is only one word that fits him perfectly, and the word is Ross.

When I agreed to work for the *New Yorker* as a desk man, it was with deep misgivings. I felt that Ross didn't know, and wasn't much interested in finding out, anything about me. He had persuaded himself, without evidence, that I might be just the wonder man he was looking for, a mistake he had made before and was to make again in the case of other newspapermen, including James M. Cain, who was just about as miscast for the job as I was. Ross's wishful thinking was, it seems to me now, tinged with hallucination. In expecting to find, in everybody that turned up, the Ideal Executive, he came to remind me of the Charlie Chaplin of *The Gold Rush,* who, snowbound and starving with another man in a cabin teetering on the edge of a cliff, suddenly beholds his companion turning into an enormous tender spring chicken, wonderfully edible, supplied by Providence. "Done and done, Thurber," said Ross. "I'll give you seventy dollars a week. If you write anything, goddam it, your salary will take care of it." Later that afternoon he phoned my apartment and said, "I've decided to make that ninety dollars a week, Thurber." When my first check came through it was for one hundred dollars. "I couldn't take advantage of a newspaperman," Ross explained.

By the spring of 1928 Ross's young *New Yorker* was safely past financial and other shoals that had menaced its launching, skies were clearing, the glass was rising, and everybody felt secure except the skipper of the ship. From the first day I met him till the last time I saw him, Ross was like a sleepless, apprehensive sea captain pacing the bridge, expecting any minute to run aground, collide with something nameless in a sudden fog, or find his vessel abandoned and adrift, like the *Mary Celeste.*

When, at the age of thirty-two, Ross had got his magazine afloat with the aid of Raoul Fleischmann and a handful of associates, the proudest thing he had behind him was his editorship of the *Stars and Stripes* in Paris from 1917 to 1919.

As the poet is born, Ross was born a newspaperman. "He could not only get it, he could write it," said his friend Herbert Asbury. Ross got it and wrote it for seven different newspapers before he was twenty-five years old, beginning as a reporter for the Salt Lake City *Tribune* when he was only fourteen. One of his assignments there was to interview the madam of a house of prostitution. Always self-conscious and usually uncomfortable in the presence of all but his closest women friends, the young reporter began by saying to the bad woman (he divided the other sex into good and bad), "How many fallen women do you have?"

Later he worked for the Marysville (California) *Appeal,* Sacramento *Union,* Panama *Star and Herald,* New Orleans *Item,* Atlanta *Journal,* and San Francisco *Call.*

The wanderer—some of his early associates called him "Hobo"—reached New York in 1919 and worked for several magazines, including *Judge* and the *American Legion Weekly,* his mind increasingly occupied with plans for a new kind of weekly to be called the *New Yorker.* It was born at last, in travail and trauma, but he always felt uneasy as the R of the F-R Publishing Company, for he had none of the instincts and equipment of the businessman except the capacity for overwork and overworry. In his new position of high responsibility he soon developed the notion, as Marc Connelly has put it, that the world was designed to wear him down. A dozen years ago I found myself almost unconsciously making a Harold Ross out of one King Clode, a rugged pessimist in a fairy tale I was writing. At one point the palace astronomer rushed into the royal presence saying, "A huge pink comet, Sire, just barely missed the earth a little while ago. It made an awful hissing sound, like hot irons stuck in water." "They aim these things at me!" said Clode. "Everything is aimed at me." In this fantasy Clode pursues a fabulously swift white deer which, when brought to bay, turns into a woman, a parable that parallels Ross's headlong quest for the wonder man who invariably turned into a human being with feet of clay, as useless to Ross as any enchanted princess.

Among the agencies in mischievous or malicious conspiracy to wear Ross down were his own business department ("They're not only what's the matter with *me*, they're what's the matter with the country"), the state and federal tax systems, women and children (all the females and males that worked for him), temperament and fallibility in writers and artists, marriages and illnesses—to both of which his staff seemed especially susceptible—printers, engravers, distributors, and the like, who seemed to aim their strikes and ill-timed holidays directly at him, and human nature in general.

Harold Wallace Ross, born in Aspen, Colorado, in 1892, in a year and decade whose cradles were filled with infants destined to darken his days and plague his nights, was in the midst of a project involving the tearing down of walls the week I started to work. When he outlined his schemes of reconstruction, it was often hard to tell where rationale left off and mystique began. (How he would hate those smart-aleck words.) He seemed to believe that certain basic problems of personnel might just possibly be solved by some fortuitous rearrangement of the offices. Time has mercifully foreshortened the months of my ordeal as executive editor, and only the highlights of what he called "practical matters" still remain. There must have been a dozen Through the Looking Glass conferences with him about those damned walls. As an efficiency expert or construction engineer, I was a little boy with an alarm clock and a hammer, and my utter incapacity in such a role would have been apparent in two hours to an unobsessed man. I took to drinking Martinis at lunch to fortify myself for the tortured afternoons of discussion.

"Why don't we put the walls on wheels?" I demanded one day. "We might get somewhere with adjustable walls."

Ross's eyes lighted gloomily, in an expression of combined hope and dismay which no other face I have known could duplicate. "The hell with it," he said. "You could hear everybody talking. You could see everybody's feet."

He and I worked seven days a week, often late into the night, for at least two months, without a day off. I began to lose weight, editing factual copy for sports departments and those dealing with new apartments, women's fashions, and men's wear.

"Gretta Palmer keeps using words like introvert and extrovert," Ross complained one day. "I'm not interested in the housing problems of neurotics. Everybody's neurotic. Life is hard, but I haven't got time for people's personal troubles. You've got to watch Woollcott and Long and Parker—they keep trying to get double meanings into their stuff to embarrass me. Question everything. We damn near printed a newsbreak about a girl falling off the roof. That's feminine hygiene, somebody told me just in time. You probably never heard the expression in Ohio."

"In Ohio," I told him, "we say the mirror cracked from side to side."

"I don't want to hear about it," he said.

He nursed an editorial phobia about what he called the functional: "bathroom and bedroom stuff." Years later he deleted from a Janet Flanner "London Letter" a forthright explanation of the long nonliquid diet imposed upon the royal family and important dignitaries during the coronation of George VI. He was amused by the drawing of a water plug squirting a stream at a small astonished dog, with the caption "News," but he wouldn't print it. "So-and-so can't write a story without a man in it carrying a woman to a bed," he wailed. And again, "I'll never print another O'Hara story I don't understand. I want to know what his people are doing."

He was depressed for weeks after the appearance of a full-page Arno depicting a man and a girl on a road in the moonlight, the man carrying the back seat of an automobile. "Why didn't somebody tell me what it meant?" he asked. Ross had insight, perception, and a unique kind of intuition, but they were matched by a dozen blind spots and strange areas of ignorance, surprising in a virile and observant reporter who had knocked about the world and lived two years in France. There were so many different Rosses, conflicting and contradictory, that the task of drawing him in words sometimes appears impossible, for the composite of all the Rosses should produce a single unmistakable entity: the most remarkable man I have ever known and the greatest editor. "If you get him down on paper," Wolcott Gibbs once warned me, "nobody will believe it."

I made deliberate mistakes and let things slide as the summer wore on, hoping to be demoted to rewriting "Talk of the Town," with time of my own in which to write "casuals." That was Ross's word for fiction and humorous pieces of all kinds. Like "Profile" and "Reporter at Large" and "Notes and Comment," the word "casual" indicated Ross's determination to give the magazine an offhand, chatty, informal quality. Nothing was to be labored or studied, arty, literary, or intellectual. Formal short stories and other "formula stuff" were under the ban. Writers were to be played down; the accent was on content, not personalities. "All writers are writer-conscious," he said a thousand times.

One day he came to me with a letter from a men's furnishing store which complained that it wasn't getting fair treatment in the "As to Men" department. "What are you going to do about that?" he growled. I swept it off my desk onto the floor. "The hell with it," I said. Ross didn't pick it up, just stared at it dolefully. "That's direct action, anyway," he said. "Maybe that's the way to handle grousing. We can't please everybody." Thus he rationalized everything I did, steadfastly refusing to perceive that he was dealing with a writer who intended to write or to be thrown out. "Thurber has honesty," he told Andy White, "admits his mistakes, never passes the buck. Only editor with common sense I've ever had."

I finally told Ross, late in the summer, that I was losing weight, my grip, and possibly my mind, and had to have a rest. He had not realized I had never taken a day off, even Saturday or Sunday. "All right, Thurber," he said, "but I think you're wearing yourself down writing pieces. Take a couple of weeks, anyway. Levick can hold things down while you're gone. I *guess.*"

It was, suitably enough, a dog that brought Ross and me together out of the artificiality and stuffiness of our strained and mistaken relationship. I went to Columbus on vacation and took a Scottie with me, and she disappeared out there. It took me two days to find her, with the help of newspaper ads and the police department. When I got back to the *New Yorker,* two days late, Ross called me into his office about seven o'clock, having avoided me all day. He was in one of his worst God-how-I-pity-me moods, a state of mind often made up of monumentally magnified trivialities. I was later to see this mood develop out of his exasperation with the way Niven Busch walked, or the way Ralph Ingersoll talked, or his feeling that "White is being silent about something and I don't know what it is." It could start because there weren't enough laughs in "Talk of the Town," or because he couldn't reach Arno on

the phone, or because he was suddenly afflicted by the fear that nobody around the place could "find out the facts." (Once a nerve-racked editor yelled at him, "Why don't you get Westinghouse to build you a fact-finding machine?")

This day, however, the Ossa on the Pelion of his molehill miseries was the lost and found Jeannie. Thunder was on his forehead and lightning in his voice. "I understand you've overstayed your vacation to look for a dog," he growled. "Seems to me that was the act of a sis." (His vocabulary held some quaint and unexpected words and phrases out of the past. "They were spooning," he told me irritably about some couple years later, and, "I think she's stuck on him.") The word *sis*, which I had last heard about 1908, the era of *skidoo*, was the straw that shattered my patience. Even at sixty-four my temper is precarious, but at thirty-two it had a hair trigger.

The scene that followed was brief, loud, and incoherent. I told him what to do with his goddam magazine, that I was through, and that he couldn't call me a sis while sitting down, since it was a fighting word. I offered to fight him then and there, told him he had the heart of a cast-iron lawn editor, and suggested that he call in one of his friends to help him. Ross hated scenes, physical violence or the threat of it, temper and the unruly.

"Who would you suggest I call in?" he demanded, the thunder clearing from his brow.

"Alexander Woollcott!" I yelled, and he began laughing.

His was a wonderful, room-filling laugh when it came, and this was my first experience of it. It cooled the air like summer rain. An hour later we were having dinner together at Tony's after a couple of drinks, and that night was the beginning of our knowledge of each other underneath the office make-up, and of a lasting and deepening friendship. "I'm sorry, Thurber," he said. "I'm married to this magazine. It's all I think about. I knew a dog I liked once, a shepherd dog, when I was a boy. I don't like dogs as much, though, and I'll, by God, never run a department about dogs—or about baseball, or about lawyers." His eyes grew sad; then he gritted his teeth, always a sign that he was about to express some deep antipathy, or grievance, or regret. "I'm running a column about women's fashions," he moaned, "and I never thought I'd come to that." I told him the "On and Off the Avenue" department was sound, a word he always liked to hear, but used sparingly. It cheered him up.

It wasn't long after that fateful night that Ross banged into my office one afternoon. He paced around for a full minute without saying anything, jingling the coins in his pocket. "You've been writing," he said finally. "I don't know how in hell you found time to write. I admit I didn't want you to. I could hit a dozen writers from here with this ash tray. They're undependable, no system, no self-discipline. Dorothy Parker says you're a writer, and so does Baird Leonard." His voice rose to its level of high decision. "All right then, if you're a writer, write! Maybe you've got something to say." He gave one of his famous prolonged sighs, an agonized protesting acceptance of a fact he had been fighting.

From then on I was a completely different man from the one he had futilely struggled to make me. No longer did he tell White that I had common sense. I was a writer now, not a hand-holder of artists, but a man who needed guidance. Years later he wrote my wife a letter to which he appended this postscript: "Your husband's opinion on a practical matter of this sort would have no value." We never again discussed tearing down walls, the Central Desk, the problems of advertisers, or anything else in the realm of the practical. If a manuscript was lost, "Thurber lost it." Once he accused me of losing a typescript that later turned up in an old briefcase of his own. This little fact made no difference. "If it hadn't been there," he said, "Thurber would have lost it." As I become more and more "productive," another of his fondest words, he became more

and more convinced of my helplessness. "Thurber hasn't the vaguest idea what goes on around here," he would say.

I became one of the trio about whom he fretted and fussed continually—the others were Andy White and Wolcott Gibbs. His admiration of good executive editors, except in the case of William Shawn, never carried with it the deep affection he had for productive writers. His warmth was genuine, but always carefully covered over by gruffness or snarl or a semblance of deep disapproval. Once, and only once, he took White and Gibbs and me to lunch at the Algonquin, with all the fret and fuss of a mother hen trying to get her chicks across a main thoroughfare. Later, back at the office, I heard him saying to someone on the phone, "I just came from lunch with three writers who couldn't have got back to the office alone."

Our illnesses, or moods, or periods of unproductivity were a constant source of worry to him. He visited me several times when I was in a hospital undergoing a series of eye operations in 1940 and 1941. On one of these visits, just before he left, he came over to the bed and snarled, "Goddam it, Thurber, I worry about you and England." England was at that time going through the German blitz. As my blindness increased, so did his concern. One noon he stopped at a table in the Algonquin lobby, where I was having a single cocktail with some friends before lunch. That afternoon he told White or Gibbs, "Thurber's over at the Algonquin lacing 'em in. He's the only *drinking* blind man I know."

He wouldn't go to the theater the night *The Male Animal* opened in January, 1940, but he wouldn't go to bed, either, until he had read the reviews, which fortunately were favorable. Then he began telephoning around town until, at a quarter of two in the morning, he reached me at Bleeck's. I went to the phone. The editor of the *New Yorker* began every phone conversation by announcing "Ross," a monosyllable into which he was able to pack the sound and sign of all his worries and anxieties. His loud voice seemed to fill the receiver to overflowing. "Well, God bless you, Thurber," he said warmly, and then came the old familiar snarl: "Now, goddam it, maybe you can get something written for the magazine," and he hung up, but I can still hear him, over the years, loud and snarling, fond and comforting.

2

The First Years

I had never heard of the New Yorker *when I sailed from New York* on the *Leviathan* in May, 1925, for a year in France. My unawareness of Harold Ross's "little magazine" (as Sam Goldwyn has always called it, in spite of its increasing wealth and matronly girth) was not surprising. Only a dozen meager issues had then reached the stands, all of them nervous and peaked, and most of them pretty bad. ("There's that goddam 'pretty' again," Ross would say. The easy overuse of "pretty" and "little" exacerbated his uneasy mind. Once, to bedevil him, I used them both in a single sentence of a Talk piece: "The building is pretty ugly and a little big for its surroundings." After stumbling upon these deliberate oxymora, Ross poked his head into my office, made a pretty ugly sound with his tongue and lips, and withdrew. We had been discussing the goddam pretty-little problem earlier that same day.)

The *New Yorker* was the outstanding flop of 1925, a year of memorable successes in literature, music, and entertainment, and the only flop that kept on going. Its continued existence may accurately be called life after death. The *Leviathan* was still at sea on that eastward voyage of thirty-four years ago when the weekly was officially declared dead at an executive luncheon in New York, presided over by its chief backer, Raoul Fleischmann. Then miracle, in the form of chance encounter, resurrected the deceased. Several hours after the coroner's verdict, Ross ran into Fleischmann at the wedding of Franklin Pierce Adams, and, in that atmosphere of hope, beginning, and champagne, they decided to have another go at it. It was hard for the F and the R of the F-R Publishing Company to believe that their cherished infant could die in such a season of viability.

In 1925, the greatest of war plays, *What Price Glory?,* was still running at the Plymouth, and two young men named Rodgers and Hart wrote the music and lyrics for the unforgettable *Garrick Gaieties,* whose big song hit, "Manhattan," still gaily rides the national airwaves. It was the year of *The Great Gatsby* and of *Arrowsmith* and *An American Tragedy.* In 1925, the new Madison Square Garden was opened, and presented its popular monstrosities to an eager public: the six-day bike race, the marathon dance, an indoor flagpole sitter, and strange men and women who took part in rocking-chair and gum-chewing contests, indefatigably entertaining the insatiable addicts of endlessness. *The Poor Nut,* starring its co-author Elliott Nugent, was a hit at the Henry Miller. Elliott came down to the ship to see me off. He was then making, we figured the other day, approximately a hundred times as much money as the twelve dollars a week I was going to get on the Paris edition of the Chicago *Tribune.*

Meanwhile, the *New Yorker* kept going downhill. From an original runoff of fifteen thousand copies in February, its circulation fell to a pernicious-anemia low of twenty-seven hundred copies in August. One evening, during that summer of Harold Ross's greatest discontent, the harried editor ran into Dorothy Parker somewhere. "I thought you were coming into the office to write a piece last week," he said. "What happened?" Mrs. Parker turned upon him the eloquent magic of her dark and lovely eyes. "Somebody was using the pencil," she explained sorrowfully. It gave a fair enough picture of the goings on in West 45th Street, where a small inexperienced staff strained to bring out a magazine every Thursday.

This is a memoir of my years with Ross, and so I shall take up, as tenderly and as briefly as may be, the troubles that beset the founder of the *New Yorker* before I became a party to his predicament and a witness of his woe. Ross could never have seriously believed his constantly reiterated "Writers are a dime a dozen." A great many writers were in Hollywood during his early struggles, others were in Paris—among them two future *New Yorker* authors, Robert Coates and Joel Sayre (Sid Perelman joined them in 1926)—and most of those he knew personally in New York were a million dollars a dozen and more amused by the *New Yorker*'s flounderings than by its contents.

There is little doubt that Ross's famous and busy writer friends of the Algonquin Round Table and its fringes took his fond enterprise lightly, as a kind of joke on him and Fleischmann. A few of them helped now and then, with left hand, and tongue in cheek. "The part-time help of wits is no better than the full-time help of half-wits," a great wit named Herman Mankiewicz is reported to have said at the time. When I reminded Ross of this line years later, all he said was, "God knows I had both kinds."

He couldn't pay anybody much money, in an era when magazine word rates were extremely high. (Nunnally Johnson got ten times as much for his humorous stories in the *Saturday Evening Post* as Ross could have paid him.) When Elwyn Brooks White came to work for the *New Yorker,* part-time, in 1926, he got thirty dollars a week, with an additional five dollars for each of his first-page comments, which were soon to become one of the *New Yorker*'s best-known contributions to American letters.

The record of contributions by the men and women Ross must have expected to help him, out of the goodness of their

hearts, during the first year is disheartening to look back upon. In 1925, Dorothy Parker turned in only one piece and two poems, and her celebrated book reviews, signed "Constant Reader," did not begin until October, 1927.

Robert Benchley waited ten months to lend a hand, and his first casual was printed in December, 1925. He didn't take over the *New Yorker*'s theater criticism until 1929, the same year that Ross's close friend Alexander Woollcott started his page called "Shouts and Murmurs." Ross's good friend Ring Lardner sent in one piece in 1925 and was not heard from again for two years. Marc Connelly and Arthur Kober got around to writing for Ross in 1926, and George Kaufman's name was first signed to a *New Yorker* casual as late as 1935.

It wasn't until 1930 that the names of Perelman and Ogden Nash showed up in the magazine's pages; Sally Benson's first story had been printed the year before. Clarence Day's reminiscences of a New York life were published in 1933. "If I had never printed anything but Clarence Day's stuff, it would have been enough," Ross once told Frank Sullivan, who, incidentally, wrote only three pieces for Ross in 1925; it would be ten years before his Cliché Expert first took the witness stand.

The *New Yorker* was a year old before Gluyas Williams began drawing for it. Peter Arno, who had sold Ross a spot in June, 1925, was first represented by a captioned drawing in September of that year of ordeal. Helen Hokinson's first captioned drawing brightened the *New Yorker* in November, 1925. It showed a saleslady at a perfume counter holding up a small phial to a woman customer and saying, "It's *N'Aimez Que Moi,* madam—don't love nobody but me." The woman customer, glory be, was the original garden club dowager whose hilarious ilk became before long one of the ornaments of *New Yorker* humor. This first Hokinson was, it seems to some of us now, the funniest thing that Ross's tremulous magazine printed in the year of our Lord 1925. The little magazine that died and came to life in the same day had the invaluable help and guidance of Rea Irvin from the start. He was responsible for its format, its special type that bears his name, and the famous figure that adorned its first issue and every succeeding anniversary number, that of the nineteenth-century dandy inspecting a butterfly through his haughty monocle.

Nothing is so dated as an old prospectus, unless it be a faded love letter to a lady who many years later divorced its author, so I shall spare you the *New Yorker*'s prospectus, drawn up in the chill winter of 1924, except for a couple of sentences that are pertinent here: "There will be a personal mention column—a jotting down in the small-town newspaper style of the comings, goings and doings in the village of New York. This will contain some josh and some news value."

The word "josh," smelling remarkably of Ross's old-fashioned vocabulary, and the phrase "the small-town newspaper style" were unhappily lifted out of context and magnified into motto by Ross and his helpers. They got the young magazine off on the wrong foot, wearing the wrong shoe. Its early issues went in for a frivolous and curiously small-town kind of joke, an almost subcollegiate flippancy, and a self-conscious, intramural urbanality, all of which show up bleakly now in an old *New Yorker* folder labeled "Office Gazette," kept in a secret vault in the present offices and accessible only to those of us who are going on a hundred.

The contents of the Office Gazette consist of fragile and yellowing notes, suggestions, letters, and interoffice memos, stained with sweat and blood, mainly Ross's. Herein we encounter a great deal of tittering about the Optimist Joke, a two-line joke that was accidentally printed like this:

> "A man who thinks he can make it in par."
> "What is an optimist, Pop?"

This sentimental souvenir of the old days was reprinted in every anniversary issue of the *New Yorker* for twenty-five years before it was abandoned. Even right side up it shows what was the matter—a kind of youthful lack of loving care. One poem was accidentally printed in two different issues in 1925; a building located by the *New Yorker* at Sixth Avenue and 55th Street was actually at Sixth Avenue and 54th Street; the name of George Eliot was spelled with two *l*'s, and Carolyn Wells was called Caroline, two mistakes that were pointed out by that old precisionist, F.P.A., whose hawk eye was ever alert for inaccuracies. When a verse of Philip G. Wylie's, signed with his initials, was reprinted in the New York Sunday *World,* it was credited to Pelham Grenville Wodehouse, and the Gazette had much rueful fun with this.

Among the notes in the old folder is one beginning "At a mass meeting of the two contributors to this magazine" and another reads "The magazine for people who cannot read." The intramural joshing turns up everywhere in the crumbling documents. Someone suggested a drawing showing "Harold Ross calling at the Martha Washington Hotel on his aunt from Dubuque." There is a lot of high school levity about the idea of using the face of Ben Turpin in burlesque reproductions of famous paintings, or to replace the countenance of Jimmy Walker, Calvin Coolidge, and others, in a series of cartoons.

The Gazette reveals that *New Yorker* readers were instructed, in one issue, how to pronounce Rea Irvin's fist name and Helen Hokinson's last name.

One 1927 item is worth reprinting in full, since it deals with two *New Yorker* immortals who soon rose above all the joshing:

> Lois Long, who writes under the name "Lipstick," was married to Peter Arno, creator of the Whoops sisters, last Friday. The bride wore some things the department stores had given her from time to time, and Mr. Arno wore whatever remained after his having given all his dirty clothes to a man who posed as a laundry driver last week. The romance had its beginning in The New Yorker office, and was greatly advanced by a summer spent abroad, the contrast between the two places being noticeable. Immediately after the wedding the couple left for 25 West 45th Street, where they will spend their honeymoon trying to earn enough money to pay for Mr. Arno's little automobile.

My own favorite item in the ancient collection is a suggestion from a reader, which goes like this:

> March 20, 1927
>
> The New Yorker
>
> I have an idea for a cartoon. The cartoon is entitled, "Pouring over his Books." This is a pun. Have a student sit by a desk with a stack of books before him and reading out of one book. In the meantime have him pour some gin in a glass and is ready to drink it. All about him on the floor have bottles thrown about.
>
> The humor in this cartoon is in the words "pour" and "poir" one means to drink and the other means to study careful.

In the margin of this wondrous note, Ross had written "Too subtle."

Ross's sweating and straining to keep his faltering magazine above the level of Dubuque and in the sophisticated tonality of cosmopolitan New York both puzzled and annoyed some readers. One of them, objecting to a facetious piece about the Barnard Cloisters, wrote testily, "Flippancy in an elephant might be amusing, but flippancy in a flea doesn't even amuse its canine host." Ross's agitated reply to this began, "We are young." And young they were. Every effort to sound metropolitan in viewpoint and background brought the breath of Aspen, Colorado, to the journal's perspiring pages.

Ross was apparently intensely devoted to a continuing department called "Are You a New Yorker?", a series of questions such as "Where is the morgue?" and "On what days is admission charged to the Bronx Zoo?" Clipped to this particular questionnaire was a tart note from a male subscriber which read, simply, "Who gives a damn?"

But it was in this turgid area of odds and ends and beginnings that I found a refreshing letter to Ross from Elmer Davis, dated May 19, 1926. After a decade on the New York *Times,* Mr. Davis had resigned in 1924 to free lance and to write books. He sold the *New Yorker,* in its first three years, some twenty-five pieces, and in this letter he enclosed a contribution for "Are You a New Yorker?" In it there were ten questions, of which the ninth went like this: "Who was Josh DeVore? Bridgie Webber? James A. O'Gorman? Pat Kyne? Hugh McAtamney? Anna Aumuller? Lieutenant Percy Richards?" Mr. Davis's tenth question made my heart leap up. It said, simply, "Where Are They Now?" That was to be the standing title, ten years later, of a series of twenty-five pieces I wrote for the magazine under the name Jared L. Manley. For a whole decade Ross had fretted and fussed about this project, excited by the idea but dissatisfied with the title, as he was usually dissatisfied with everything, sometimes for weeks, sometimes for years. In the end, of course, he came back, as he often did, to the original suggestion, but I doubt that Elmer Davis was remembered as the originator of the idea for

"Where Are They Now?" or that Ross's debt to him was ever acknowledged. The editor was always conscientious about giving credit where credit was due, but his head continually buzzed with a thousand different ideas, and in the flutter the Davis letter must have been forgotten.

The carelessness and confusion of the first two years, echoed and reflected in the Office Gazette, are undoubtedly responsible for Ross's later intense dedication to precision, order, and system. He studied the New York Telephone Company's system of verifying names and numbers in its directories, and used to say that, despite the company's careful checking, it had never got out a phone book with fewer than three mistakes. He found out about the *Saturday Evening Post*'s checking department, which he said consisted of seven women who checked in turn every fact, name, and date. He must have set up a dozen different systems, during my years with him, for keeping track of manuscripts and verifying facts. If the slightest thing went wrong, he would bawl, "The system's fallen down!"

He lived always in the wistful hope of getting out a magazine each week without a single mistake. His checking department became famous, in the trade, for a precision that sometimes leaned over backward. A checker once said to me, "If you mention the Empire State Building in a Talk piece, Ross isn't satisfied it's still there until we call up and verify it." When Robert Coates, in a book review, said that Faulkner sometimes seemed to write about the woodland of Weir instead of the American South, checkers ransacked postal guides, maps, and other sources looking for the Weir that existed only in the imagination of Edgar Allan Poe. When, in a piece I sent in from the French Riviera in 1938, I mentioned the Hotel Ruhl, the checkers found out that it was actually the Hotel Ruhl et des Anglais, and changed it to that in my copy. I wrote Ross a sharp note saying, "Where shall we meet for five o'clock tea—at the Waldorf-Astoria or the Ritz-Carlton?"

But overchecking was better than underchecking, in his opinion, even if it did sometimes lead to the gaucherie of inflexibility. Ross's checkers once informed Mencken that he couldn't have eaten dinner at a certain European restaurant he had mentioned in one of his *New Yorker* articles, because there wasn't any restaurant at the address he had given. Mencken brought home a menu with him to prove that he was right, but he was pleased rather than annoyed. "Ross has the most astute goons of any editor in the country," he said.

While Ross was sweating blood and baying the moon during that awful summer of 1925, I was in a farmhouse in Normandy trying to write a novel. It didn't work out because I got tired of the characters at the end of five thousand words, and bade them and novel-writing farewell forever. In September I got my job as a rewrite man on the Paris *Tribune*.

"I got thirty men ahead of you who want jobs," the city editor said when I went to see him. "What are you, by the way, a poet, or a painter, or a novelist?"

I told him I was a newspaperman with five years' experience, and I knew how to get it and write it and put a headline on it, and he hired me on the spot. That first month I wrote about the crash of the dirigible *Shenandoah* in Ohio, and in October the editor handed me six words of cable from America and said, "Write a column about that." The six words were "Christy Mathewson died today at Saranac," and I wrote a column about it.

It wasn't until the following month, November, 1925, that I first heard of the existence of a magazine called the *New Yorker*. I was sitting on the *terrasse* of the Café Dôme, reading our rival paper, the Paris *Herald* (which had wanted no part of my services), when I came upon a first-page story about a flutter in the dovecotes of Park Avenue. The story said that Ellin Mackay, daughter of the millionaire head of Postal Telegraph, and later Mrs. Irving Berlin (he dedicated two songs to her that year, *Always* and *Remember*) had written an "exposé" of

Park Avenue society for a weekly magazine called the *New Yorker*. Miss Mackay's short article, called "Why We Go to Cabarets" and subtitled "A Post-Debutante Explains," seems as quaint and dated now as its title, but it got the *New Yorker* on the front pages of New York newspapers and gave it its first big shot in the arm circulationwise, as they say in American business circles. Miss Mackay slapped with her fan the wrists of all the sad young men in the Park Avenue staglines, whose dullness drove American society girls with stars in their eyes to cabarets, where they danced to jazz music on the same floor with "drummers" and other interesting barbarians from the hinterland.

After thirty-four years, the dusty pages of Miss Mackay's once vital prose seem less a souvenir of the Jazz Age than a dying echo of the days of silent movies and the era of Rudolph Valentino. That great matinee idol, incidentally, was to collapse outside a New York cabaret in 1926 with an agony in his stomach that turned out to be a fatal perforating ulcer. When he fell, his opera hat rolled into the street, and was rescued by one of those who rushed to his aid, none other than Harold Ross, the young editor of the *New Yorker*. Several months before Valentino's collapse in New York, I had interviewed him at the Hotel Ruhl (et des Anglais) in Nice, where I had gone from Paris in the winter of 1925 to be assistant editor of the *Tribune*'s Riviera edition. I remember that Valentino proudly showed me the hundred pairs of shoes he always took with him on his travels, or it may even have been two hundred. Ross kept his opera hat, intending to return it to him when he left the hospital, which he never did alive. The hat was accidentally thrown out when Ross and his first wife moved from their house on West 47th Street in 1928. "I thought it was an old hat of Aleck's," Jane Grant, Ross's first wife, told me. Alexander Woollcott had shared the coöperative house in the West Forties.

The loss of Rudolph Valentino's opera hat might well

stand as a kind of symbol of the ending of the *New Yorker*'s infancy and the beginning of its maturity. In 1928 Oliver Wolcott Gibbs joined the staff of the magazine, and in one issue of that year a short first piece, called "Alumnae Bulletin," appeared away back on page 101. It was written by a young man named John O'Hara, who was then twenty-three years old and whose short stories were to help set up a lasting literary barrier between the town of Dubuque and the city of New York.

I got back to New York in early June, 1926, with ten dollars, borrowed enough to hold on to until July in a rented room on West 13th Street, and began sending short pieces to the *New Yorker*, eating in doughnut shops, occasionally pilfering canapés at cocktail parties (anchovies, in case you don't know, are not good for breakfast). My pieces came back so fast I began to believe the *New Yorker* must have a rejection machine. It did have one, too. His name was John Chapin Mosher, a witty writer, a charming man, and one of the most entertaining companions I have ever met, but an editor whose prejudices were a mile high and who had only a few enthusiasms. It was in the always slightly lunatic tradition of the *New Yorker* that he had been made first reader of the manuscripts of unknown writers. In the years that followed, we became friends, but I never had lunch with him that he didn't say, over his coffee, "I must get back to the office and reject."

In 1943 he rejected a story by Astrid Peters (then known

as Astrid Meighan), called "Shoe the Horse and Shoe the Mare," which its author later read aloud to me one day. I sent it to Ross with a note saying it should have been bought, and he bought it. It was one of the stories included in *The Best American Short Stories 1944*. Mosher's only comment on it had been a characteristic: "A tedious bit about an adolescent female." I sometimes wonder what Mosher would say, if he were alive now, about the *New Yorker*'s flux of stories by women writers dealing with the infancy, childhood, and young womanhood of females. "We are in a velvet rut," Ross once said many years ago, and this was amended not long ago by a sardonic male writer to read, "We are now in a tulle and taffeta rut."

I first called at the *New Yorker* office late in June, 1926, to find out what had happened to the only piece of mine that had not been returned like a serve in tennis. It was about a man named Alfred Goullet, the greatest of all six-day bike riders, with whom I had shared a stateroom on a liner returning from France in 1920. (I had been a code clerk in the American Embassy for two years.) Mosher came out into the reception room, looking like a professor of English literature who has not approved of the writing of anybody since Sir Thomas Browne. He returned my manuscript saying that it had got under something, and apologizing for the tardy rejection. "You see," he said, "I regard Madison Square Garden as one of the blots on our culture."

I didn't ask to meet Ross that day, but I did inquire if Mr. White was in. On the *Leviathan* going to France, I had met a married sister of White's with the lilting name of Lillian Illian. She had often talked about her talented brother, whose name I remembered as Elton Brooks White. His real first name, of course, is Elwyn, but he had been lucky enough to go to Cornell, where every male student named White is nicknamed Andy, after Andrew White, the university's first president. White wasn't in that day, and so nearly eight months went by before I met him and Ross. I must have seen him, however, without recognizing him, for he also lived on West 13th Street then, sharing an apartment with three other Cornell graduates. One of them, Gustave Stubbs Lobrano, later became an editor of the *New Yorker*.

By July first my money had run out again, but I didn't take the reporting job on the *Evening Post* that had been offered me by its city editor, whom I had met in Paris while he was on vacation. I had an idea for a parody of current best sellers, to be called "Why We Behave Like Microbe Hunters," and to finish it I threw myself upon the hospitality of Clare Victor Dwiggins, called Dwig, a well-known comic-strip artist, who was spending the summer at Green Lake, New York, with his family. (I had met him in Nice.) The wonderful Dwigginses took me in, and I finished the twenty-five thousand words of the book by the end of August. In September I peddled it about New York. It was rejected suavely by Harper's, and without a word by Farrar and Rinehart, unless you can count the "Here" of the secretary who handed me the manuscript when I called at the office. Herschel Brickell, rest his soul, almost persuaded Henry Holt to take the parody, but was overruled by the sales department: "We can't publish a first book of humor by an unknown writer." I sent the six chapters of the book piecemeal to the *New Yorker* and got them all back. Then I went to work on the *Evening Post,* but still kept trying to sell something to Ross's magazine.

In December I had about given up, and was thinking of going back to Columbus, when I sent one of my many rejections to F.P.A. on the *World*. It was the story of Hero and Leander done in newspaper headlines, and Mr. Adams printed it. It filled up one whole column of "The Conning Tower." I think it was ten years later that I told the conductor of "The Conning Tower" that I had written the thing. He had no way of knowing because I had signed it, for reasons too obscure to remember, Jamie Machree.

I now lived in a basement apartment on Horatio Street, near the Ninth Avenue El, with my first wife, who has somehow got lost in the shuffle of these reminiscences. She was convinced I spent too much time on my *New Yorker* efforts, and so one night I grimly set the alarm clock to ring in forty-five minutes and began writing a piece about a little man going round and round and round in a revolving door, attracting crowds and the police, setting a world's record for this endurance event, winning fame and fortune. This burlesque of Channel swimming and the like ran to fewer than a thousand words, and was instantly bought by the *New Yorker*. For the first time out of twenty tries I got a check instead of a rejection slip.

With the money we bought a Scottie, the same Jeannie that was later to be lost in Columbus and to cause the dog fight between Ross and me. The proof that no permanent scars resulted from that brief snarling and fateful encounter lies in an old incident I like to remember. In 1929 my wife began raising Scotties and poodles in Silvermine, and one day Ross asked me if he could buy one of her Scottie pups. "I don't want it myself, for God's sake," he explained hastily, "but Helen Hokinson said the other day that she would like to have a Scottie, and I thought I'd give her one for Christmas." Ross did countless thoughtful and generous things for the men and women he loved, often going far out of his way and spending a great deal of time hunting for gifts, arranging introductions, smoothing paths, and lightening personal burdens.

One of Jeannie's male offspring, three months old, was selected by my wife and, with a wide red ribbon around its neck and a card attached, was delivered by messenger to Miss Hokinson on Christmas Day. She loved the dog but said she couldn't possibly keep it in town, where she was then living, and returned it sadly to my wife. It had cost Ross seventy-five dollars, and my wife made out a check for this amount. He flatly refused to take it and promptly sent it back. Thus the strange story of Ross and Jeannie and me came, in its curious and somehow satisfying way, full circle.

It was easy for me to sell things to the *New Yorker* after the first one was taken, although, in rereading some of the earliest ones, I marvel that Ross put his approving R on "Villanelle of Horatio Street, Manhattan" and a short parody called "More Authors Cover the Snyder Trial." In this last I tried to imitate the style of James Joyce and that of Gertrude Stein, and Ross could never have read a single line of either author. The Stein part went like this:

> This is a trial. This is quite a trial. I am on trial. They are on trial. Who is on trial?
> I can tell you how it is. I can tell you have told you will tell you how it is.
> There is a man. There is a woman. There is not a man. There would have been a man. There was a man. There were two men. There is one man. There is a woman where is a woman is a man.
> He says he did. He says he did not. She says she did. She says she did not. She says he did. He says she did. She says they did. He says they did. He says they did not. She says they did not. I'll say they did.

In gritting his teeth, swallowing hard, and buying that, Ross must have depended upon the counsel of his literary editor, Mrs. Katharine Angell, graduate of Bryn Mawr, wife of a lawyer, and the author of articles and reviews for the *New Republic,* the *Atlantic, Harper's,* and other magazines before she was hired in 1925 as assistant to Fillmore Hyde, the magazine's first literary editor. Mrs. Angell, who hired Andy White in 1926 and was later married to him, was one of the pillars upon which Ross could lean in his hours of uncertainty about his own limitations. "She knows the Bible, and literature, and foreign languages," he told me the day I first met him, "and she has taste."

That day in February, 1927, when I first saw Ross plain and talked to him, I had been brought to his office by White. Andy had called me on the phone one day to say that his sister had mentioned meeting me on the *Leviathan* and that he was, like myself, a friend of Russell Lord, a man who had gone to both Ohio State and Cornell, later wrote *The Wallaces of Iowa,* and somewhere in between, like practically everybody else, took his turn as managing editor of the *New Yorker.* I didn't meet White until five minutes before he took me in to see Ross, but Ross always believed that White and I had been friends for years.

When he got an idea fixed in his head, it usually stayed fixed, and time and truth could not dislodge it. He had decided thirty years ago that Wolcott Gibbs was Alice Duer Miller's nephew, and the fact that Gibbs was actually her cousin never registered in Ross's mind, although he was told this fact a dozen times. Gus Lobrano had worked for *Town and Country* before coming to the *New Yorker,* but Ross got the notion that he had been on *Harper's Bazaar,* and nothing Lobrano said through the years could correct this misconception. Ten years before Lobrano died in 1956, Ross said to him about something, "I suppose you learned that on *Harper's Bazaar.*" Gus sighed resignedly and said, "Yes, and it wasn't easy."

Harold Ross had an exasperating way of pinning quick tags and labels on people he met, getting them cozily pigeonholed, and sometimes completely wrong. Ben Hecht, for example, was a police reporter at heart, Elmer Davis a corn-belt intellectual, Alan Dunn "the only recluse about town I know." When

Morris Markey, the *New Yorker*'s first reporter-at-large, was assigned to write a piece about what goes on behind the gates at Grand Central, he had to postpone his visit because of the illness of the station master, but for ten years Ross would say, when someone suggested an assignment for Morris, "He couldn't get into Grand Central."

After Ross found out, the hard way, that I was not an administrative editor, he had to think up a tag for me to make my task of writing the "Talk of the Town" department as hard as possible for both of us.

"Thurber's worked too long on newspapers," he told somebody. "He can't write Talk the way I want it. He'll always write journalese." I don't think Ross had ever read anything I had written outside the *New Yorker*. It wasn't much at the time, but I did have a scrapbook of unjournalese pieces I had sold to *Harper*'s "Lion's Mouth," the *D.A.C. News, Sunset Magazine,* and the Sunday *World* and *Herald Tribune*. What stuck in Ross's head was that I had covered City Hall for the Columbus *Dispatch,* been central Ohio correspondent for the *Christian Science Monitor,* worked for the Chicago *Tribune* in France and the *Evening Post* in New York, and once contributed weekly jottings on Ohio politics to the Wheeling *Intelligencer*. So it was that in the new Ross-Thurber relationship of editor and rewrite man there were several months of another kind of ordeal, full of thrust and parry, doubt and despair, sound and fury. It wasn't until the issue of December 24, 1927, after three months of slavery, that a Talk piece of mine appeared which Ross had praised and not rewritten. It was a "personality" piece called "A Friend of Jimmy's," about William Seeman, intimate of Mayor Walker, brother-in-law of Rube Goldberg, canner of White Rose salmon, and crony of Harold Ross. It is no more worth bothering with than that old prospectus, and sticks in my mind only as the second turning point in my relationship with Ross.

3

Every Tuesday Afternoon

The earliest New Yorker *ritual that any oldster can remember was* the weekly Tuesday afternoon art meeting. Philip Gordon Wylie was the second person in the history of Harold Ross's magazine to "hold the artists' hands," as the editor always described the task of dealing with artists and their drawings. Before Wylie, there had been a young woman, but, like most women, she made Ross nervous and he asked Wylie to fire her, while he (Ross) was at lunch. Two hours later Ross phoned Wylie to ask if the deed had been done, and he was told the lady had left with two weeks' salary, and then Ross came back to the office. He never had, to put a blunt point on it, the guts to fire anybody himself, with one exception. In the early thirties, Scudder Middleton, then the official handholder, was emboldened one night at the Players Club to say to Ross, "How am I doing at the office?" and Ross, emboldened by Scotch, snapped, "You're fired!" Then, to cover his own embarrassment, he blustered that he was going to get Peter Arno on the phone and fire him, too. It was way after midnight, and Ross's call aroused Arno from sleep. He promptly bawled Ross out and ordered him never to wake him up again.

In the very beginning, the art meeting was attended by

Ross, Wylie, and Rea Irvin. The invaluable Irvin, artist, ex-actor, wit, and sophisticate about town and country, did more to develop the style and excellence of *New Yorker* drawings and covers than anyone else, and was the main and shining reason that the magazine's comic art in the first two years was far superior to its humorous prose. At the art meetings, Wylie would hold up the drawings and covers, and Irvin would explain to Ross what was good about them, or wrong, or old, or promising. Rea had done the first cover—the unforgettable dandy with the monocle, known intramurally as Eustace Tilley, a name invented by Corey Ford—and for months it remained the composition most like the sort of thing Ross was after, the sort of thing Rea Irvin spent several hours every Tuesday teaching the "corny-gag editor-hobo" (Wylie's description) to understand. Ross learned fast, didn't always see eye to eye with Irvin, often stubbornly had his own way, but was never truly comfortable if his art editor was not at the meetings.

Phil Wylie remembers that Al Frueh did the second cover, and a pretty, shy girl named Barbara Shermund the third one. He recalls, too, the advent of Reginald Marsh, Johan Bull, and Covarrubias, and above all, Curtis Arnoux Peters, a young man not long out of Yale and playing the piano in a jazz orchestra in the West Fifties, who came into the office one day wearing sneakers and carrying a sheaf of drawings signed Peter Arno. Ross was later to write him a note that read, "You're the great-est artist in the world." Under Irvin's supervision and encour-agement, other now famous cartoonists began appearing with their work, changed some of it at his quiet suggestion, took his ideas about their future stuff.

One of the last parties Ross ever gave was a cocktail affair at the Barberry Room in honor of Rebecca West, whom he always considered one of the two finest journalists of her sex. The other was Janet (Genêt) Flanner, the *New Yorker's* Paris correspondent almost from the start. I remember only one art-ist at the West party, the late Helen Hokinson, for whom Ross had great admiration and affection. "Artists don't know anybody and they never go anywhere," he was still grumbling. "They stay home at night, drinking soft drinks in cold sitting rooms, and watching home movies." This Ross exaggeration was, and is, certainly applicable to many *New Yorker* cartoonists but there were several others who went everywhere and knew everybody. The editor himself was socially close to Arno, Al Frueh, John Held, Jr., Rea Irvin, Gluyas Williams, Rube Goldberg, Wallace Morgan, and Ralph Barton, whose suicide in 1931 was a grievous blow to the editor ("When I called on Barton it was like talking to a man with a gun in his hand").

One of my 1927 chores, on top of everything else, was that of holding the artists' hands, but I didn't like it and was not good at it, and soon told Ross the hell with it. I think my first assignment in this touchy area came when Ross asked me to phone Al Frueh and tell him his caricature of Gene Tunney was not a good likeness. Frueh and I had never met, and when I gave him Ross's message he said, "You can go to hell," and hung up on me. Later I got to know and, like the rest of us, to love Al Frueh, who once came upon me in my garage in Connecticut, sitting ten feet in front of my Ford and trying to draw it head on. "You can't do that, Thurber," said Frueh, out of his vast knowledge and experience as a draftsman. "You'd better draw it from the side." I took his advice.

For several months in 1927 I was one of the editors that attended the art meetings, and every now and then after that year I used to drop in as an unofficial observer. In 1929 a sense of order was brought to the meetings by the advent of Miss Daise E. Terry, who comforted Ross by keeping track of covers and drawings (at one time with the assistance of a youngster named Truman Capote). Miss Terry ("She's vigilant about art," said Ross) also took down his comments and criticisms, mainly unfavorable, in shorthand. The art meetings began after lunch and often lasted until nearly six o'clock. One week, during the thirties, finished drawings, rough sketches, and typed suggestions reached a total of some twenty-five thousand. "We got a bank of drawings big enough to last two years," Ross once said, "but there aren't enough casuals to last three weeks."

In the center of a long table in the art meeting room a drawing board was set up to display the week's contributions from scores of artists, both sacred cows and unknowns. It was never easy, and still isn't, for a new artist to break into the *New Yorker.* Some of those whose names have become well known tried for months, or even longer, sending in dozens of rough sketches week after week. If an unknown's caption, or sketch, seemed promising, it was often bought and turned over to an established staff cartoonist. Arno usually got the cream of the crop; the wonderful Mary Petty has never worked from any idea except her own; James Reid Parker did most of Helen Hokinson's captions; and other artists either had their own gagmen or subsisted on original inspiration, fortified by captions and ideas sent in by outsiders or developed by the staff. In the early years, Andy White and I sent to the meeting scores of captions and ideas, some of them for full-page drawings, others for double-page panels for Gluyas Williams and Rea Irvin. If a caption didn't suit Ross—and he was as finicky about some of them as a woman trying on Easter bonnets—it was given to White to "tinker." Gibbs and I did tinkering, too, but White was chief tinkerer to the art meeting.

No phone calls were ever put through to the meeting room on Tuesday afternoon, and only three or four of us could enter unannounced and watch without upsetting Ross. A dozen years ago I began writing a play about Ross and the *New Yorker,* a comedy whose three acts took place in the art room. When I showed the first draft of Act I to a famous man of the Broadway theater he said, "I have a sense of isolation about that meeting room, as if the characters were marooned there and there was nobody else in the building. There must have been people in the other offices on the floor, but I don't feel them."

There were plenty of people outside the quarantined room, surging about the offices and up and down the corridors. If there was an unusual racket of some kind, Ross would say to Miss Terry, "Go out and stop that, and don't tell me what it was." Once it was a workman with a pneumatic drill, who had begun tearing up the floor of the reception room. The area he was ripping up had been marked off by chalk lines. I think Ross wanted a staircase put through to the floor below. The work was not supposed to start until after office hours, but the man with the drill had begun too soon, not realizing that the magazine's working day was from ten to six. According to Ralph Ingersoll, I increased the racket by banging metal wastebaskets up and down the halls, as a form of protest. Miss Terry managed to quiet the drill and me, and to clear the corridors of bystanders.

Ross at one time had his own office soundproofed and thought of extending the system to the art meeting room, but someone at Riggs Sanitarium, where he had spent a couple of weeks resting up from the wrangle and jangle of life, advised him against it. Ross told White and me when he came back, " 'You can exclude noise by soundproofing your mind,' this man said. You don't hear racket if you know how to concentrate. Soundproofing walls is catering to weakness." One summer day, to demonstrate how this theory worked, he called me into his office. "They're putting up a building on the corner," he said, "and there must be twenty automatic drills going right now." He dismissed this tiny irritation with a jaunty wave of his hand and began discussing some office problem that annoyed him. Suddenly he whirled and bawled at the racket outside, "Stop that!"

The art meeting always began with the display of finished covers in color, one at a time. They were bought and scheduled six months in advance, so that in June we were studying Christmas covers. Ross sat on the edge of a chair several feet away from the table, leaning forward, the fingers of his left hand spread upon his chest, his right hand holding a white knitting needle which he used for a pointer. Miss Terry remembers the day he brought it in, having picked it up nobody knows where. She later bought a dozen more of them, so everybody could have one. Ross liked to have a lot of everything he needed, for nothing irritated him so much as not to be able to put his hand instantly on what he wanted. There was always a full carton of Camels, for instance, in the drawer of the long table, and it was kept replenished by his secretary, like the carton in the drawer of his office table. For a while he had used a pencil as a pointer, but he was afraid of marking up the drawings. Then he tried a ruler, but the goddam thing wasn't right, and fate directed him to the knitting needles that solved this little problem.

He became, I think, by far the most painstaking, meticulous, hairsplitting detail-criticizer the world of editing has known. "Take this down," he would say to Miss Terry, and he would dictate a note of complaint to the creator of the drawing or cover under consideration. The memory of some of his "sharpshooting"—I don't know who applied the word, but it was perfect—will last as long as the magazine, and perhaps even longer. I cannot vouch for the truth of his query about a drawing of two elephants gazing at one of their offspring with the caption, "It's about time to tell Junior the facts of life," but, valid or apocryphal, it has passed into legend. "Which elephant is talking?" he is supposed to have asked. I was on hand, though, when he pointed his needle at a butler in a Thanksgiving cover depicting a Park Avenue family at table, and snarled, "That isn't a butler, it's a banker." Suddenly, the figure was, to all of us, a banker in disguise, and Ross dictated a note asking the artist to "make a real butler out of this fellow." He once complained of a blue sky, "There never was a sky like that." It is not true, as rumor has it, that he said, "It's delft, or Alice, or some goddam shade." The only blues Ross could have known are light, sky, and navy.

On another day, he doubted that the windows of the United Nations Building were anything like those shown in a drawing, and he ordered that a photographer be sent to take pictures of the windows. My favorite of all his complaints, in a career of thousands of them, was reported to me by Peter De Vries, who for years attended the art meetings and still helps go through the "rough basket," skimming off the best of hundreds or thousands of sketches. The cover on the board showed a Model T driving along a dusty country road, and Ross turned his sharpshooting eye on it for a full two minutes. "Take this down, Miss Terry," he said. "Better dust."

Idea drawings, as they were called to distinguish them from captionless spots, were raked by Ross's sharpshooting fire from the wording of the captions to the postures and expressions of the figures and the shape and arrangement of furniture or trees, or whatever else was in them. Sometimes it seemed to me and the rest of us that Ross was bent on wringing the humor out of a drawing by his petulant objections to details. This attitude reminds me of Gibbs's celebrated single-sentence criticism of Max Eastman's book, *The Enjoyment of Laughter,* whose advance proofs Ross had asked him to read. Gibbs wrote in a memo to Ross: "It seems to me Eastman has got American humor down and broken its arm."

Ross rarely laughed outright at anything. His face would light up, or his torso would undergo a spasm of amusement, but he was not at the art meeting for pleasure. Selecting drawings was serious business, a part of the week's drudgery, and the back of his mind ever held the premonition that nothing was going to be funny. Just as he searched writers' copy for such expressions as Dorothy Parker's office-celebrated "like shot through a goose," he scanned drawings for phallic symbols and such, and once found one, he thought, in a hat I had drawn on a man in one of my covers. He was imagining things, but I had to change it anyway.

The most prudish neighbor woman in H. L. Mencken's

Bible belt could not have taken exception to any *New Yorker* drawing I can remember, including Arno's husbands and wives in bed and the series he did of a man and a woman on, or near, a porch swing in what was intended to be a compromising clinch, the while they talked such passionless words as "Have you read any good books lately?" Arno's first conception of this entanglement was warm without being torrid, it seemed to me, but it gave Ross the galloping jumps, and under his coaching and coaxing Arno finally drew a couple approximately as sexually involved as a husband and his sister-in-law at a christening.

One realistic detail of the kind that upset Ross was overlooked by him and the others, out of understandable ignorance. It was a Garrett Price that was published in the issue of December 20, 1930, and it showed a young woman on an operating table saying to a young surgeon entering the room, "Why, Henry Whipple, I thought you were still in medical college!" The scrub nurse in the drawing is holding a tray upon which lies what is known to the surgical profession as a doublespoon curette, an instrument used in, as Ross might put it, you know what. Wylie later wrote Ross kidding him about this, but if old Afraid-of-the-Functional exploded, I didn't hear about it. For one thing, the scene was what he called "clinical," which took some of the curse off the realistic and functional. However, he did direct Scudder Middleton to ask Price, "Were you trying to put something over on us?" Price is not that kind of man or artist, and just the other day he told me that his father was a doctor and he had drawn the curette from memory of instruments in his father's office. "I didn't know what it was for," he said on the phone (like many other famous *New Yorker* artists, Garrett Price is one I've never met).

Every drawing was a task for Ross, and a few were real problems. It took courage for a humorous magazine to publish the grim Reginald Marsh that showed a woman holding up her little child so that, over the heads of an assembled crowd, it could witness a lynching. Among the submissions that were too much for Ross was a full page of two Arab fighters leaving a field upon which bodies are scattered, one of the Arabs saying, "Some of my best friends are Jews," and there was another, whose central figures were two divinity students, their eyes bright with recognition, walking toward each other in Grand Central Station with outstretched hands, above the caption "Well, Judas Priest!" I substitute the name for that of the deity because I share Ross's deep conviction that major blasphemies have no place in comedy. Ross hated to lose this drawing, though, and he sent it to White for tinkering. Andy tinkered it into a line that he told Ross comfortingly would not offend the church. It was "Well, I'll be a son-of-a-bitch!" Ross chuckled about that all day and then sent White a memo reading, "No, but I'm afraid it would offend American mothers."

I never saw the editor of the *New Yorker* get more enjoyment out of anything than he derived from a Gluyas Williams full page showing a board meeting room in which all the chairs at the long table are empty while the chairman and the members of the board are crouched in a football huddle in one corner of the office. That one lingered lovingly in his memory along with the famous Williams drawing of the day a cake of Ivory soap sank at Procter & Gamble's, and the picture captioned "Oops, sorry," in which one trapeze artist misses the outstretched hands of another, high in the air—the work of George V. Shanks. There were hundreds of others, too, but I haven't got all year.

A magazine that has published nearly twenty thousand drawings was bound to run into repetitions and formulas years ago, and they formed another nightmare for Ross. There were too goddam many men and women on rafts and on desert islands, and too many talking animals, and too many guys in a jail cell—on and on the calendar of formula ran. I once made a series of drawings especially for Ross about the trials and tortures of the art meeting. One showed the scowling Ross himself shoving a drawing at a timid office employee and snarling, "Is that funny?" He was a great man for what he called the outside opinion, and sometimes sent a questionnaire to five or six of us on which we were to say yes or no about a drawing, or a casual, or a poem. Two of the other art meeting drawings I did for Ross ("You tease him too much," my mother once told me sternly. "You shouldn't tease him so much.") showed, respectively, an old woman asking for a cup of cold water at a storage dam, and the same old woman asking a fireman for a match at a great conflagration. The editor had the drawings framed and hung on the walls of his office to remind him of the threat of formula. That was Harold Ross. He could not only take a joke at his own expense, he could perpetuate it. Not long before he died, I discovered, in going through my scrapbook of drawings in the office library, that I had drawn one with the caption "The magic has gone out of my marriage—has the magic gone out of your marriage?" and another with "Well, who made the magic go out of our marriage—me or you?" I sent tear sheets of the two drawings to Ross, and he sent me a note that read, "Well, who's responsible for the magic going out of your marriage twice—you or me?"

It would not have surprised Ross if the sanity had gone out of any artist at the very moment he was saying good morning to the editor. Ross regarded writers as temperamental mechanisms, capable of strange behavior, and artists were just as bad, or even worse. Complexes, fixations, psychological blocks, and other aberrations of the creative mind had him always on the alert. "They have *sinking* spells," he would say. "They can't ride on trains, or drive after dark, or live above the first floor of a building, or eat clams, or stay alone all night. They think automobiles are coming up on the sidewalk to get them, that gangsters are on their trail, that their apartments are being cased, and God knows what else." This dissertation, with variations, always gave Ross his saddest look and his darkest sigh. After one of these enumerations of his woes, he and I had lunch at the Algonquin. It was in the years when I could see, and I suddenly stared blankly at the bill of fare as if I had never seen one before, got slowly to my feet, and began trembling. I tried to turn pale, too, but I doubt if I managed that. Ross's alarm bell rang. "Are you all *right?*" he demanded nervously. I kept on staring at the bill of fare. "What the hell is this thing?" I croaked.

"It's the goddam menu," Ross said, and then he got it. "Don't do that to me, Thurber," he pleaded. "Too many people I know are *really* ready for the bughouse." That was his invariable word for rest home, sanitarium, and such.

For Ross's developed taste and sense of humor in selecting cover art and idea drawings I have a firm and lasting respect. Sitting and staring at a hundred pictures, one after the other, week after week, can become a tedious process that dulls perception, but Ross's eager, unflagging desire to get the best and the funniest kept a sharp edge on his appreciation. Picking drawings at a lengthy meeting is somehow comparable to producing a play. You're not going to know for sure whether something is good until the readers or the audience see it in print or on the stage.

One afternoon in the winter of 1928, when I was sharing an office with White, Andy interrupted my typing to ask my opinion of a caption he had just worked out for a drawing. He was a little solemn about it, and clearly uncertain that he had hit on the right idea. I looked at the drawing and the caption and said, "Yeh, it seems okay to me," but neither of us cracked a smile. This drawing, by Carl Rose, appeared in the issue of December 8, 1928, and it carried one of the most famous and laughed-at captions in the history of the magazine, the one in which the mother says, "It's broccoli, dear," and the little child replies, "I say it's spinach, and I say the hell with it." The youngster's expression of distaste was to become a part of the American language. A song was written about it called "I Say It's Spinach," it has been mentioned in hundreds of editorials and newspaper columns, and it was worked into the title of a book by Elizabeth Hawes, which I illustrated, called *Fashion Is Spinach*. (In *An American Dictionary of Slang* the definition of the word "spinach" as "nonsense or bunk" is attributed to J. P. McEvoy, who used it in his book, *Hollywood Girl,* in 1929.)

The experience of that winter afternoon so long ago, when Andy tossed the famous caption up for grabs and both of us darn near let it fall, served to moderate my disappointment whenever a caption drawing of mine was later turned down, or bought without comment, as a matter of routine. I suppose the best known of my own scrawls is the one of the seal on the headboard of a bed in which a wife is snarling at her husband, "All right, have it your way—you heard a seal bark." I hadn't thought enough of it to show it to anybody before submitting it, and I was as surprised as I was delighted when its appear-

"All Right, Have It Your Way—You Heard a Seal Bark!"

ance in the magazine in January, 1932, brought me a truly ecstatic telegram from Bob Benchley, than whom there was nobody whose praise a cartoonist or humorist would rather have had. I gave him the original of the drawing, and named my first book of pictures *The Seal in the Bedroom* because of what he had said.

The incredulous eye of Harold Wallace Ross fell for the first time upon a drawing of mine in the spring of that troubled year 1929. For years I had been scrawling drawings on pieces of yellow copy paper and throwing them on the floor or leaving them on my desk. I began drawing at seven, mostly what seemed to be dogs, and carried the practice into the years of so-called maturity, getting a lot of good, clean, childish fun out of filling up all the pages of memo pads on the office desks of busy friends of mine, seeking to drive them crazy. Ingersoll recalls that he was a frequent victim of the ubiquitous dogs when he tried to find a blank page to write down an address or a phone number, but he maintained his reason like a veteran of the artillery of infantilism. After all, he had gone through worse than dogs with Ross.

It was White who got the mad impetuous idea that my scrawls should be published and, what is more, paid for with money. I didn't think he could make it. It is true that, a dozen years earlier, I had filled up a lot of space with dogs and an improbable species of human being in the Ohio State *Sun-Dial,* but I was its editor-in-chief then (one of my predecessors was Gardner Rea, a *New Yorker* artist since its first issue), and nothing could be done to stop me. Some of the *Sun-Dial* drawings were about the same as those I had done when I was seven and the ones I did for the *New Yorker,* but others were elaborate arrangements of solid black and crosshatching. When White caught me trying this same style again one day, he spoke a sound word of warning that has gained a small deserved fame: "Don't do that. If you ever got good you'd be mediocre."

One spring day in 1929 I had done, in approximately thir-

teen seconds, a pencil sketch on yellow copy paper of a seal on a rock staring at two tiny distinct specks and saying, "Hm, explorers." White inked it in, a task for which rough tremor disqualified me, and sent it to the art meeting. Anything that had the strong backing of Andy White was likely to impress Ross, who had bought and printed the year before my first serious casual, a thing called "Menaces in May," only after getting White's favorable opinion on it. I don't know what Ross said upon first gazing at a Thurber drawing, but he probably dismissed it lightly as a gag, a single buzzing fly that one could swat and then there wouldn't be any more. Rea Irvin drew a picture of a seal's hand on the same paper with my seal and wrote under it, "This is the way a seal's whiskers go." Promptly the following Tuesday White sent the drawing back to the meeting with a note attached that read, "This is the way a

Thurber seal's whiskers go." It came back again, this time without a word. As the weeks went on, White kept inking in and
sending on other drawings of mine, and they were all rejected.
All that Ross ever said during this preliminary skirmishing was
a gruff "How the hell did you get the idea you could *draw?*"

Soon Andy and I began writing *Is Sex Necessary?,* for
which he insisted that I do the illustrations. We finished the
book in the late summer and sent it to Harper's, who had published White's book of verses, *The Lady Is Cold.* Then one day
we called on the publishers with a big sheaf of my drawings.
White laid them out on the floor, and three bewildered Har-
permen stared at them in dismay, probably murmuring to
themselves, "God, how we pity us." One of them finally found
his voice. "I gather these are a rough idea of the kind of illustrations you want some artist to do?" he said. White was firm.
"These are the drawings that go into the book," he said. There
was a lot of jabber then about sales ceilings, the temper of the
time, reader assistance, and the like, but the drawings went
into the book, and the book was a success, and Ross kept hearing about it and about the drawings. He was mightily disturbed. Something created in his own office, something he had
had first shot at, had been printed by a publisher, a species of
freak with whom Ross never ceased to do battle. He came into

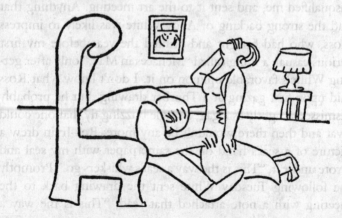

my office, looking bleak. "Where's the goddam seal drawing, Thurber?" he demanded. "The one White sent to the art meeting a few months ago." I told him that he had rejected it and I had thrown it away. "Well, don't throw things away just because I reject them!" he yelled. "Do it over again." I didn't do it over again for two years, although he kept at me.

The first drawings of mine to appear in the *New Yorker* were of animals, illustrating a 1930 series called "Our Own Pet Department." In one of these, incidentally, a drawing of a horse's head with antlers strapped to it, the horse's teeth had been put in by a girl friend of mine. Everybody took liberties with my drawings. In one of them, showing a man and his wife and another woman at a table, a charming editrix blacked in the other woman's shoes with India ink to make it clear to readers that the designing minx was playing footy-footy with the husband. The startled husband, strained and bolt upright in his chair, had drawn from his wife the line "What's come over *you* suddenly?" Benchley, always a kind of jealous guardian of my art, such as it was, was annoyed by this monstrosity of explicitness, and said so to Ross. My goddam drawings were beginning to close in on Ross. Now he had something new to fret and fuss about, something he had never dreamed God would let happen to him.

It wasn't until January, 1931, that I sent another idea drawing to the *New Yorker*'s art meeting. I had begun drawing straight away in India ink, without pencil foundation. Ross bought the drawing and asked for more. This was easy, since I could do a hundred in one week end, but I usually submitted only two or three at a time. (In 1939 I did all the drawings for *The Last Flower* between dinner and bedtime one evening. but spared Ross this flux of pictures, because I didn't want to be responsible for his having a seizure of some kind.) He still kept pestering me about the seal drawing, and one evening in December, 1931, I tried to recapture it on the typewriter paper I always used. The seal was all right, atypical whiskers and all, but the rock looked more like the head of a bed, so I turned it into a bed, and put the man and his wife in it, with the caption Benchley so generously wired me about. With its purchase and printing in the magazine, I became an established *New Yorker* artist, still to Ross's mixed bewilderment and discomfiture.

He never asked me if the couples I put in beds were married, but some of the drawings aroused his Sunday alarm or perplexity. There was the one known around the office as "The Lady on the Bookcase," a nude female figure on all fours, about whom a man is saying to a visitor, "That's my first wife up there," and adding, "and this is the *present* Mrs. Harris." I have often told about what happened when *that* hit Ross squarely between his fretful editorial eyes. He telephoned me in the country to say, "Is the woman on the bookcase alive, or stuffed, or just dead?" I told him I would give the matter my gravest consideration and call him back, and I did. "She has to be alive," I told him. "My doctor says a dead woman couldn't support herself on all fours, and my taxidermist says you can't stuff a woman." He thought about it for a few seconds and then roared into the phone, "Then, goddam it, what's she doing naked in the house of her former husband and his second wife?" I told him he had me there, and that I wasn't

"That's my first wife up there, and this is the *present* Mrs. Harris."

responsible for the behavior of the people I drew. Just the other day I turned up a note of amplification that I had sent to him. In it I explained that I had tried to draw a wife waiting for her husband on top of a flight of stairs, but had got the perspective all wrong and suddenly found I had a woman on a bookcase. This led naturally, I said, to the unnatural domestic situation I had drawn. "Thurber's crazy," Ross told someone later, but it wasn't the first time he had so diagnosed my condition.

There was another drawing that set off a memorable display of fireworks between the editor and me. It showed three hound dogs in the window of a pet shop, one of them, sitting between the other two, having unusually sad eyes and gentle expression. A would-be woman purchaser is talking to the proprietor of the store, who is saying, "I'm very sorry, madam, but the one in the middle is stuffed, poor fellow."

"I don't think they have stuffed dogs in pet shops," Ross said. "Not in the show window, anyway."

"*This* shop has one in the show window," I said stubbornly.

"You have me there," Ross growled. Then I got into deeper difficulty. "It's a variant of that old story about the three men on the subway train late at night," I said. "They were sitting across from a fourth man, who is left alone on the train with the three others after still a fifth passenger hands him a note and gets off at the next stop. The note says, 'The man in the middle is dead.'" I never saw Ross look unhappier about anything. He said so much then, in such a splutter, that it doesn't come back to me coherently now. "I'll send that drawing in to every art meeting until it's bought and printed," I told him. I think it was bought on its third resubmission. Some of my drawings were held up much longer than that, and one night I got into Ross's office with a passkey, faked his R on three drawings I especially liked, and sent them through the works the next day. Nothing was ever said about that, but for weeks I expected all hell to break loose.

Ross's tormented forehead was always in creases of worry about some art problem. When, early on, he had decided to put captions in italics—bang! there was the problem of what to do about emphasizing words and phrases that needed it. Clearly they would have to be set up in roman, thus reversing an ancient convention, and Ross was not fond of being the first by whom the new idea is tried. Several times I tried to sell him the idea of romanizing only part of an emphasized word, on the ground that Americans, particularly females, often do that; a case in point is the caption I sent in (my last one, I think) for which Whitney Darrow did the drawing, an ardent girl saying to her gloomily intellectual young man, "When you say you hate your own species, do you mean *everybody?*" Actually, it seemed to my ear, our young ladies stress only the "ev" in that word, but this was a kind of hybrid that would have driven Ross into a new ulcer.

Since the great warrior was a worshiper of the gods of Clarity and Explicitness, that devotion sometimes led him into overelaboration of captions. I remember an early Arno of a husband and wife arguing *en boudoir,* the wife saying, "And after I've given you the best years of my life," and the husband snapping back, "Yes, and who made them the best years?" The point would be sharper if only the husband's speech were used, and Ross soon gave up dialogue for monologue in most captions. He could torture single lines, though, as in the case of a Hokinson dowager complaining to her pampered Pomeranian, *couchant* on a soft cushion in his cage at a dog show, "I'm the one that should be lying down." The caption had come in that way, but Ross changed it to "I'm the one that should be lying down somewhere," so readers wouldn't get the idea the dog's owner wanted to climb in and lie down on its cushion. I made my own mistakes in the same area, too, once drawing a tipsy gentleman, fallen prone at the feet of a seated lady and saying,

"This is not the real me you're seeing, Miss Spencer." It should, of course, have been simply, "This is not the *real* me."

The editor was also often on the edge of panic about suspected *double entendre,* and after thirty-one years I recall his concern about an Arno drawing of one of his elderly gentlemen of the old school dancing with a warmly clinging young lady and saying "Good God, woman, think of the social structure!" Ross was really afraid that "social structure" could be interpreted to mean a certain distressing sexual phenomenon of human anatomy. He brought this worry to me, pointing out that "social diseases" means sexual diseases, but I succeeded in quieting his fears, and the caption ran unchanged. He was wary of fatality in drawings, sharing Paul Nash's conviction that "not even Americans can make death funny," and when Carl Rose, in 1932, submitted a picture of a fencer cutting off his opponent's head and crying *"Touché!"* Ross thought it was too bloody and gruesome, and asked Rose to let me have a swing at it, because "Thurber's people have no blood. You can put their heads back on and they're as good as new." It worked out that way. Nobody was horrified.

In the early thirties all the *New Yorker* cartoonists had to put up for months with the havoc and bother of a new Ross apprehension. He became convinced that somebody was giving away our captions to rival magazines before they could be used. The trouble began when two similar drawings with identical captions appeared in the *New Yorker* and the old *Life.* A snowbound traveler in the Alps is taking the brandy cask from a Saint Bernard and saying, "What, no White Rock?" The line had been invented by Donald Ogden Stewart, who told it to somebody, who told it to somebody else, and thus both magazines heard about it before long. After that alarm had sounded through the offices like a somber bell in Macbeth's castle, the originals of drawings the *New Yorker* bought came back to the artists with heavy strips of butcher's paper pasted over the captions. This ruined some of the drawings, since the paper often stuck to the caption like a collie's tongue to a frosty hitching post. A drawing of mine with the caption "What have you done with Dr. Millmoss?" got the super-secret treatment, and was obliquely described in the office records as "Woman with strange animal." The strange animal was a hippopotamus, but the *New Yorker* wasn't going to let any spy find out about that. This panic, like many another office panic, died down and was forgotten.

If I wrote of Ross's constant concern and kindliness about my eyes, it would embarrass him in heaven, as it would embarrass him on earth if he were still here. He was not a demonstrative man, or he thought he wasn't, but anyone who knew him well could see through the profane bluster and gruffness that covered great solicitude for men and women he loved when they were in peril, or in any kind of trouble. He began by taking my drawings as a joke, went through a phase in which he dismissed them as "a passing fancy, a fad of the English," and ended up doing his darnedest, as my disability increased, to keep the drawings going by every kind of ingenious hook and crook. After I got so I could no longer see to draw, even with black grease crayon on large sheets of yellow paper, Ross began a campaign, recorded in a series of letters he wrote me, to reprint old drawings of mine with new captions. First he suggested reversing the old cuts, a simple mechanical maneuver; then, with the aid of others in the office who knew about such things, he experimented with taking figures or furniture out of one drawing and putting them in another, arriving at a dozen permutations of men, women, and dogs, chairs, bridge lamps, and framed pictures, upon which he must have spent hours of thought with his confederates in this conspiracy of consolation.

I did think up a few new captions for old drawings, but whatever device of recomposition was used, some readers got on to it. The first publication to point out what was going on was the *News Chronicle* in London. The interest of the English, or some of them, in my drawings both pleased and puzzled Harold Ross. He was puzzled by Paul Nash's enthusiasm for my scrawls, although he was delighted by Nash's having singled me out at a luncheon in the Century Club in 1931 from the very forefront of American painters, all present and lined up for introduction to the visiting British painter and critic. He loved my story of how Nash insisted that I be put on his right (on his left was a bottle of whiskey we had snatched from a sideboard), and by the distinguished visitor's asking a formidably bearded connoisseur of art, seated across from him, "What do you think of Milt Gross?"

When Nash was art critic for the *New Statesman and Nation* in London, he once wrote a piece about American comic art in which he mentioned that I apparently began drawing without anything particular in mind, in the manner of the early drawings of the great Matisse. This remarkable and somewhat labored comparison was distorted by word of mouth until some careless columnist printed the news that Henri Matisse was an admirer of my scrawls. So it came about that in 1937, when two bold young gallery men in London put on a one-man show of my drawings, one of them telephoned Monsieur Matisse, over my dead body, to try to arrange a meeting. The poor chap came back from the phone a little pale, and stammering, "Matisse's secretary says that Matisse never heard of Mr. Thurber *or* the *New Yorker*." That same year a short-lived magazine called *Night and Day,* too imitative of the *New Yorker* for its own good, was published in London, and it bought and printed a series of my drawings called "The Patient," which the *New Yorker* had rejected. I saw to it that Ross was immediately notified of the sale, and I sent him a copy of the magazine. That's when he really began telling people, "Thurber's drawings are a fad of the English, a passing fancy." He thought that some of my drawings were funny, all right, but what really got him, I could tell from his tone and look when he first mentioned it to me, was the praise they got from Ralph Barton and Wallace Morgan when Ross asked these friends of his about them. There was one *New Yorker* cartoonist, perhaps one of many that felt the same way, who yelled at Ross one day during the thirties, "Why do you reject drawings of mine, and print stuff by that fifth-rate artist Thurber?"

"Third-rate," said Ross, coming promptly and bravely to the defense of my stature as an artist and his own reputation as an editor.

In the last seven years of his life Ross wrote me dozens of letters and notes about my drawings. In one he said he had found out that the *New Yorker* had published three hundred and seven of my captioned drawings, of which one hundred and seventy-five had been printed in one or another of my books. He wanted to know if I would permit new captions by outsiders on those rearranged originals of mine. "There is a caption here on a sketch by an idea man," he wrote me, "that it is thought might do for a re-used drawing of yours, as follows: (Two women talking) 'Every time she tells a lie about *me,* I'm going to tell the truth about *her.*' Now that I've got it on paper, it may not sound so hot, but it might do. The women in your drawings used to say some pretty batty things." He wanted to pay me for the full rate I had got for originals, but I said no on a project in which I would have no real creative part.

The whole idea was abandoned after I told Ross that I didn't grieve about not being able to draw any longer. "If I couldn't write, I couldn't breathe," I wrote him, "but giving up drawing is only a little worse than giving up tossing cards in a hat. I once flipped in forty-one out of the whole deck, at twelve feet." I may have been straining a point to cheer up Ross, but cheering up Ross was a good deed, like lighting a lamp.

He was fond of two series I had drawn, "Famous Poems Illustrated" and "A New Natural History," and here are some of the things he wrote me about them. "Why in God's name did you stop doing the illustrated poems? There are forty million other verses in the English language, many of them unquestionably suitable for Thurber illustration." "I hereby suggest the Blue Funk as an animal or bird in the Natural History series. Also, I suggest the Blue Streak and the Trickle, and mention the fact that you might get a few more animals out of the bones of the human skeleton." "There might be a name for something in the Natural History series in 'Lazy Susan,' a flower or a butterfly, or something. Would 'antimacassar' be possible? I guess not."

Some of his written comments on the Natural History series show the old sharpshooter at work. "The checking of the names in your Natural History series revealed that one name is a real name: there is an actual fish called the pout. You have a bird called a shriek. In real life there is a bird called a shriker and also one called a shrike. I should think the approximation here does not matter. There is a bee called a lapidary, but you have drawn an animal. You have a clock tick. There is, of course, a tick. No matter, I say. There is a bird called a ragamuffin. You have drawn a ragamuffin plant. No real conflict." I wrote Ross that, for temperamental reasons, and such, I could draw only creatures suggested to me by my own thoughts and words, and said, "I've come to the end of this series, unless you want a man being generous to a fault—that is, handing a small rodent a nut. And I know you won't want a female grouch nursing a grudge. As for the illustrated poems, they began when I sent St. Clair McKelway, from Frederick, Maryland, the Barbara Frietchie drawings, and they ended when I tried Poe's Raven, and it turned into a common cornfield crow."

In 1955 my London publishers brought out a small paperback of some forty selected drawings of mine, with a short preface. It was called *A Thurber Garland* and cost five shillings, or about seventy cents. That year only thirty-seven copies of it were sold, and I can hear Ross now, as I so often hear him, pacing the chalcedony halls and complaining. Perverse, unpredictable, H. W. Ross is grumbling to some uninterested angel, "What the hell's the matter with the English? Thurber's drawings are not a fad, or a passing fancy, they are here to stay. Don't they know that?"

The paragraph above is the way this installment ended when it was printed in the *Atlantic Monthly*. After it appeared, I got a reproachful letter from my English publishers, Hamish Hamilton, Ltd., telling me that *A Thurber Garland* had sold more than five thousand copies during its first year. I don't know how I made such an appalling mistake, but it wouldn't have surprised Ross. It wouldn't have surprised the late Gus Kuehner, either. He was my city editor on the Columbus *Evening Dispatch* when I covered City Hall for that newspaper in the early 1920's, and he once put up a kidding notice on the bulletin board announcing that I would no longer be allowed to deal with sums running into more than five figures—it now turns out it should have been four, or maybe three. As I recall it, I'd written a story in which I magnified the municipal debt by some six million dollars.

Ross and Kuehner, incidentally, had a great deal in common. They had both started in as part office boy and part reporter when they were in their teens; they both got along well with cops; their frowns and snarls and moods were similar, and they talked the same language. One day in 1928 the phone rang in my office at the *New Yorker* and a voice as loud as Ross's tried to disguise itself, with about as much success as Ross would have had. "Are they serving tea and lady fingers at the *New Yorker* now?" said a strong falsetto that I recognized instantly. Kuehner could never get it out of his head that the *New Yorker* was a fancy pants place, with thick carpets on the office floors, and editors who smoked cigarettes in long holders. He said he had been in town for a convention of newspapermen, but was on his way back to Columbus. I told him to come over so I could introduce him to Ross. "I want you to meet him," I said. "He's a guy like you. In some ways he *is* you." Kuehner was unimpressed. "I'm taking a train in about ten minutes," he said. "Don't let your tea get cold. Kiss Ross for me." And that was the last time I ever heard his voice. He died one Christmas Day in Columbus, at the age of forty-nine. If heaven were a place in which guys could get together and talk, Ross and Kuehner would have a fine time exchanging newspaper and editorial experiences and taking Thurber apart, the guy who didn't know the difference between thirty-seven and five thousand.

4

Mencken and Nathan and Ross

The questions most often asked me by outsiders during my early New Yorker years were: "What is Dorothy Parker like?" and "How old is Peter Arno?" Later on, at home and abroad, more and more people, in bars and drawing rooms, wanted to know: "What manner of man is this Harold Ross?" To this I could only reply, "What Harold Ross do you mean? There are so many of him. On the other side of every Ross is still another Ross. I keep finding new ones myself." In the drawing rooms I have frequented, people usually inquired, over their tea or gin and tonic, "What kind of mind does he have? What is his literary background?"

Faced with these formidable questions, any of his intimates, unstimulated by a third Martini, might easily murmur, even now, "God knows," or "Search me." Having undertaken the task of describing Ross, I shall reach for the brandy bottle and, for the purposes of this chapter, the anecdotes marked "literary," perhaps the richest and easily the most bewildering section of my memory files. Ross wouldn't like any part of it. The man who gave the dictionary a new definition of "profile" was never entirely secure about the formula, especially when it was tried on complex personalities he knew well. When Joe

Bryan announced that he was planning to write about Bench-ley for the *Saturday Evening Post,* Ross said, "It won't work." Months after the piece was printed, Ross caught sight of Bryan in Grand Central Station one day and yelled at him, "I told you it wouldn't work."

Starting high, as they say in the theater, I shall take you first to Harold Ross's Park Avenue apartment. The time is 1948, after dinner of a spring evening. Ross had asked me (to shift tenses suddenly in a manner that always irked him) to sit around and talk with him and H. L. Mencken and George Jean Nathan. (Mayor O'Dwyer had been asked to join the party, but he didn't show up.) Ross felt, I think, that he could depend upon me to redirect the traffic of conversation if it got onto boulevards where the going might make him uneasy. Mencken had then been writing for the *New Yorker* for a dozen years, and until his final illness he wrote a total of fifty-six pieces for Ross, about his travels in Europe, his life, and the American language. After twenty years of editing, Mencken had given it up to devote himself to prose, meditation, and the companion-ship of good minds.

The ex-editor of *Smart Set* and the *American Mercury* and the editor of the *New Yorker* had both helped to revitalize native literature, humor, and journalism in the half century then drawing to its close. They had seen the decline and fall of such relics of the somnolent carriage years as *Everybody's, Munsey's, Ainslee's,* and *Pearson's,* the disappearance of *Puck,* the old *Life,* and *Judge* (of which Ross had once been editor), the collapse of *Vanity Fair* upon the bosom of *Vogue,* the silent stealing away of many a so-called little magazine, and the advent of Henry Luce's *Time, Life,* and *Fortune* and DeWitt Wallace's *Reader's Digest.* They had viewed, through widely different lenses, the amazing and disturbing and exhilarating American scene, Mencken aiming his binoculars and his bung starter at those well-known and badly battered objects of his eloquent scorn and ridicule, the booboisie, the Bible belt, the professor doctors, the lunatics of the political arena, and the imbeciles infesting literature; while Ross, fascinated by many things that would have bored Mencken, took in the panorama and personalities of New York City and finally the whole American spectacle, interested in everything from a swizzle stick he picked up one day ("There's a story in this damn thing") to the slight swaying of the Empire State Building in a stiff gale.

The long newspaper experience of the two men, certain of their likes and dislikes, and their high and separate talents as editors formed basis enough for an evening of conversation. They were both great talkers and good listeners, and each wore his best evening vehemence, ornamented with confident conclusions, large generalizations, and dark blue emphases. Nathan and I were, for the most part, just spectators. The session was richly monogrammed with Mencken's M and Ross's R. The man from Baltimore announced that heads of authoritarian governments who discouraged religion were feeble-minded, or else they would go from door to door giving everybody the choice of joining the state church or being led to the gallows. On theories of international politics Ross could be both hazy and positive. He had once asked me, "Is Communism the same as Marxism?" and on another occasion he had said, with finality, "All Communists had unhappy childhoods." That night he said nothing on the subject. "Taft is a good man," Mencken said suddenly. "If he had Dewey's voice he would sweep the convention." He pinned an orchid, in passing, on Alf Landon, for whom he had a perverse and persistent liking.

Ross rarely talked about domestic politics, and when he did it was on a curiously personal basis. He said he had been against Roosevelt because "Morris Ernst could get in to see him any time of the day or night" and because "Roosevelt called Ralph Ingersoll by his first name. Jim Forrestal worked for him, too," he added morosely, "and I have little confidence in a government run by friends of mine." Mencken then applauded some Southern newspaper publisher who had boldly turned his plant into a non-union shop. Ross said, gloomily, that he was satisfied if the unions let him get out his magazine. He couldn't understand why the men who printed the *New Yorker* didn't have a special loyalty to it, somewhat comparable to his own.

Now and then that evening the tone and color of their thoughts seemed to blend perfectly; once when they discussed the parlance of railroading—deadhead, highball, whistle stop, gandy dancer—for Ross wanted Mencken to write an article about it, which Mencken was eager to do, and when they discussed newspapers ("All managing editors are vermin," said Mencken) and literary-minded reformers who kept writing social-conscious pieces ("It's a city of Abraham Lincolns," said Ross).

Mencken began talking about Will Durant, for whom he had conceived a recent and unexpected admiration. "How could an imbecile suddenly become a great man?" he demanded, meaning, in Menckenese, how could the author of *The Story of Philosophy* have written *Caesar and Christ?* Mencken regarded this step, "from balderdash to excellence," as little short of miraculous. Ross could add nothing to this discussion, for if Will Durant meant anything to him at all it was as the unhappy victim of a bizarre public banquet in his honor, given in 1930, which Andy White had written up for the *New Yorker's* "Talk of the Town." This banquet, at the Fifth Avenue Hotel, had degenerated into an embarrassing charade in which several actors in masquerade, one of them representing Molière, had appeared from nowhere around midnight to place a laurel wreath upon the agonized brow of the American philosopher. Herbert Spencer was the only philosopher Ross ever quoted, and it was always the same quote: "A genius can do readily what nobody else can do at all," which precisely described the editorial genius Ross kept dreaming about.

The conversation split in two at this point, and Mencken and I began talking about Willa Cather. We were still discussing "the old girl" when Ross caught the name, turned it over in his mind a couple of times, and then said, "Willa Cather. Willa Cather—did he write *The Private Life of Helen of Troy?*" I couldn't see Mencken's face, but I felt the puzzled quality of his silence, and hastily came to the rescue of a situation hopelessly snarled by Ross's incomprehensible confusion of Willa Cather and John Erskine. "Ross hasn't read a novel since *When Knighthood Was in Flower,*" I said, "or *Riders of the Purple Sage.* He doesn't read anything except what goes into his magazine."

"I haven't got time to read novels," Ross admitted. That evening, as always, he had brought home from the office a briefcase stuffed with manuscripts and proofs. There was hardly ever a night that he didn't bring work home with him, or go back to the office after dinner to take up where he had left off between six and seven o'clock. The Cather-Erskine confusion was never cleared up. We just let it die there.

Among the writers Mencken liked to talk about—I had listened to him several times while he smoked an after-breakfast cigar in the Rose Room of the Algonquin—were Cabell and Dreiser, about whom Ross could have had nothing to say, and Sinclair Lewis and Scott Fitzgerald. The *New Yorker* files reveal only two pieces by Lewis, both printed in 1937, one of them a "That Was New York" article and the other a profile of an imaginary character called Effie Kayshus. Fitzgerald (whom Mencken fondly called Fitz) is represented in the files by three casuals and two poems. Faulkner, Dos Passos, and Mencken's great friend Hergesheimer never wrote for the magazine, for Ross did not seek big established names. Thomas Wolfe sent in three pieces, unsolicited, which were bought, but Hemingway contributed only one, a short parody of Frank Harris's autobiography, away back in 1927 when the author of *The Sun Also Rises* was just another writer to Ross. Mencken had once described the Hemingway stories of *In Our*

Time as "cloacal," a judgment he never modified. He and Ross might well have been of one mind about *Death in the Afternoon,* which had been reviewed for the *New Yorker* by Robert M. Coates when he was its book critic. After reading the review, Ross had phoned Coates in the country to say, "Woollcott tells me there's a hell of a bad word in the book—bathroom stuff." Coates wanted to know what the word was. "I can't tell you over the phone," Ross said.

About American novels Mencken could talk endlessly—he thought *Tom Sawyer* and *Babbitt* were the best—but Ross was soon lost and floundering. He had said to me, after reading Peter De Vries's accurate parody of Faulkner, "Does Faulkner still write this way?" The sentence structure and punctuation dismayed him, and he could have got little further in any Faulkner than in Joyce's *Ulysses.* He was always wary of his own book department, approaching it with curiosity, respect, and trepidation, the way I once saw a Scottie approach a turtle. He couldn't understand why one critic refused to review the last of the Thomas Mann "Joseph" books, and I tried to explain that the distinguished man of letters then serving as literary critic for us had not read the others in the series or the body of Mann's work. "I don't care about the body," Ross said. "I don't see what that has to do with it." To him, a new novel whose publication had been heralded and talked about had a timely news value. Clifton Fadiman, the *New Yorker's* book reviewer for ten years, was probably the one with whom Ross felt most at ease. The editor had been attracted by Fadiman's lively and penetrating essay on Ring Lardner in the *Nation* and had hired him in 1933 when Robert Coates dropped out as critic.

"I agreed in part with Ross that books are news," Fadiman has told me. "I always reviewed a book on publication, even when I was reviewing as many as thirty a week; and I never considered that a book should be a springboard for personal theorizing." Ross probably did not concur in Fadiman's belief that the key to Lardner was to be found in "his ability, even talent, for hating," for Ross had a deep affection for Lardner, as well as great admiration. He once told me, "I asked Lardner the other day how he writes his short stories, and he said he wrote a few widely separated words or phrases on a piece of paper and then went back and filled in the spaces." Ross had fallen for one of the great humorist's famous deadpan gags. Fitzgerald wrote of his close friend Ring, "He had a face like a cathedral." Lardner had obviously turned his somber Gothic gaze upon Ross and made him believe the nonsense about his method of composition. Ross's keen, almost boyish, enthusiasm for novel bits of information could disarm, for a while, his mature shrewdness and skepticism which, on clear days when the mental visibility was good, functioned as sharply as any man's.

Ross was unembarrassed by his ignorance of the great novels of any country, and one of the indestructible items of Rossiana tells how he stuck his head into the checking department of the magazine one day to ask, "Is Moby Dick the whale or the man?"

When he found out that I had spent several months writing a parody of Henry James and heard that Edmund Wilson had suggested I send it to the *Atlantic*—I had already promised it to Cyril Connolly for his now defunct *Horizon* in England—he said he wanted to read it. He gave it back a few days later with a sigh, saying, "I only understood fifteen per cent of the allusions." But he printed a nostalgic piece I had written after rereading James's *The Ambassadors* and what Ross might have called Willa Cather's *The Private Life of a Lost Lady*. It had interested him even though he had no knowledge of Madame de Vionnet or of Marian Forrester. "It's about a man and two women," he said, "and it comes over." If a literary essay had a narrative scheme that held his attention, it got by, but he kept a bludgeon ever handy for the literary exercise or *tour de force*. "Nobody's going to make me arty," he would say. "This is not the old *Dial*."

Ross's general reading was like a trip into darkest Confusia, without a map. It had neither discipline nor direction. He talked, fitfully and at long intervals, about Twain's *Life on the Mississippi*, the short stories of O. Henry, especially "The Ransom of Red Chief," Jack London, certain war books, H. G. Wells—not the novels—the memoirs of doctors and surgeons, *True Detective* magazine, a book about the migration of eels, whose way of life never lost its fascination for him, and Kipling—not the poems. (He said once to a secretary of his, "Never leave me alone with poets.") Sometime during the thirties, in a memo complimenting his literary editor, Gus Lobrano, on a deft piece of rewriting, he said, "This is a swell job. Kipling couldn't have done it better."

One afternoon Sherwood Anderson was brought into Ross's office and introduced to the editor. On such occasions, when there was time, Ross was briefed by one of us as to the nature and stature of a visiting author's work—not that it ever did much good. Ross stood in awe and reverence of no writer. He had been through too much with too many of them. I am sure that, after the introduction, he said, "Hi, Anderson," in his large freewheeling way, and then launched into whatever came into his mind. This meeting was notable for one of his reckless literary pronouncements: "There hasn't been a good short story writer in America, Anderson, since O. Henry died." I wasn't there and I don't know how this affected Anderson, but he later sold Ross five short stories.

I was present, though, when Ross met Paul Nash, having ushered the English painter into the editor's office myself one morning in 1931. The day before, I had explained to Ross that Nash was on his way to Pittsburgh to serve as one of the three foreign judges of the annual Carnegie Exhibition of Modern Art, but had stopped over in New York to meet Otto Soglow, Milt Gross, and other favorite cartoonists of his, for he was easily admirer-in-chief of American comic art and artists. I had also told Ross that Nash was a keen collector of human curiosa, and had long wanted to talk with the editor of the *New Yorker*.

"Hi, Nash," Ross began. "There are only two phony arts, painting and music." Nash was a man of humor and imagination, whose eyes twinkled, and never darkened, when outrageous opinion raised its aggressive head. He was pretty good at holding untenable positions himself. When Nash and I finally left Ross's office, the Englishman said, "He is like your skyscrapers. They are unbelievable, but there they are."

Ross's knowledge of the two phony arts was, it is safe to say, flimsy. I never heard of his going to a show of paintings, and he would have been as unhappy at a symphony concert as at a lecture on dialectical materialism. He had certainly encountered modern painting in colored reproductions and on the walls of the apartments of some of his friends and acquaintances, but he must have viewed them disconsolately, as if they were jumbled paragraphs of prose that needed straightening

out. Nobody ever heard him sing, or even hum, a single bar of any song, and whistling set his teeth on edge. "His mind is uncluttered by culture," said a man at the Players Club, during one of those impromptu panel discussions of Harold Ross that often began when writers and artists got together. "That's why he can give prose and pictures the benefit of the clearest concentration of any editor in the world." It wasn't as simple as that, for there was more than clear concentration behind the scowl and the searchlight glare that he turned on manuscripts, proofs, and drawings. He had a sound sense, a unique, almost intuitive perception of what was wrong with something, incomplete or out of balance, understated or overemphasized. He reminded me of an army scout riding at the head of a troop of cavalry who suddenly raises his hand in a green and silent valley and says, "Indians," although to the ordinary eye and ear there is no faintest sign or sound of anything alarming. Some of us writers were devoted to him, a few disliked him heartily, others came out of his office after conferences as from a side show, a juggling act, or a dentist's office, but almost everybody would rather have had the benefit of his criticism than that of any other editor on earth. His opinions were voluble, stabbing, and grinding, but they succeeded somehow in refreshing your knowledge of yourself and renewing your interest in your work.

Having a manuscript under Ross's scrutiny was like putting your car in the hands of a skilled mechanic, not an automotive engineer with a bachelor of science degree, but a guy who knows what makes a motor go, and sputter, and wheeze, and sometimes come to a dead stop; a man with an ear for the faintest body squeak as well as the loudest engine rattle. When you first gazed, appalled, upon an uncorrected proof of one of your stories or articles, each margin had a thicket of queries and complaints—one writer got a hundred and forty-four on one profile. It was as though you beheld the works of your car spread all over the garage floor, and the job of getting the thing together again and making it work seemed impossible. Then you realized that Ross was trying to make your Model T or old Stutz Bearcat into a Cadillac or Rolls-Royce. He was at work with the tools of his unflagging perfectionism, and, after an exchange of growls or snarls, you set to work to join him in his enterprise.

Ross's marginal questions and comments were sometimes mere quibbling or hairsplitting, and a few of them invariably revealed his profound ignorance in certain areas of life and learning and literature, while others betrayed his pet and petty prejudices. You had to wade through these and ignore them, as you did his occasional brief marginal essays on unrelated or completely irrelevant subjects. One or two of his trusted associate editors would sometimes intercept a proof and cross out the impertinent and immaterial Rossisms, but I always insisted that they be left in, for they were the stains and labels of a Ross that never ceased to amuse me.

The blurs and imperfections his scout's eye always caught drew from his pencil such designations as *unclear, repetition, cliché, ellipsis,* and now and then blunter words. He knew when you had tired and were writing carelessly, and when you were "just monkeying around here," or going out on a limb, or writing fancy, or showing off. His "Who he?" became famous not only in the office but outside, and ten years ago was the title of a piece on Ross written by Henry Pringle. Joe Liebling once had "Who he?" painted on the door of his office, to the bewilderment of strangers who wondered what kind of business Liebling could be in. Sometimes this query put a careful finger on someone who had not been clearly identified, and at other times it showed up the gaps in Ross's knowledge of historical, contemporary, or literary figures. (He once said that only two names were familiar to every reader in the civilized world: Houdini and Sherlock Holmes.)

I remember that Ross once told me, after reading a casual of mine, "You must have dropped about eight lines out of this in your final rewrite." The thing ran smoothly enough, it seemed to me when I reread it in his office, but I went back and checked my next to last draft. Ross had been wrong. I had dropped only seven lines.

When he worked on a manuscript or proof, he was surrounded by dictionaries, which he constantly consulted, along with one of his favorite books, Fowler's *Modern English Usage*. He learned more grammar and syntax from Fowler than he had ever picked up in his somewhat sketchy school days. He read the *Oxford English Dictionary* the way other men read fiction, and he sometimes delved into a volume of the *Britannica* at random. One of the funniest moments in Wolcott Gibbs's *Season in the Sun* showed the actor who played Ross calmly looking up the word "hurricane" in *Webster's Unabridged* while the advance gales of a real hurricane swept toward him like a cavalry charge.

When Ross got up from his desk late in the afternoon, with a deep reluctant sigh, often after everybody else had left, for he always hated to stop work and turn to the affairs of the outside world that had been designed to wear him down, he sometimes found that he had a dinner and theater date with his wife or a friend or colleague. One night Wolcott Gibbs took him to see the Old Vic Company's production of *King Henry IV, Part II*. Ross wore an attitude of discomfort at plays, and you felt that he might get up at any moment and start pacing the aisle, ironing out some office problem in his mind. He often seemed more antagonist than spectator. On this particular night it was raining and he "had an umbrella and rubbers and a wet trench coat in addition to that briefcase," Gibbs remembers. "Everything kept dropping off his lap." Ross was annoyed by the female character called Rumour, whose long speech opens the play, and Gibbs recalls that the aggrieved Ross said to him, "What kind of writer would put in a dame like that just to muck me up?" As in his editing, he looked first for faults and flaws, and he would have been more amused by

Falstaff if he hadn't been upset by two characters in the play named Bardolph.

The editor's curious critical awareness, likely to strike from any quarter, pounced upon the lightly confessed promiscuity of the heroine of *The Voice of the Turtle*. A few days after we had gone to see it together, he asked me if I would want my daughter to attend the play. I said she wasn't old enough to understand it, and he snapped, "I mean if she were sixteen or seventeen." I said certainly, why not? "Because the girl stands up there and admits she has slept with several men she wasn't married to," said Ross.

"Compared to the amorous activities of certain persons we could hit from here with this ash tray," I told him, "the characters in that play are virtuous to the point of chastity."

"I don't want to hear any names," growled Ross, and he turned away.

He never gave up going to the theater, but as the years went on, he practically had to be dragged to opening nights, because he knew and would have to talk to almost everybody in the audience. I think he was comforted by Mencken's overt opposition to the stage as a medium that distorted human life and magnified the distortions. And yet a great many of Harold Ross's closest friends were theater people—actors and actresses, playwrights, directors, and producers. Jed Harris at one time was a crony of his, and once Ross actually began writing a profile of his friend, but he never got past the first page. In the old days you might meet at his apartment one or more of half a hundred theater people whom he liked and admired, including Noel Coward, Harpo and Groucho Marx, Bert Lahr, Bert Wheeler and Bob Woolsey, Joe Cook and Dave Chasen, S. N. Behrman, Charles MacArthur and Helen Hayes and Ben Hecht, Beatrice Lillie, Madge Kennedy, Phyllis Povah, Ina Claire—the list seems endless as I begin recalling the names. Men and women of outstanding importance in the theater, all good friends of Harold Ross, dominated the list of ten advisory editors who got up the prospectus for the *New Yorker* in the winter of 1924, several months before the magazine was first published in February, 1925. This informal board of advisers consisted of Ralph Barton, Heywood Broun, Marc Connelly, Edna Ferber, Rea Irvin, George S. Kaufman, Alice Duer Miller, Dorothy Parker, Laurence Stallings, and Alexander Woollcott. Rea Irvin, who remained the magazine's chief art adviser for many years, had been an actor, and a good one, before he turned to cartooning. A few of the others became well-known contributors—Ralph Barton, Dorothy Parker, Woollcott—but the editorship of all except Irvin was purely nominal.

I don't know who wrote the prospectus, but the old museum piece bears neither the stamp of Ross's hand nor, read aloud, the sound of Ross's voice. Only one sentence has survived the years: "The *New Yorker* will be the magazine which is not edited for the old lady in Dubuque."

The *New Yorker* was, whatever else, first and foremost the magazine of the young man from Aspen. Many helped him, a little or a lot, in the trial take-offs of his frail craft. Its name was suggested, I am told, by John Peter Toohey; John Hanrahan, a professional counselor in such matters, is said to have staffed the business and advertising departments; and Raoul Fleischmann, as everybody knows, rashly financed and kept refinancing the infant project; but the hand on the editorial controls was the stubborn, impulsive hand of H. W. Ross, who was by no means absolutely sure where he was going in his tremulous flying machine, but knew he would recognize the place when he got there. The boy from Aspen, Colorado, finally came in for a landing, and I was glad to join him and to be one of the lucky men who went along with him on his adventures for a quarter of a century that went too fast and ended too soon.

5

The Talk of the Town

One of the already well-established rituals aboard the New Yorker when I joined its jittery crew in the wayward weather of 1927 was what skipper Harold Ross, alternately dauntless ("Don't give up the ship!") and despairing (" 'We are lost!' the captain shouted.") called the weekly Talk meeting. I survived hundreds of them—physically, at any rate. Named for "The Talk of the Town," the front-of-the-book department that was Ross's favorite and gloomiest preoccupation in the early years, the Wednesday morning meetings rambled on for anywhere from one to three hours, depending upon the mood of the master.

When Ross's secretary informed him that the rest of us— Katharine Angell, Andy White, Ralph Ingersoll, and I—were gathered around the table in the meeting room, Ross would saunter in, sometimes with the expression of a man who has heard an encouraging word but oftener with the worried brow of a bloodhound that is not only off the scent but is afraid it's losing its sense of smell. ("You're lousing up your metaphors," I can hear Ross grumbling. "Now you got a goddam blood-hound commanding a ship!") He would plop his briefcase on the table, sit down, sigh darkly, and open the meeting with some pronouncement, either a small fact about a big man:

"William Randolph Hearst still has all his teeth," or a derogatory comment about an institution: "Medical science doesn't even know how to cure dandruff," or a running broad jump to some despondent conclusion: "Maude Adams lives in town now, but I haven't got anybody that can find out what she does and where she goes and who she sees."

Then the regular order of business began with a safari through the darkest regions ("Now, by God, I'm Stanley!") of the X issue, the one that would reach the stands the following day. It never satisfied Ross, and it rarely put him in a good humor. There weren't enough laughs in Talk, or any interesting facts; two drawings in the issue were too much alike; and "White and Thurber both mentioned novocain in their casuals. We're getting neurotic."

There was always, tossed in somewhere, a brief lecture about something: the lack of journalistic sense in the female of our species, everybody's ignorance of the rules of grammar and syntax, the wasting talent of a certain artist who was making a career of sex, or the incompetence of some doctor who was treating a friend of Ross's. He affected a disdain for doctors and other professional men, and once when I introduced him to a great eye surgeon, he shook hands with him and said, "I have little respect for professional men." He actually had great respect for this particular doctor, and for several others, but his rude generalization was prompted by the little boy in him, or the partly educated adult envious of specialized training and skeptical of technical knowledge, or some orneriness of mood aggravated by the peptic ulcers that bothered him during the last thirty years of his life. Alexander Woollcott explained the ungracious phase of the fabulous editor in ten words: "Ross has the utmost contempt for anything he doesn't understand."

Ross had a kind of mental file of prejudices and antipathies, some momentary, others permanent, and most of them of unrevealed origin. At one Talk meeting he scrawled on a memo pad "Hate Southerners," handed it to Ingersoll, and growled, "Keep bringing that up every week." It was brought up every week until Nancy Hoyt wrote a sharp satirical piece about a fictional Southern girl. Ross liked and admired many Southerners, among them Laurence Stallings and Nunnally ("Where I come from the Tobacco Road people are the country club set") Johnson. In 1926 Johnson had told Ross he would like to review motion pictures for the magazine. "For God's sake, why?" Ross demanded. "Movies are for old ladies and fairies. Write me some pieces." Ross had early conceived a violent dislike of movies, and hoped his cinema critic would have at them with a cudgel. His feeling was moderated somewhat after he saw *Public Enemy* and *Viva Villa*. On several visits to Hollywood he became a friend of James Cagney and Frank Capra, among others, and, a dozen of his letters prove, tried for years to interest Hollywood producers in my "The Secret Life of Walter Mitty," whose film possibilities he was the first to detect.

Ross almost never got through a Talk meeting without contriving to make Ingersoll say something to irritate him. When Ingersoll suggested a dope piece about the enormous ball that surmounts the Paramount building, Ross glared at him and snarled, "I wouldn't print a piece about that ball if Lord Louis Mountbatten were living in it." On another Wednesday, when Ingersoll told him, "I have the stuff you wanted on Thaw," Ross's eyes brightened darkly. Ingersoll always pronounced *Thaw* as if it were *Thor,* and Ross knew this, but he said, "I don't want a piece about Thor, or Mercury, or any of the other Greek gods." Ingersoll was the main target of his gripes, and I was next. "There isn't a single laugh in the Talk of the Town," he snapped one day, and I snapped back, "You say that every week," and he snarled, "Well, there are even fewer this time." Ross was not Ross until he had churned the hour, any hour, into a froth of complaint and challenge, and this was part of the inexhaustible, propulsive force of the magazine. I took up the challenge about Maude Adams, and a few days later laid on his desk her private phone number and enough data on her goings and doings for two separate pieces in "Talk of the Town." Ross stared at the stuff as if it had been dug up by a little child, and all he said was, "Well, I'll be damned!" It was a long time before he accepted me as a dependable reporter, but I was used to this because I had had the same experience of trial by ordeal with three different city editors of newspapers.

Russell Maloney, who took over from me in 1935 the task of writing most of Talk, once wrote in the *Saturday Review* that Harold Ross regarded perfection as his personal property, like his hat or his watch. This observation could be carried further without straining its soundness. In the first few years of his magazine Ross sometimes had as many as three men, in separate offices, writing pieces for Talk, each one unaware of the competition of the others. Most of them "went out like matches in the wind of Ross's scorn," as Ralph Ingersoll once put it. When the editor of the *New Yorker* became convinced that writers did not possess the perfection that was rightfully coming to him, out they went. Even when he decided that a writer probably did have his perfection, he liked to believe the fellow would never come across with it. He always hoped he would find perfection lying on his desk when he came to work, but he was pretty sure there would be no such luck.

Fifteen years ago I brought him a sheaf of some miscellaneous writings by Peter De Vries, whom I had met in Chicago, where he was then editor of *Poetry,* and told Ross I had found a perfect *New Yorker* writer. He stared at the material glumly, and said, "I'll read it, but it won't be funny and it won't be well written." Two hours later he called me into his office. Hope had risen like a full moon and shone in his face. "How can I get DeVree on the phone?" he demanded, his enthusiasm touched with excitement. Not many days after that Ross and I had lunch at the Algonquin with Peter DeVree—the name had become wedged in Ross's mind as French, not Dutch, and he was sure the sibilant should go unsounded, as in *debris,* and he never got it straightened out. I had warned Pete, since I was a veteran of such first meetings, that Ross's opening question might go off in any direction, like an unguided missile. "Hi, DeVree," said Ross as they shook hands. "Could you do the Race Track department?" This was the kind of irrelevancy I had in mind, and Pete was prepared for it. "No," he said, "but I can imitate a wounded gorilla." He had once imitated a wounded gorilla on a radio program in Chicago. Ross glared at me, realizing I had briefed De Vries, and then his slow lasting grin spread over his face. "Well, don't imitate it around the office," he growled amiably. "The place is a zoo the way it is." Thirty years ago Ross would probably have opened up on De Vries with "Maybe you could run the magazine" or "Could you write the Talk department?"

Ross couldn't have described perfection, because his limited vocabulary got tangled up in his fluency ("I don't want you to think I'm not incoherent," he once rattled off to somebody in "21"), but he recognized it when he saw it. He handled White's invaluable contributions as if they were fine crystal, and once stuck this note in Andy's typewriter: "I am encouraged to go on." Surely no other editor has ever been lost and saved so often in the course of a working week. When his heart leaped up, it leaped a long way, because it started from so far down, and its commutings over the years from the depths to the heights made Ross a specialist in appreciation. In spite of preliminary ordeal, of which there was always plenty, it became a pleasure to write for a man whose praise was so warm and genuine when it came. Dozens of us cherish old memos from him, and letters, and the memory of phone calls, and it is surprising how quickly they come to mind. I often remember a single sentence he scribbled and sent to me about one of the drawings I had done, illustrating Leigh Hunt's "The Glove and the Lions." It read, "It's the goddamdest lion fight ever put on paper." But this is about "Talk of the Town," of whose significant figures White was perhaps the most important, because of his superb handling of the first, or editorial, page of that department.

Elwyn Brooks White, who had been God's gift to the Cornell *Sun* and to that university's English professors, gentlemen used to perfection in books but not in classroom themes, was getting thirty dollars a week writing automobile advertising in New York when Ross's magazine began. He sold Ross his first piece two months later, and then half a dozen light verses and some more "oddities," as he calls them. He did not meet Ross until after he was hired by Katharine Angell in the fall of 1926. I might as well admit, right here, that I have done a lot of brooding about the mystery that some literary scholars have wrought out of, to quote one of them, the central paradox of Harold Ross's nature; that is, his magic gift of surrounding himself with some of the best talent in America, despite his own literary and artistic limitations. Without detracting from his greatness as an editor, it must be pointed out that the very nature of his magazine, formless and haphazard though it was to begin with, did most of the attracting. Writers and artists of the kind Ross was looking for decided that here was a market for their wares, and to say that the head of such an enterprise, personally unknown to most of those who came to work for him, was the attracting force is to say that the candle, and not the flame, attracts the moths. I think the moths deserve most of the credit for discovering the flame.

White "brought the steel and music to the magazine," according to Marc Connelly, famous among his colleagues for such offhand lyrical flights. Others, White among them, have not been quite so definite about what it was that the *New Yorker*'s "number one wheel horse" (Ingersoll's phrase) brought to the magazine from Cornell by way of the advertising business. In 1926 White began working part time for the *New Yorker* at thirty dollars a week. "I hung on to my advertising connection because I had no confidence in my ability in the world of letters," White has written me. "Nothing that has happened in the last thirty years has shaken my lack of confidence—which is why I still hang on to newsbreaks." Nobody else in the world of letters shares White's lack of confidence in White.

Andy quickly cured one of Ross's early persistent head-aches, caused by the problem of newsbreaks, those garbled and often hilarious items from American journals and magazines which conveniently fill out, or "justify," *New Yorker* columns. For more than thirty years White has written the taglines for these slips of the linotype machine, and some thirty thousand of them have brightened the *New Yorker*'s pages. Nobody else, and many have tried, ever caught the difficult knack of writing the tags, or inventing the various newsbreak categories such as "Raised Eyebrows Department," "Neatest Trick of the Week," and a score of others. My one contribution to the categories was "How's That Again? Department," but I was baffled by the task of writing taglines.

Once when White was on vacation I tried my hand at it, and it turned out to have five thumbs. I invented a phony newsbreak, to see if I could get it past Ross. The item, which I credited to a mythical newspaper, went like this: "Oswego, New York, birthplace of William Tecumseh Sherman, has no monument or other memorial to the great Civil War general." Under this I had written, "Oswego marching through Georgia?" Sherman, of course, was born in Ohio, and this fact flickered into flame in the back of Ross's mind when the issue containing the fake break came out. Then he checked the newspaper and found out I had made it up. He banged into my office crying, "Goddam it, Thurber, don't kid around with the newsbreaks."

It would be like hunting for a broken needle in a hayfield to try to find a given newsbreak published long ago, and I doubt that even Miss Ebba Jonsson, the *New Yorker*'s incomparable librarian, could locate my own favorite newsbreak in the roughly seventeen hundred issues of the weekly that have been published so far. Fortunately it was printed in 1931 in a little book of *New Yorker* newsbreaks, called *Ho Hum,* with a foreword by White and drawings by Soglow. It goes like this:

> The Departure of Clara Adams
> [From the Burbank (Cal.) Post]
> Among the first to enter was Mrs. Clara Adams of Tannersville, Pa., lone woman passenger. Slowly her nose was turned around to face in a southwesterly direction, and away from the hangar doors. Then, like some strange beast, she crawled along the grass.

Ross had been in the habit of peddling the newsbreaks around the office, letting everybody try his hand at writing lines of comment to round them out. White turned in his first batch one day in the fall of 1926, and then went out to his parents' home in Mount Vernon, New York, where he came down with chicken pox. Ross instantly knew he had found the one and only man who could handle newsbreaks perfectly, and he got White on the phone in Mount Vernon. "I had never heard such a loud voice over any telephone," White wrote me, "and I had never been encouraged before by an employer, so it was a memorable occasion. Then Ross asked me to come right back into the office and I had to tell him I had chicken pox. 'You have *what?*' bellowed Ross." It was one of those innumerable petty irritations that bedeviled him in his early life as an editor. He just couldn't believe that he had at last found someone who was willing to endure the boredom and triviality and fine print of newsbreaks—and then this man had contracted a child's disease. It was the kind of experience that used to make him bang his hand on the table and scream, "That's my life!"

The handling of newsbreaks, White and Ross soon found, had its special perplexities, of the kind that made the editor nervous: a couple, instead of a coupé, found in a ditch; a hippy in place of a happy bride; a ship's captain who collapsed on the bride, instead of the bridge, during a storm at sea; and a certain percentage of items skillfully counterfeited. There were also a few fanatics who made a hobby, or even a lifework, out of reading newspapers and sending in breaks, and most of them were touchy and temperamental. One of these career men wrote, "Do not put paper clips on my rejections. They leave marks." This complaint happened to Andy on a gloomy day. He poured Glyco-Thymoline on the breaks, instead of putting clips on them, and a few days later showed me a letter from the newsbreaker, thanking him for his care. "That's *my* life," said White.

White's "Notes and Comment," the first page of "Talk of the Town," through the years has left its firm and graceful imprint on American letters, and every now and then has exerted its influence upon local, or even wider, affairs. It was responsible for the moving of the information booth in the Pennsylvania Station out into the center of the main floor; for the changing of the lights, from colored to white, in the tower of the Empire State Building; and for directing attention to the captive audiences in Grand Central Station, where passengers had been forced to listen to broadcast commercials. This practice was officially abandoned after hearings by the Public Service Commission. The editor made few public appearances in his lifetime, but this was one of his finest hours, and he enjoyed every minute of it. It was White, though, who had inaugurated the campaign to free the captives of commercialism.

"Notes and Comment," called simply "Comment," did more than anything else to set the tone and cadence of the *New Yorker* and to shape its turns of thought, and White's skill in bringing this page to the kind of perfection Ross had dreamed of intensified Ross's determination to make Talk the outstanding department of the magazine. It was a great help when God sent him an efficient and tireless young reporter named Charles

H. Cooke, the magazine's first "Our Mr. Stanley," who was often up at dawn and abroad at midnight, digging up data.

The prospectus had declared, "The *New Yorker* will be what is commonly called sophisticated, in that it will assume a reasonable degree of enlightenment on the part of its readers." Ross found it hard to keep in mind this assumption of enlightenment, and sometimes seemed to be editing Talk for a little boy or an old lady whose faculties were dimming. When I used *axe-haft,* Ross followed it, in parentheses, with "the haft is the handle of the axe." His profound uneasiness in the presence of anything smacking of scholarship or specialized knowledge is perpetuated in dozens of small changes he made in my copy. In the following excerpt from a Talk piece, which I wrote after a visit to the Metropolitan Museum, I have italicized his insertions: "For those who exclaim over armour, *a thing pretty rare with us,* the three new suits the museum has just come by will prove enthralling. One of them, a righly ornamented Spanish war harness, has more pieces of réchange, *or you might say accessories,* than any other battle suit in the world. . . . Among other prizes of the New Accession Room is the lid of an amphora, *but we never did find out what an amphora is.*" In another Talk item about the demands upon his hosts of the difficult and imperious Count Keyserling, I wrote that he had to have, around midnight, after his lecture, "champagne or claret," and Ross had to explain to his sophisticated readers that claret was "French red wine," so they would not confuse it with its prizering meaning of "blood."

Harold Wallace Ross, who secretly enjoyed being thought of as raconteur and man about town, was scared to death of being mistaken for a connoisseur, or an aesthete, or a scholar, and his heavy ingenuous Colorado hand was often laid violently upon anything that struck him as "intellectual." Thus his avid mental curiosity balked at whatever seemed to him redolent of learning. I find I once wrote of him in a letter to White, "What are you going to do about a man who would rather listen to Jim Farley discuss Coca-Cola than to Robert Frost describing rings of lantern light?"

Ross had the enthusiasm of a youngster at a circus for a thousand different things, but none of them was in the realm of the recondite or the academic. One day, a year before he died, I brought him together at the Algonquin with an old friend of mine who had never met him but had always been eager to find out what he was like. Ross launched immediately into a breathless discussion of his enthusiasm of the moment, the history of Bull Durham tobacco. My friend sat entranced for a quarter of an hour and, after Ross had departed, exclaimed, "He's a Gee Whiz guy!" Ross was fascinated by facts and statistics about the big and costly, but he didn't like his facts bare and stark; he wanted them accompanied by comedy— you unwrapped the laugh and there was the fact, or maybe vice versa.

The Gee Whiz Guy was forever enchanted by the size and saga of the fabulous city's great buildings. He had long wanted a profile on Jacob Volk, a building wrecker out of Herculean mythology, who tore down two hundred and fifty big struc-

tures in Manhattan during his lifetime and never passed the Woolworth Building but what he dreamed of the joys of razing it. I had wanted the piece for Talk, where it seemed to me it belonged, but Ross assigned Robert Coates to do the profile. (Ross also took Shipwreck Kelley, the flagpole sitter, away from me and profiled him. These enlargements into profiles of snapshots that belonged in Talk marked the beginning of Ross's interest in long pieces instead of sharp vignettes.) I got Jake Volk for Talk, in spite of Ross, because the famous wrecker died while the Coates profile was in the works, and we never ran profiles about dead men. I broke the sad news to the editor. "Dammit," mourned Ross, "why couldn't he have waited a week?" Ross believed that God and nature owed the *New Yorker* a reasonable amount of consideration in the matter of life and death. We laid Jake Volk to rest in "Talk of the Town," which dealt with the dead as well as the quick.

He had died two months before another wrecker began taking down the old Waldorf, on whose site the Empire State Building was erected. The original Waldorf was a toughly constructed building, and the wrecker who took it apart was paid nine hundred thousand dollars for the job—old Jake had paid for the privilege of tearing structures down, and made his profit by selling intact sections, but the debris of the Waldorf was all taken out to sea and dumped. I wrote about the last day of the famous hotel, and eighteen months later climbed the still unfinished tower of the Empire State.

Jake shook his head at mention of Stanford White. "When he built 'em they stayed built," he would say sadly. One that stayed built has been made over into apartments for fifteen or twenty families. It's the great Italian Renaissance mansion in East 73rd Street where Joseph Pulitzer spent his last years and died without ever having been in forty-five of its sixty rooms. My bones still feel the cold of the mansion's deserted sprawl of rooms and halls littered with trash and covered with dust when I shivered in them one wintry day in 1934. The legends of

Pulitzer and Stanford White are growing dim, but the famous mansion is as staunch as ever. I trust that the ghost of Jacob Volk, seeming to munch one of the caviar sandwiches he so loved, does not mournfully stalk the corridors of the old mansion just off Fifth Avenue.

In Columbus, or in France, or for the *Evening Post,* I had interviewed many celebrities: Eddie Rickenbacker, who had little to say; General Pershing, who had nothing to say; Harry Sinclair, who mumbled tonelessly; Thomas A. Edison, who kept repeating, "The radio will always distort the soprano voice." Interviews for "Talk of the Town" were easier, because most of the characters of that period were colorful and voluble: Jimmy Walker, always eager to say something; Al Smith, a born speaker; Huey Long, who paced the four rooms of his hotel suite delivering a political speech for an hour to an audience that consisted of me; Jack Johnson, who talked about himself in the third person—"Jack Johnson don't approve of the immorality of the Broadway theater." If the principal celebrities of the time were to be seeded, like tennis players, on the basis of number of mentions each got in Talk, the listing of the first seven would go like this: Jimmy Walker 63, Al Smith 60, Calvin Coolidge 43; Lindbergh 33, J. P. Morgan 29, Gene Tunney 25, Otto Kahn 21. Ross once tacked an order on the bulletin board which read: "Otto Kahn has been mentioned six times in Talk recently. There will be no more mentions of him for six months." Ross was sternly opposed to anecdotes about the Algonquin group, and when an excellent one required the use of the name Alexander Woollcott, he cursed awhile and said, "I'll tell you what we'll do—we'll misspell it," and we left out one of the "l's." He worried about overmention of others, too: Admiral Byrd, Rudy Vallee, Grover Whalen, and Fiorello La Guardia.

Harold Ross, ever hot for certainties in this our life, was also, being a true newspaperman, avid of exclusive stories for Talk. It wasn't easy, though, to get them, because of the danger of their being leaked out between press time and publication day. Once we broke to the world the news of the vast Rockefeller Center project, only to find that the world knew all about it. Alva Johnston had written it up in a Sunday newspaper article before we hit the stands. We did manage what I called in my lead "A little miracle of secrecy" in reporting the first meeting of Gene Tunney and Charles A. Lindbergh, which took place at the studio of the artist Charles Baskerville in 1928. Ross and Tunney had become friends during the *Stars and Stripes* days in France. Ross got a great kick out of making me believe for a time, after the Tunney-Lindbergh story, that I had been hoaxed and that no such meeting had taken place—he himself had been out of town when I wrote the piece. But Gene Tunney has recently verified the old meeting in a letter to me, which he ended with, "Hal Ross was a great American," and Mr. Baskerville, riffling through the years, recently found a photograph of himself and Tunney and Lindbergh taken that day at his studio.

Every press agent in town dreamed of getting into Talk by throwing his fast ball past Ross (one day a story reached my desk about a cockroach race at the Nut Club in Greenwich Village), but Ross was struck out only once, by, of all people, Texas Guinan. She telephoned him one day to say, in a fine imitation of breathless excitement, that Ella Wendel, last of the three wealthy Wendel sisters, who lived in the gaslit past in a mysterious Fifth Avenue mansion, had visited her night club, accompanied by two elderly gentlemen out of the carriage days of old Gotham. "She talked to me about it for half an hour," Ross told me. I stared at the wise old newspaperman in disbelief. "She talks to everybody for half an hour on the phone," I told him. "She talked to me for half an hour one day when I was on the *Post.*" Ross then went on to say that a few days after Miss Ella's visit Tex had received from her an elegant specially made handbag worth forty-five hundred dollars, to replace one given her by Larry Fay, which she had lost. "You can't believe that!" I yelled. "It's obviously a phony. Ask any woman you know, ask any little girl." But Ross ordered me to write the story—I told him he would have to make it an order—and it was printed, and Miss Wendel's attorneys called on Ross and demanded a retraction of the story. H. W. Ross gave up hard. He sent out three different reporters to call on every handbag maker in the East, and they all came back with the word that he had been royally humbugged.

One of the clearest pictures in my mental memory book of the old days is that of Ross pounding away on his typewriter, trying, by speed and finger power, to get facility and felicity into his writing of Talk. "It should be like dinner-table conversation," he used to repeat, but although he could be an entertaining dinner-table conversationalist, he was unable to hammer it into written prose. This was because he became an unreal Ross when he tried writing for the magazine, a strained and artificial personality, completely different from the undisguised and articulate one that still breathes in almost every line of the thousands of personal letters he wrote. He simply was not a *New Yorker* writer, never got better at it, and in the thirties gave it up, although he persisted in sticking into my copy now and then such pet expressions of his as "and such" and "otherwise." His "and such" spots old "Talk of the Town" pieces like flyspecks. It was his idea of achieving ease. In one story, "The studio walls are hung with oils and watercolors, with here and there a gouache and silverpoint" became "The studio walls are hung with oils and watercolors, and such." His sense of rhythm, often orally effective, failed him on the typed page.

Sometimes I secretly rewrote his clumsier rewrites of my Talk pieces and faked his R, which every piece of copy had to bear when it went to the printers. He was capable of awkward sentences that would have made him bellow if he had found them in someone else's copy; such a prize monstrosity, for instance, as "A man in a brown suit named Jones came into the room." Once he hastily changed "colloid" to "collide," and I sent him a note of reproof and told him to look up the word in the dictionary. He did and wrote back, "It's a hell of a complicated world." Our clashes over Talk, frequent and lengthy in the beginning, gradually quieted down with his increasing interest in other departments of the magazine. But the late twenties were full of scraps between us. When, as something of an expert on the haunts of O. Henry in his beloved Bagdad-on-the-Subway, I wrote that he had last lived at the Hotel Caledonia, 28 West 26th Street, Ross yelled that I was wrong. F.P.A. had told him that it was the Hotel Chelsea, and to Ross the great Frank Adams was infallible. He sent a reporter to City Hall to check the vital statistics on Porter, William Sidney, and then slouched into my room to say grudgingly, "Okay on the Caledonia, Thurber," not so much pleased that I had been right as sorry that Adams had been wrong. If I was a man who lost things, and he was sure I was, he couldn't understand how the hell I could get facts straight.

The harassed editor, always beset by anxieties, worried about the rigor mortis of formula in "Talk of the Town" style, the repetition of "a gentleman of our acquaintance," "a man we know," "a Park Avenue lady," and such. Anecdotes, of which we have printed thousands, many of them flat, some of them memorable, were like mosquitoes that pestered him continually. "Nobody in this whole goddam city seems to say anything funny except taxi drivers, children, and colored maids." "We get too damn many about telephones and Macy's." And he would stick up a notice on the bulletin board beseeching everybody to turn in some fresh anecdotes. Once he paced for days, off and on, wondering what to do about a story my brother had sent in from Columbus, Ohio, dealing with Calvin Coolidge. It seemed that Mr. Coolidge had lost a nightgown in a Pullman sleeper and had written the company asking that it be returned or that he be reimbursed for his loss. This one never did reach print, because Ross could not figure out how to "hang it," that is, how to account for our knowing about a fact that had originated in the Near Far West.

With rue my heart is laden for one anecdote printed in Talk. It reported an incident that occurred during a convention of monumentalists, or tombstone cutters, in White Plains. A local member of the craft had shown off his own handiwork during a tour of a cemetery with a visiting headstonist. As they left the cemetery, a whistling boy walked past them. "Son of that big granite job I showed you back there," said the White Plains man. Ross loved it and ruined it with his rewrite. He not only dragged Rotary into it, for no good reason, but tinkered clumsily with the pay-off line, so that it came out: "Son of that big granite and iron job I showed you back there." Ross had turned a deaf ear to the speech and, for all I know, may also have found out that there is always some ironwork in a granite monument.

When another superior anecdote was sent in—it is still known around the office to old-timers as the "grison anecdote"—I rewrote it and commanded Ross not to touch a single word. He read it, brought it into my office, said it was swell, looked as sad as if he had just lost a friend, and said, "Can't I please put a comma after 'My God'?" That comma, the record shows, is there. Here is the grison anecdote:

> The Harold Wilcoxes, of Nutley, New Jersey, have a grison, which they keep in a cage on their porch. A grison is a very odd-looking South American weasel-like carnivore. The other day a house-to-house salesman for a certain brand of dainty soap rang the bell (without noticing the grison) and Mrs. Wilcox answered. He launched right into his well-rehearsed praises of the soap, in the course of which he finally did see the grison. He blanched, but kept right on: "It preserves the fine texture of the most delicate skin and lends a lasting and radiant rosiness to the complexion my God, what *is* that thing?"

One day in 1931 Ross came into my office to say, after a lot of silent pacing, "Are we *important*?" The voice was not that of the man who had kept repeating a year before, "We're getting *grim*." I didn't encourage his implied ambition for higher things and longer pieces, but said, "We're just a fifteen-cent magazine." He left the room without saying anything, but half an hour later stuck his head in my door again. "I don't think so," he said, and went away.

The Talk meetings grew wearisome in the end and ran down like an old clock and stopped. "Thurber and White are sulky or surly or silent," Ross once told somebody, "and we're not getting anywhere."

Once, at meeting's end Ross said to me, "Have you got anything else to bring up, Thurber?" and I said I had, and I brought it up, and it turned out the others had just been discussing it. "Thurber is the greatest unlistener I know," Ross later complained. Then there was the day, very near the end, when I wrote doggerel during a meeting and shoved it across to White. Ross had figured I was making notes on something he had said, but the thing got into the magazine, I can't remember why, and there it is in the files, entitled "Bachelor Burton." It runs like this:

> Allen Lewis Brooksy Burton
> Went to buy himself a curtain,
> Called on Greenburg, Moe, and Mintz,
> Bought a hundred yards of chintz
> Stamped with owls and all star-spangled,
> Tried to hang it, fell, and strangled.

My eight years of wandering the city for Talk ended in 1935, and my last visit piece was about a melancholy stroll along 14th Street a few days before Christmas that year. It ends like this: "We missed this year the vendors of those old-fashioned German Christmas cards with the tinsel snow and the rich colors. There used to be several of them around, and a sad man who played 'O Little Town of Bethlehem' on a flute. Nobody seemed to know what had become of them." Most of the personalities of the Crazy Years between Lindbergh's flight and Hitler's heyday are dead and gone, and I had forgotten most of the tinsel snow and the colorful trivialities I gathered for "Talk of the Town" so long ago until I looked them up in the files the other day. There was a lot of stuff to hold the interest of the Gee Whiz Guy: Ely Culbertson pondering for forty-three minutes before playing a certain card in his celebrated bridge match with Sidney Lenz; the signature of Count Felix von Luckner, fourteen inches long and two inches high, in an enormous guest book; and an item about the thirty-six-ton meteorite that Admiral Peary brought back from Greenland and presented to the Museum of Natural History. "Gee-zus!" said Ross. "I hope they were expecting it."

There was always something to catch and hold his eager interest in the foibles, frailties, and wonders of human nature. When a certain toothpaste's "Beware of Pink Toothbrush" campaign was on, it pleased but did not surprise him when we found out that a drugstore on Broadway had received more than forty requests for pink toothbrushes in one week. He was

also tremendously amused when the Schrafft restaurants stopped selling Lucky Strikes because of the far-flung slogan, "Reach for a Lucky instead of a sweet," only to discover, at the end of the year, that the sale of all kinds of sweets had gone up, not down, as the result of the cigarette advertising.

There were, also, many things that made him scowl and fret. One week I nodded, and rewrote an anecdote that someone had stolen from Homer's *Odyssey*, one about the weary seafarer who starts walking inland with an oar over his shoulder and says he is going to keep going until he comes to a land where nobody knows what the thing is for, and there he will settle down. "Now Thurber's falling for anecdotes a thousand years old," Ross complained, after some classical scholar had written in about it. But I also caught several old ones that Ross had sent me to rewrite, among them the one about the little colored girl called Femily who, her parents told a visitor, had been named by the family doctor. The name which the doctor had put on the birth certificate was, as you may know, Female. Everybody knows now the story of the woman at the zoo who asked the caretaker, "Is that a male or a female hippopotamus?" to which the man replied, "Madam, I don't see how that could interest anybody except another hippopotamus." It was Harold Ross who brought that anecdote into my office, and it was the *New Yorker* that printed it first. Everybody in town stopped him and told him stories, and he became an expert in telling the old from the new. And how, in those years, he loved a fact—a great big glittering exclusive fact! When the King of Siam was operated on for cataract in 1933, Ross wanted to know if I could find out how much he had paid the great surgeon who performed the operation. He said it was rumored around town that the amount was as high as a hundred thousand dollars. It wasn't until about seven years later that I brought him this particular fact, and laid it on his desk. The chamberlain of the king had inquired of the surgeon's secretary what was the largest fee a commoner had ever paid him and was told the answer was ten thousand dollars. Thereupon the chamberlain wrote out a check for twenty thousand dollars and gave it to the secretary. The fact fascinated Ross, but the story was cold and seven years old, and he wouldn't use it.

Ross gradually lost his high interest in "Talk of the Town," but the best of it, carefully selected, would be a valuable record of the Wonderful Town in the bizarre second quarter of this century. In 1950 I wanted to write for Talk two or three pieces about Houdini, but Ross wrote me that he didn't want to "piddle Houdini away on Talk of the Town." This was the epitaph for the old journalistic department as I had known it. Four years earlier he had written me a letter that clearly reveals the dying of an old passion of his. It begins "Dear Jim." (Ross rarely called men by their first names in talking to them in the office, but he often used first names in letters, and at social gatherings at his apartment, and otherwise. Like me, both White and Gibbs were always a little surprised by the intimate salutation, and once Gibbs was disturbed. He had been in the hospital for several weeks, and Ross had visited him there. "I was about to have a third of my right lung taken out," Gibbs wrote me, "and, as I know now, without a very good chance of surviving the operation. He came to see me the afternoon before they were going to work on me, and he called me Wolcott, pronouncing it almost right, and I swear to God it was the first time it really occurred to me that I might be going to die. I called him Harold back, but it was quite an effort in my condition.") Here is the Ross letter, dated November 12, 1946:

The fault with Talk is mainly ideas. When you were doing the rewrite, we were getting better ideas. Shawn (peerless as an idea man) was on the job, and if I do say it myself, I was sparking some too. I was younger then. I've been very uneasy about the idea end of Talk for some time, now that the war is over and things aren't so obvious. I look over the ideas every week and am discouraged. If you should know of a man who can spark ideas, there's a job open for him, God knows.

It isn't true that there are many reporters. At the moment, we are weak there too, unless two or three absolutely new men should develop a flair, like Charles Cooke's (he also was peerless). We've had a couple of very good girls, but one got married and left town, and the other has gone on to working on longer pieces. We use reporters on long pieces more than we used to, but no more on Talk, I think, except for people trying out. We're trying to find young talent of all kinds and it's hard. And as to the writing, no one writer is making it a principal interest now, and I think that makes a difference. All the boys are doing Talk along with other things. Give me you, Shawn, and Cooke and I'll get out a Talk department. . . . It's up to God to send some young talent around this place, and He's been neglecting the job. That's the trouble.

When Ross wrote that, Bill Shawn, now editor of the *New Yorker,* was top man on the totem pole and remained there the rest of Ross's life, thus setting a world's endurance record. It was characteristic of H. W. Ross to forget that the two idea men in my day were Ralph Ingersoll and Bernard A. Bergman, who were never excelled, that Russel Crouse and Bob Coates had been two of the earliest and ablest Talk writers, and that the remarkable Haydie Eames Yates had been one of the first and liveliest reporters. Once, thirty years ago, I incorporated a line of her notes intact in one of my rewrites and sent it on to Ross. It was about a certain colorful celebrity and reported simply: "His love life seems as mixed up as a dog's breakfast." Ross blue-penciled it, of course, but the phrase remained a part of office lingo. As the years rode by, the love life of more and more *New Yorker* people became as mixed up as a dog's breakfast—but that's another story for another time.

Russel ("Buck") Crouse had been doing most of the Talk rewrite when I joined the staff. He would attend the Talk meetings, and then take a folder of stuff home with him to do in his spare time. As conductor of a column on the *Evening Post* called "Left at the Post" he had a job he didn't want to give up for the full-time anonymity of Talk, which in those days was signed *"The New Yorkers."* When Ross piled most of the Talk rewrite on me, in addition to my other work, he decided to save money by letting Crouse go and, as often happened, he did this while Crouse was on vacation. It wasn't until Buck came back and called at the office for his weekly folder of data that he found out that he wasn't going to do Talk any more. "I phoned Ross and asked him why he hadn't let me know I was out," Crouse says, "and Ross said, 'I was too embarrassed.' "

Buck Crouse had started two *New Yorker* departments, "That Was New York" and "They Were New Yorkers," and he had astounded Ross one day by telling him there were too many profiles about big successful Americans, and there ought to be one about a failure. Ross glared at him and said, "You're crazy," but Crouse turned in a profile of a typical Bowery dere-lict, and Ross read it and liked it and printed it. That was H. W. Ross—the editor who said you were crazy one day and then agreed with you the next.

Charles H. Cooke's career on the *New Yorker* was unique, which means it was like everybody else's, only different. The time of each of us there was peculiar in its own way, to come as close to definition as may be. Cooke was hired by Ingersoll at thirty-five dollars a week, worked twelve years, day and night, and never got more than sixty dollars. He turned in some twelve hundred Talk stories. No other reporter ever equaled his energy, or came close to his output. To Ross, whom he has called "the irascible, lovable genius," he was, more than most other men, a prize and a puzzle, a person to praise one day and lash out at the next. "I'm surrounded by piano play-ers," Ross once said to me. "Why we haven't got a piano in this joint I'll never know." He meant not only Cooke, who wrote a book on piano playing, but Peter Arno, a real profes-

sional; Shawn, who once played a piano in a place in Mont-
martre; John McNulty, who had been a pianist in a silent movie
theater; and Andy White, a parlor performer on the keys.

Cooke has sent me a long, fascinating summary of his Talk
experiences, and the places he visited and the men he interviewed would make a book in itself, a book he has now and
then started to write, but given up for the dozens of other
activities he has crammed into his life, as novelist, short story
writer, lieutenant-colonel in the Air Corps, and researcher in
Washington. After the war, he wanted to get back on the *New
Yorker,* but Ross told him, "I long ago decided not to keep any
reporter for more than five years." What he meant by that I'll
never know. Cooke had been a peerless reporter for him for
twelve years. I'll never know, either, why he told Cooke, in
1946, he was going to give him the job of Talk editor, and
then didn't do it. This happened at one of the many times
when Ross admonished God for not sending him just such a
man as Charles Cooke. Maybe Cooke will solve it all when he
gets around to his own history of the *New Yorker,* and I hope
he does.

I can't leave out a wondrous three-cornered exchange of
notes involving Cooke and Ross and McKelway. Charles had
turned in a piece about a performing dog, and it contained this
sentence, "He stared at us and smiled affably." Ross read that
and sent this note to McKelway, then managing editor (one of
the fifteen Cooke worked for in his time): "Tell Cooke to for
God's sake stop attributing human behavior to dogs. The dog
may have stared but Cooke knows damn well he didn't smile."
McKelway sent the memo to Cooke, and appended this: "Ross
wants you to for God's sake stop attributing human behavior
to dogs. O.K.?" Cooke sent it back to McKelway with this
added: "O, for God's sake K." Later that same day Cooke got
this message from McKelway: "Ross says your dog piece is
swell. He put it through as is and left in the smile. Bow for
God's sake wow."

6

Miracle Men

"Hell, I hire anybody," Harold Ross told Ralph Ingersoll in the summer of 1925 when Ingersoll called on the editor of the *New Yorker,* asked for a job, and got one. It wasn't as simple as it sounds, though. Ingersoll had appeared in the editor's office dressed in a Palm Beach suit he had bought for the occasion, and Ross had talked to him for only a few minutes, gesticulating widely, when his big right hand struck an inkwell. Suddenly Ingersoll's new suit was dripping with ink and Ross was covered with embarrassment. Ingersoll had almost reached the office door on what he was sure was his way out of Ross's life when the editor shouted, "You're hired!" And then, a few moments later, sighed, "Hell, I hire anybody."

From then on Ross hired anybody, and everybody, in his frantic and ceaseless search for the Fountain of Perfection. A few of us came to realize that he didn't really want to find it, whether he knew it or not; that the quest itself was what kept him going. If he had found the Redeemer who, in Cabell's words, would make everything as "neat as a trivet or an apple-pie," he would have grasped his own starry scheme of things entire, smashed it all to bits, and then remolded it nearer to his heart's desire, or his mind's illusion, or whatever it was. A team of Freuds would have a hard time putting a finger on the Imp of the Perverse in Ross's psyche. I think he was looking for two separate kinds of Miracle Men: (1) the administrative genius who would sit at a Central Desk, push buttons, and produce Instant Perfection of organization, and (2) a literary wizard who would wave a magic wand over writers and artists and conjure up Instant Perfection in prose, drawings, and all other contents of the magazine.

H. W. Ross, being neither artist nor poet, was not equipped to bring "grace and measure" out of the chaos of man on earth, for his heart's ease or his peace of mind, but there was in him something of the powerful urge that has animated the human male from Sir Percival to Pasteur, from Marco Polo to Admiral Peary. He never knew exactly what he was after, since he didn't have much self-knowledge and was afraid of introspection, but I think he hoped it would be as shining as the Holy Grail, or as important as the Northwest Passage, or as rewarding as the pot of gold. He was afraid, though, that a Gorgon would pop up at any time to frustrate him, or a Questyng Beast, or a Gordian knot, and he realized that he damn well better have a Perseus on hand to help him, or a Palamedes, or an Alexander the Great. These romantic comparisons would, I am sure, move psychiatrists to ridicule; they would find in Sir Harold not a romantic, but a mixed-up modern man driven by the well-known compulsion to build with one hand and tear down with the other. Well, that urge was in him, too, along with fixation, defense mechanism, inferiority complex, and all the rest.

Many of us who went with him on his Quest, part of or all the way, often became bored or infuriated, and wanted to quit, and there were scores who did quit and found an easier way to live and make a living. A few of us could not quit. We had put on the armor and strapped on the sword and we were stuck with them. Once, when E. B. White had taken all he could, or thought he had, he said he was quitting and went home. Ross paced his office all afternoon and then got White on the phone at his apartment. "You *can't* quit," he roared. "This isn't a magazine—it's a Movement!" Andy did not leave the Movement.

The limits and limitations of Sir Harold's quest were defined by the very nature of his magazine, and no matter how high, and ever higher, he set his goal, it was ludicrously low compared with the objectives of the great pioneers and pathfinders whose listing above would nevertheless give Ross, I think, more comfort than discomfiture. He had humor, but he was never able to see clearly the essential comedy of a shining quest confined and constricted by mundane office walls and all the mean mechanics of magazine production. Once in a while he would say that he didn't really give a damn, and that the only thing he had ever liked doing was getting out the *Stars and Stripes* in Paris. "Every magazine has its cycle," he would say, "and this one has its cycle, too. It's a precarious enterprise, at best, and I wouldn't encourage anybody to invest in it." But if you concurred in his depressive views and pretended to share his mood, he would snap out of it like a switch blade.

In the last months of his life, when he was trying to lean back and take it easy at his home near Stamford, on doctor's orders, one of those who called on him was Hobart Weekes, since 1928 a big cog in the *New Yorker* magazine, a Princeton and Oxford man whose knowledge of and familiarity with make-up, proofreading, fact checking, English, and English literature frequently amazed his boss. Once Ross was about to scribble "Who he?" in the margin of a proof opposite the name William Blake, but one of those hunches or intuitions that stayed his hand made him send for Weekes. "Who's William Blake?" he demanded, and Weekes told him. "How the hell did you know that?" Ross said. He was also astonished by Weekes's knowledge of the differences, ecclesiastical and otherwise, between a virgin and a verger. (A virgin, instead of a verger, had crept into a Talk story about some church ceremony, but was hustled out by the learned Princeton-Oxford man before she could get into the magazine and mortify its editor.)

The day Weekes called on him at Stamford, Ross was lying on his bed, restless and disconsolate, smoking cigarettes against orders. "They don't need me at the office any more," said the man who had sometimes protested he didn't want to be there. Weekes straightened him out on that, implementing and underlying the *New Yorker*'s need for its founder. That night, I am sure, H. W. Ross slept better.

Nothing throws a stronger light on Ross's eternal questing, his incurable discontent, and his psychological, if not indeed almost pathological, cycle of admiration and disillusionment than the case history of Ralph McAllister Ingersoll from 1925 until he quit in 1930 to become a Luce editor, later the founder of *PM*, a controversial front-page figure during the war, a lieutenant-colonel in the U.S. Army, and the author of half a dozen books. In 1942 he was the subject of a two-part profile in the *New Yorker* written by Wolcott Gibbs.

When Ingersoll was on the magazine, Ross would have bet a cool million to one that no such profile would ever be published. (Thirty years ago, when Ingersoll kept suggesting a profile of Walter Winchell, Ross said, "Dismiss it from your mind. There'll never be a profile of Winchell in this magazine." St. Clair McKelway's *New Yorker* profile of Walter Winchell in 1940 ran to six parts.)

Ingersoll, not yet twenty-five when he was hired by Ross, was a graduate of Yale's Sheffield, and he had been a reporter and a mining engineer, but all this meant little to his employer. What meant a lot was that Ingersoll was a grandnephew of Ward McAllister and knew his way around Park Avenue and Long Island. "He knows what clubs Percy R. Pyne belongs to, and everybody else," Ross once told me. "He has entree in the right places. He knows who owns private Pullman cars, and he can have tea with all the little old women that still have coachmen or footmen or drive electric runabouts. It's damned important for a magazine called the *New Yorker* to have such a man around." Ross had sent him, for opinion, Ellin Mackay's "Why We Go to Cabarets," and it was Ingersoll's terse, emphatic "It's a must" that persuaded Ross to print it.

When I reached the *New Yorker* in March, 1927, Ross's enchantment with Ingersoll was undergoing its inevitable decline. Ross cast his own spells and broke them himself, and nobody has ever known just how or why. The great irony of Ross's quest, to me, was the simple truth that Ingersoll, who turned up when the magazine was a few months old, was the best of all the Central Desk men, the very administrative expert Ross spent his life looking for. I think he knew this unconsciously, would not admit it even to himself, and spent a lot of time after he had let Ingersoll go trying to justify and rationalize his bad judgment.

"He thinks he's a writer," he said to me when I told him he had lost his most valuable assistant. "He wrote a book called *In and Under Mexico*. I haven't read it, and don't want to, but it can't be good. The top drawer of his desk was always full of medicine. If I'd given him a thousand dollars a week to sit alone in a room and do nothing, in five days he'd have had six men helping him." Thus spake Harold Ross, the same man who kept saying, "We haven't got any manpower, we haven't got anybody who knows how to delegate anything." He had one final word the day I bawled him out for losing Ingersoll. "He brought Hush-a-phones into the office. I think he talked to brokers all the time, and people like Cornelius Vanderbilt. He knew too many people." Thus spake the man who had once boasted that Ingersoll knew everybody and that the *New Yorker* needed just such a man.

One of the hundred little things that plagued Ross was the postal regulation that requires all periodicals to print, at certain intervals, the names of their editors and principal stockholders. To satisfy this requirement, Ingersoll was listed as managing editor, all alone for several years, and then as co-managing editor with Katharine White. "Ross never stopped taunting me about it," Ingersoll says. "He would tell me that it didn't mean a thing, and that he was thinking of listing his butler as managing editor—'the way French newspapers name janitors or elevator men as their editors, so they can be the patsies in libel suits and such.'"

Ross kept bringing in other men, me among them, partly for the purpose of sticking pins in Ingersoll's pride. He told me, when I was "in charge," to give Ingersoll orders. "Don't let him write anything," he once said. "He did the captions on covering art this week. That's your fault. Change them." By "covering art" he meant a double-page spread of drawings that used to illustrate horse racing, open air concerts, and other goings on. Ingersoll had done the captions for a yacht race spread, drawn by Johan Bull: "The Start," "Midway," and "The Finish." Being sane at the time, or fairly so, I let them stand. "Did you change those captions?" Ross asked me later.

"All you have to do is read them," I said. "They have my touch, it's unmistakable." He was satisfied.

Ralph Ingersoll and I became friends and nothing, even his passing into legend, has changed that. He spends his weekends now at his home in Castleton, Virginia, and is editor-publisher of the Middletown, New York, *Times-Herald* and the Pawtucket, Rhode Island, *Times*. Without his help and direction, always efficient and untiring, I could never have got "Talk of the Town" off the ground. He took care of a thousand managerial details that I was supposed to handle, couldn't have, and didn't want to, and Ross never knew about it. When Ingersoll began publishing *PM* in 1940, I wrote a brief column for it, called "If You Ask Me," twice a week until I went into a nervous tail spin following my fifth eye operation. Ross read a few of these columns and objected because, he said, "You're throwing away ideas on *PM* that would make good casuals." But I was out from under the strict and exacting editing for which the *New Yorker* was and still is famous, and I needed this relaxation and the hundred dollars a column Ingersoll paid me.

One column I wrote in 1941 dealt with an old *New Yorker* Talk item some contributor had sent to the magazine twelve years before, in 1929. My wife had turned it up in going through some old stuff of mine in the early summer of 1941 when we went to Martha's Vineyard. In my column I referred to the lost and found contribution, which had never got into print, as "an ancient fragment of urgency." It was a letter from a woman reader, and on it was clipped a pink memo reading "Must go this week" and signed with the initials of Arthur Samuels, one of the Miracle Men of 1929. When my wife found the thing, the item was not only a dozen years old, but Arthur Samuels had been dead for three years. Ross read that *PM* column, all right, but all he said to me was, "God knows how we got out a Talk department when you were writing it." Ingersoll could have told him how we managed it, and Bernard A. Bergman could have told him, too, and Raymond Holden, and Ogden Nash. All of them belonged to the Big Parade of Miracle Men that came and went across the years.

The pink memo slip for urgency is said to have been put into effect by Holden, and later to have been abandoned because one of the editors in charge of urgency was color-blind. Ross took as capricious, and laughed about it only grudgingly, my suggestion that we use shape instead of color to denote urgency. "Let's make the urgent memos round, like an alarm clock, and use rectangular or coffin-shaped ones for less immediate matters," I said. Some way or other, in the notable confusion of all *New Yorker* systems, first things usually came first and others trailed along. Ross, at bottom, had about as much grasp of system as I had, which was perilously close to zero, but the difference was that he worried about it constantly and it was the least of all my concerns. We needed a guiding hand, there is no doubt about that, but often a competent secretary or a well-trained office boy could have brought about the order and pattern that Ross was confident could be achieved only through the agency of a genius sent to him by God.

After Ingersoll left in 1930, Ross realized, but never said so, that he had left behind an empty space it would take at least two men to fill. In the next few years Ross brought in at least eight hopefuls. As Ingersoll put it, in *Fortune* in 1935, "Ross has hired them out of advertising agencies, from behind city desks, from the Social Register, from the Players Club. He brings them back from lunch, he cables for them." One day, in 1930, Ross brought Ogden Nash into my office and said, "I'm thinking of letting Nash here take a swing at running the Talk department." Ogden himself, in a letter to me, has told, better and more succinctly than I could, what happened to him, and I quote his letter:

My experience with Ross was brief but unfortunate. He started buying my stuff early in 1930; later that year we

met for the first time—not in the office—but in a speakeasy.

I don't need to tell you that in many ways he was a
strangely innocent man and he assumed that my presence
in a speakeasy meant that I was a man about town. He
was, I believe, still in mourning over the departure of
Ingersoll, who had apparently been the ultimate in men
about town, and was looking for a suave and worldly editor. He hired me practically on the spot. It took him less
than three months to discover that it takes more than a
collection of speakeasy cards to make a man about town.
Besides this, he didn't need an editor anyhow, as anything
he didn't do himself was capably handled by Raymond
Holden and Mrs. White. The end of the third month,
therefore, found me in the employ of what was then Farrar
and Rinehart.

Shortly after I moved to Baltimore, where I remained
for some twenty years; I was living there at the time of his
death. I saw him occasionally when I visited the office.

He was an almost impossible man to work for—rude,
ungracious and perpetually dissatisfied with what he read;
and I admire him more than anyone I have met in professional life. Only perfection was good enough for him, and
on the rare occasions he encountered it, he viewed it with
astonished suspicion.

I suppose that in the twenty-odd years of our relationship I had half a dozen grudging kind words from him.
Once, toward the end, he sat down and wrote me a letter
of congratulation on a certain piece that was almost fulsome; those rare kind words meant more to me than any
compliments from reviewers, and I wish I could afford a
tombstone large enough to hold the letter.

Office legend has it that the first of the Miracle Men (they
were also known in the early years as Jesuses and Geniuses)
was Joseph Moncure March, but he soon got out from under
and from on top. Someone has told me that, after a particularly
rough session with Ross, March sat for hours in the make-up

room one night, staring out the window, but he wasn't the only one of us to do that; sometimes we sat for hours after work, alone except for a bottle of Scotch or rye, planning just how to tell Ross where to get off. There were a few men who had the good sense not to listen when Ross said, "Maybe you can run the magazine," a famous epitaph for at least two dozen miscast Geniuses.

Fillmore Hyde, the *New Yorker*'s first literary editor, was one of these wise men. He got out early, for greener and more tranquil pastures. Hyde was a sensitive, difficult, and able editor, who took no nonsense from Ross or anybody else. On my first day at the *New Yorker* he snapped at me, "Boy, take this telegram." I snapped something back at him and walked away, annoyed because he had spotted me for an office boy and not the new Redeemer. The last episode involving Fillmore Hyde at the *New Yorker* resulted from a letter to him that Bergman had dictated to a secretary. Bergman sent the letter back to her with instructions to do it over because she had misspelled Hyde's name, but he had made the mistake of writing in pencil in the margin, "For God's sake get this man's name right. Hyde is a touchy blankety blank." The secretary retyped the letter, incorporating the penciled sentence in it, and, the tale tells, Bergman signed it without rereading it and sent it off. I don't know what happened after that.

Others, besides Hyde, who turned down the Big Job included Hobey Weekes, Wolcott Gibbs, and Clifton Fadiman. Ross piled so much work on Weekes just after the war years, Big Job or not, that this invaluable editor came down with a serious illness requiring a major operation and a long siege in the hospital. Ross never seemed to know when a man had reached the limit of his endurance. If you kept taking it, he kept piling it on. His strange ambivalence—admiration and disenchantment, faith and distrust—went through a series of undulations in regard to Weekes. Once, mad about something trivial, he picked up his desk phone and threw it during a conference with Hobey.

At an earlier time, Weekes felt that he was being "put in the icebox," that some of his editorial duties were quietly being taken away from him, not to lessen the pressure of his work, but out of some Ross dissatisfaction with it. A new Genius, named Don Wharton, had appeared on the scene, and Ross had said of him, "Wharton can handle anything." Weekes sensed that the ancient formula of hiring and firing was about to be repeated again, but he didn't know what he had done to offend Ross. Hobey had started out as a checker and sometime Talk reporter, and had come up the hard way to chief of the copy desk, later taking on added heavy chores in the make-up and proofreading departments. He finally went to Ross and said, "There seems to be a move on foot to get rid of me. If I'm not wanted here, I'll leave in ten minutes." Ross didn't say anything, just sat staring at him. A good three minutes went by, during which Ross didn't move a muscle or speak a word. When Weekes couldn't stand it any longer he just got up and left the room. He wasn't fired.

When I was, at least in Ross's stubborn mind, top man, we were dealing heavily with some slight problem in his office one day (circa June, 1927), when his secretary tiptoed in and laid on the desk an enormous typescript, bound in imitation leather and seeming to me now, in retrospect, at least as thick as a desk dictionary. It was labeled "Mistakes Made by J. Thurber as Managing Editor." Ross stood up and stared at it, his tongue coming out of the corner of his mouth, his eyes getting darker and darker. Then he said to his secretary, "Get that thing out of here. Get rid of it. I don't want to know what you did with it." Since the monumental compendium of my mistakes, many of them deliberate, seemed to me a sure safe conduct out of the job I hated, I said, "Aren't you going to read it? Don't you want to find out what's in it?" What he wanted to do, it came out after a lot of silent pacing, was to fire the man he held responsible for this assumption of authority, this gross insubordination, this rude interruption of his routine. I told him he would have to fire the man himself, that he was one of the best on the magazine. After a long pause and much coin jingling, he said, "I'm mistaken for him by some people, right here in the goddam hallways. It's embarrassing. People probably think he's me, too." I laughed him out of that finally, but not out of his firing mood.

"I want you to fire So-and-so," he said, changing the object, but not the subject, of his wrath. So-and-so was a young woman, long since in heaven with the angels, who wrote one of the back-of-the-book departments. "She makes me nervous," Ross said. "Last night, at Tony's, she was damn near sitting in the lap of the man she was with." It happened that I had been at Tony's the night before, too, and had seen the couple, sitting and drinking and talking like any other couple in Tony's, and I told Ross that. Then he came out with one of his accusations that were pure, patented Ross. "They were talking in awful goddam low tones," he said. It wasn't often that I laughed in the inner sanctum in those first months, but that was too much for me. Then I said, "Don't you know your Shakespeare: Her voice was ever gentle and awful goddam low, an excellent thing in woman?" Ross turned away so that I couldn't see his grin, but his torso had one of those brief spasmodic upheavals that so often served as a sign of his amusement in the art meeting when he looked at a drawing he thought was really funny. When he turned around he was scowling. "Goddam it, Thurber, don't quote things at me," he said. The firing mood was gone.

It was at a restaurant called Martin and Mino's, that Ross rarely went to, but some of the rest of us haunted during Prohibition, that he said to Gibbs, "Maybe you can run the magazine." Gibbs quickly and sharply returned this serve, which had been both unexpected and expected, leaving Ross flatfooted. It was one of Ross's silliest attempts to get his administrative

rocket into the wild blue yonder. He should have known by
then that Wolcott was much too important a writer and copy
editor to be launched gaudily into a meaningless orbit in the
great managerial Nowhere. Years later, when somebody wrote
in an article in *Harper's* that Gibbs didn't like anything, Ross
said to me, "Maybe he doesn't like anything, but he can do
everything."

This high praise was little short of plain fact. White and
I and Gibbs had joined the *New Yorker* staff in that order
between the fall of 1926 and the end of 1927. Before Wolcott
arrived, to take on a dozen different jobs and do each one
superbly, Alexander King had done an interview with Alexander Woollcott in a now dead magazine called *Americana*. I
remember only one sentence, in which Woollcott was quoted
as having said, "The *New Yorker* is got out by a shiftless
reporter with the help of two country bumpkins." The bumpkins were White and I, and the reporter was, of course, Harold
Ross, but "shiftless" was an unintentional misquotation. What
Woollcott had actually said was "ship news reporter," a job
Ross had once had in San Francisco. " 'Shiftless' is perhaps
the only derogatory adjective that does not fit Harold Ross,"
Woollcott later said.

The two country bumpkins have been written about quite

a lot here and there, but Wolcott Gibbs has never got the attention he deserves. He was easily, not just conceivably—to use one of his favorite words—the best copy editor the *New Yorker* has ever had. For years he had to deal with the seventy per cent of *New Yorker* fiction that has to be edited, often heavily, before it reaches print. Gibbs, an accomplished parodist, was always able to fix up a casual without distorting or even marring its author's style. He was inimitable, as such word experts are, but when he quit as copy editor in the fiction department to become the magazine's dramatic critic and to write some of its best casuals and profiles, he wrote and sent to Ross—this must have been twenty years ago—what he called "Theory and Practice of Editing *New Yorker* Articles," based on his experiences, often melancholy, with the output of scores of writers, male and female. The final straw, in his editorial career, was a casual that began: "Mr. West had never been very good with machinery." Here was the little man, a genre sometimes called, around the office, the Thurber husband, popping up for the thousandth time, and it was too much for the Gibbsian nerves. The Gibbs essay on editing, which has not been published before, follows:

THEORY AND PRACTICE OF EDITING
NEW YORKER ARTICLES

The average contributor to this magazine is semi-literate; that is, he is ornate to no purpose, full of senseless and elegant variations, and can be relied on to use three sentences where a word would do. It is impossible to lay down any exact and complete formula for bringing order out of this underbrush, but there are a few general rules.

1. Writers always use too damn many adverbs. On one page recently I found eleven modifying the verb "said." "He said morosely, violently, eloquently, so on." Editorial theory should probably be that a writer who can't make his

context indicate the way his character is talking ought to be in another line of work. Anyway, it is impossible for a character to go through all these emotional states one after the other. Lon Chaney might be able to do it, but he is dead.

2. Word "said" is O.K. Efforts to avoid repetition by inserting "grunted," "snorted," etc., are waste motion and offend the pure in heart.

3. Our writers are full of clichés, just as old barns are full of bats. There is obviously no rule about this, except that anything that you suspect of being a cliché undoubtedly is one and had better be removed.

4. Funny names belong to the past or to whatever is left of *Judge* magazine. Any character called Mrs. Middlebottom or Joe Zilch should be summarily changed to something else. This goes for animals, towns, the names of imaginary books and many other things.

5. Our employer, Mr. Ross, has a prejudice against having too many sentences beginning with "and" or "but." He claims that they are conjunctions and should not be used purely for literary effect. Or at least only very judiciously.

6. See our Mr. Weekes on the use of such words as "little," "vague," "confused," "faintly," "all mixed up," etc. etc. The point is that the average *New Yorker* writer, unfortunately influenced by Mr. Thurber, has come to believe that the ideal *New Yorker* piece is about a vague, little man helplessly confused by a menacing and complicated civilization. Whenever this note is not the whole point of the piece (and it far too often is) it should be regarded with suspicion.

7. The repetition of exposition in quotes went out with the Stanley Steamer:

> Marion gave me a pain in the neck.
> "You give me a pain in the neck, Marion," I said.

This turns up more often than you'd expect.

8. Another of Mr. Ross's theories is that a reader picking up a magazine called the *New Yorker* automatically supposes that any story in it takes place in New York. If it doesn't, if it's about Christmas, Ohio, the lead should say so. "When George Adams was sixteen, he began to worry about the girls" should read "When George Adams was sixteen, he began to worry about the girls he saw every day on the streets of Columbus" or something of the kind. More graceful preferably.

9. Also, since our contributions are signed at the end, the author's sex should be established at once if there is any reasonable doubt. It is distressing to read a piece all the way through under the impression that the "I" in it is a man and then find a woman's signature at the end. Also, of course, the other way round.

10. To quote Mr. Ross again, "Nobody gives a damn about a writer or his problems except another writer." Pieces about authors, reporters, poets, etc., are to be discouraged in principle. Whenever possible the protagonist should be arbitrarily transplanted to another line of business. When the reference is incidental and unnecessary, it should come out.

11. This magazine is on the whole liberal about expletives. The only test I know of is whether or not they are really essential to the author's effect. "Son of a bitch," "bastard," and many others can be used whenever it is the editor's judgment that that is the only possible remark under the circumstances. When they are gratuitous, when the writer is just trying to sound tough to no especial purpose, they come out.

12. In the transcription of dialect, don't let the boys and girls misspell words just for a fake Bowery effect. There is no point, for instance, in "trubble," or "sed."

13. Mr. Weekes said the other night, in a moment of desperation, that he didn't believe he could stand any more triple

adjectives. "A tall, florid and overbearing man called Jaeckel." Sometimes they're necessary, but when every noun has three adjectives connected with it, Mr. Weekes suffers and quite rightly.

14. I suffer myself very seriously from writers who divide quotes for some kind of ladies' club rhythm.

"I am going," he said, "downtown" is a horror, and unless a quote is pretty long I think it ought to stay on one side of the verb. Anyway, it ought to be divided logically, where there would be a pause or something in the sentence.

15. Mr. Weekes has got a long list of banned words, beginning with "gadget." Ask him. It's not actually a ban, there being circumstances when they're necessary, but good words to avoid.

16. I would be delighted to go over the list of writers, explaining the peculiarities of each as they have appeared to me in more than ten years of exasperation on both sides.

17. Editing on manuscript should be done with a black pencil, decisively.

18. I almost forgot indirection, which probably maddens Mr. Ross more than anything else in the world. He objects, that is, to important objects or places or people being dragged into things in a secretive and underhanded manner. If, for instance, a profile has never told where a man lives, Ross protests against a sentence saying, "His Vermont house is full of valuable paintings." Should say "He has a house in Vermont and it is full, etc." Rather weird point, but it will come up from time to time.

19. Drunkenness and adultery present problems. As far as I can tell, writers must not be allowed to imply that they admire either of these things, or have enjoyed them personally, although they are legitimate enough when pointing a moral or adorning a sufficiently grim story. They are nothing to be lighthearted about. "The New Yorker can not

endorse adultery." Harold Ross vs. Sally Benson. Don't bother about this one. In the end it is a matter between Mr. Ross and his God. Homosexuality, on the other hand, is definitely out as humor, and dubious in any case.

20. The more "As a matter of facts," "howevers," "for instances," etc. etc. you can cut out, the nearer you are to the Kingdom of Heaven.

21. It has always seemed irritating to me when a story is written in the first person, but the narrator hasn't got the same name as the author. For instance, a story beginning: " 'George,' my father said to me one morning"; and signed at the end Horace McIntyre always baffles me. However, as far as I know this point has never been ruled upon officially, and should just be queried.

22. Editors are really the people who should put initial letters and white spaces in copy to indicate breaks in thought or action. Because of overwork or inertia or something, this has been done largely by the proofroom, which has a tendency to put them in for purposes of makeup rather than sense. It should revert to the editors.

23. For some reason our writers (especially Mr. Leonard Q. Ross) have a tendency to distrust even moderately long quotes and break them up arbitrarily and on the whole idiotically with editorial interpolations. "Mr. Kaplan felt that he and the cosmos were coterminus" or some such will frequently appear in the middle of a conversation for no other reason than that the author is afraid the reader's mind is wandering. Sometimes this is necessary, most often it isn't.

24. Writers also have an affection for the tricky or vaguely cosmic last line. "Suddenly Mr. Holtzmann felt tired" has appeared on far too many pieces in the last ten years. It is always a good idea to consider whether the last sentence of a piece is legitimate and necessary, or whether it is just an author showing off.

25. On the whole, we are hostile to puns.

26. How many of these changes can be made in copy depends, of course, to a large extent on the writer being edited. By going over the list, I can give a general idea of how much nonsense each artist will stand for.

27. Among many other things, the *New Yorker* is often accused of a patronizing attitude. Our authors are especially fond of referring to all foreigners as "little" and writing about them, as Mr. Maxwell says, as if they were mantel ornaments. It is very important to keep the amused and Godlike tone out of pieces.

28. It has been one of Mr. Ross's long struggles to raise the tone of our contributors' surroundings, at least on paper. References to the gay Bohemian life in Greenwich Village and other low surroundings should be cut whenever possible. Nor should writers be permitted to boast about having their telephones cut off, or not being able to pay their bills, or getting their meals at the delicatessen, or any of the things which strike many writers as quaint and lovable.

29. Some of our writers are inclined to be a little arrogant about their knowledge of the French language. Probably best to put them back into English if there is a common English equivalent.

30. So far as possible make the pieces grammatical—but if you don't the copy room will, which is a comfort. Fowler's *English Usage* is our reference book. But don't be precious about it.

31. Try to preserve an author's style if he is an author and has a style. Try to make dialogue sound like talk, not writing.

Wolcott Gibbs

Harold Ross said to me, one dark day during the 1930's, "If you and Gibbs and White ever leave this place, I'll go, too." Years later, when he didn't have long to live, he told me one day that he had stayed late at the office the night before and flipped through some back copies of the magazine, on a lonely journey through the regrets and triumphs of the past. "There wasn't anything the three of you couldn't do," he snarled. The snarled sentence was a brief preface to, "You could have got the magazine out without any other help if your private lives weren't so damn tangled up." He had made a list of the things he said the three of us had done in our time. It was written in pencil and I lost it long ago, but I remember most of what he wrote down, and it may be that I have added a few he forgot: covers, Goings On, Notes and Comment, The Talk of the Town, idea drawings, spots, captions, casuals, verse, newsbreaks, The Theatre, The Cinema, Books, Profiles, A Reporter at Large, Onward and Upward with the Arts, Where Are They Now?, Our Footloose Correspondents, fact and fiction editing, proofreading, some make-up, and The Tennis Courts.

I covered tennis for several years (and so did Gibbs), and something I wrote in January, 1937, upset Ross when Franklin P. Adams told him I had gone out on a limb and didn't know what I was talking about. (The limb was a place that scared Ross. He used to say he was going to write an autobiography called *My Life on a Limb*.) I had predicted that Donald Budge would win the singles titles at both Wimbledon and Forest Hills in 1937 and beat Baron von Cramm once or twice. I offered to bet Ross and Frank I was right, but there were no takers. In my dotage, I often sit cackling in the chimney corner when I think of my old prophecy, for Budge won at both Wimbledon and Forest Hills in 1937 and, in July that year, beat von Cramm in the Davis Cup singles. Ross didn't play or know anything about sports, unless you count croquet, and he read such departments only for mistakes in grammar, and such. Once he broke Frank Adams's heart, when Adams was doing the tennis column, by striking out the phrase "the Red Budge of Courage." He hated puns, but I once got a beauty past him: "I'm tired of seeing our tennis hopes brought back home on our Wood Shields." Ross had never heard of Sidney Wood or

Frank Shields, then our two outstanding Davis Cup players, and I'm sure he didn't know about slain warriors being brought back home upon their shields. I often wonder how he bore up under the strain of me. And vice versa.

Somebody has asked me, "Do you think the New Yorker was successful because of, or in spite of, Harold Ross?" The answer is: The New Yorker was created out of the friction produced by Ross Positive and Ross Negative. He tried, and failed, to make an executive editor out of me, and wanted to do the same thing to Gibbs. This was Ross Negative at its worst. He had the good sense, from the first, to let White alone. This was Ross Positive at its most perceptive. He got from this one trio, in the end, the "productivity" he was after from the very first. How much productivity he lost, through the years, because of the mixture in him of the perspicacious, the perverse, and the preposterous, nobody could ever measure. The files of the magazine, during his years as editor, are the only dependable record of Harold Wallace Ross Positive and Negative. My own conclusions are, at best, only one man's footnotes, personal and debatable.

7

❧

More Miracle Men

So many people have told me that Harold Ross was a simple mecha-nism, and so many others have assured me that he was a com-plex character, it is small wonder that I dreamed the other night that he was both complified and simplicated. There are those who contend that the multiple editor of the *New Yorker* never stepped off the elevator on his office floor without put-ting on an invisible military uniform. He was accused of hav-ing a secret weapon for rigid military discipline, in spite of his waggish and scalawaggish experiences in the AEF. His fre-quent and profane denunciations of all top brass were sup-posed to cover a sneaking admiration of GHQ red tape. I can't go along with this, if only because I'm unable to dispel the image of Ross as the jittery skipper of a schooner out of Cole-ridge, a ship's master with more than a dash of mutineer in him. When he is not that figure in my nightmares, he is an "aw shucks" farm boy from Colorado trying to land a 1900 biplane in the middle of Fifth Avenue.

When, as Private H. W. Ross, he was editor of the *Stars and Stripes,* the situation was more comic opera than American Army. He was once put in the guardhouse by Captain Guy T. Viskniskki for some insubordination. But he had to be released or the newspaper could not have been got out. As editor, he could give orders to Captain Franklin P. Adams and to Sergeant Alexander Woollcott, who once called him, in Paris, "the best editor in the world." Where and how he finally learned his obsessive reverence for Order and Organization nobody will ever know for sure. Although he was always scornful of American big business and big businessmen, he talked constantly of "running this place like any other business office." He was vociferous in his contempt for the way most metropolitan newspapers were run, but I always felt that his urge to tear down walls and set up a Central Desk was an unconscious tendency to create a vast city room, with everyone in full sight of everyone else. I go on feeling this in the face of his continual scoffing at all things intramurally journalistic in any writer's copy. He didn't want any stories by reporters and ex-reporters about their work on newspapers. "It makes me self-conscious," he would say, and he once went so far as to insist when I used "city room" in a Talk story that it be changed to "the room where the reporters write their stories." Whatever the origin of his driving desire for Order and Organization may have been, it satisfied two of his deepest needs: something to keep trying for, and something to keep grousing about.

When I was in Columbus, Ohio, in the summer of 1927, on vacation and on my way out of the job of "running the magazine," I got a six-word note from Andy White that read: "Thurber. The new passing system. White." The new passing system, typed on an enclosed piece of paper, went like this: "White passes to Levick who passes to Ross." I have no copy at hand and it may be that I have left out one of the passes. Perhaps it went like this: "White passes to Barnes who passes to Levick who passes to Ross." If there was a Barnes, he has long since passed and been forgotten. Sometimes I wake up at night and chant to myself, "White passes to Tinker who passes to Evers who passes to Chance who passes to Ross." This old system, indicating the official route for "Notes and Comment" from White's typewriter to Ross's desk, was one of a hundred similar systems devised by distraught executive editors in a futile effort to set Ross's organization-conscious mind at rest. These systems formed what Stanley Walker, who later got involved in them, called "the rigmaroles."

The man who had thought up a way to reroute Comment, so that Ross wouldn't worry about its getting lost between Andy's office and his, was named M. B. Levick. He lasted about as long as I had in the untenable job of mastermind and whipping boy to Harold Ross. Levick's final frantic response to the editor's demand for a method of keeping track of everything was an enormous sheet of cardboard, six feet by four, divided into at least eight hundred squares, with fine hand lettering in each of them covering all phases of the scheduling of departments and other office rigmaroles. This complicated caricature of System, this concentration of all known procedural facts, hung on a wall of the Talk meeting room until one day it fell down of its own weight. Ross had stared at it now and then without saying a word. When it crashed, he told his secretary, "Get rid of that thing." I suppose this was also what he said about a sign I made at the time and hung on a wall near the elevators: "Alterations going on as usual during business."

Bill Levick, one of the few men Ross always called by his nickname in the office, had been a friend and colleague of the editor in his San Francisco newspaper days. He had greatly impressed Ross at that time by his calm and efficient direction of a staff of reporters one day when some disaster struck the city. Levick, as I remember it, had been city editor of the paper. His calmness and efficiency, which had stood up under disaster, did not long stand up under Ross's continual badgering and heckling. After he gave up the hopeless task of trying to please Ross in the Big Job, he did not leave, like most of the others, but became the art make-up man. He was unhappy in that role, too, because he didn't like artists, and thought most of their drawings were silly. "You're the only cartoonist that can spell," he once told me sourly, "and you may be the only one that can read and write." I wasn't ever close to him, but we got along well, although he rarely had much to say beyond his invariable morning greeting, "One day nearer the grave, Thurber."

A now tottery graybeard says he saw Levick one day in the office with tears in his eyes—tears of fury or frustration were not infrequent in some of the men who worked for Ross. But Levick could be tough, too, and his faint, gentle smile could turn cold when Ross backed him into a corner. One day the editor went up in flames because of the similarity and proximity of two drawings in the front of the book, but instead of bawling Levick out himself, he sent his secretary to the make-up man with a sharp reprimand. Levick took a swing at the fellow and, when Ross sent the young man back with an even shorter message, knocked him down, resigned, went away, and was not seen again.

Bill Levick died a few years later, somewhere in New Jersey, out of work and down on his luck, and I told Ross about it. He was genuinely saddened, and the news depressed him for days. "I didn't treat him right, goddam it," he told me. "But he kept calling me 'Sir,' and standing there mocking me and grinning at me. He called Woollcott 'Foolish.' He would say, 'Foolish is late with his copy this week for "Shouts and Murmurs." ' He kept saying 'sked' for schedule and 'pix' for drawings. All he cared about was his goddam pianola rolls. He had millions of them, there wasn't anything else in his house. You don't play the pianola every night unless there's something the matter with you. He even *edited* the damn rolls, pasting them up with tissue paper, collaborating with guys like Beethoven. He was a good man, though. I was fond of him, but he didn't belong here." I thought of asking him, "Who does?" but I just went away and left him with his memories and miseries.

When a system fell down, Ross was usually dejected until

he or somebody else thought up a new one, but once in a while the mutineer in him took over. He was gleeful if the falling down or pushing over of a system disturbed, or tangled up, the business department, "those guys upstairs." Once when a rebuilt typewriter I had been using broke down, I phoned the Underwood Company at noon, ordered its most expensive machine, and charged it to the *New Yorker*. The typewriter, delivered at the office two hours later, was held up by the alert business department, and a deputy was sent to Ross with the complaint that I had got the machine without authorization or the signing of any requisition slips. The typewriter had been hidden from me in the art stock room, but an office boy told me where it was and I went and got it. The whole illegal procedure delighted Ross. "It's the only direct action there's been around here in years," he yelled at the nervous man from the business department. "I'll okay it," and he grabbed pencil and paper and okayed it.

When he found out that I was in the habit of going to the supply stock room, getting in with a passkey and taking whatever I wanted—paper, paper clips, typewriter ribbons, pencils, and wire baskets—he sauntered into my office and asked, "How do you get your supplies?" I told him, and he went away grinning. A monthly checkup by the business office had shown a discrepancy in supplies on hand, and again someone had complained to the editor and he had suspected me. I was thwarted for a while when the guys upstairs installed new locks on all doors, but I smuggled the master key to a locksmith and had a dozen keys made from it. I told Ross about that myself, adding that I had given a few of the extra keys to girls I knew for souvenirs. Ross didn't believe that, even though it was true. The heartiest laugh of the mutinous skipper came the day I found out, and told him, that the master key to the former system of locks had been retained and hung on a hook beside the new one. I showed it to him. Attached to it was a small wooden plaque on which someone had printed in India ink "master key" and, under that, "doesn't work." Ross told the story all over town. It represented to him not merely the bewilderment of some office boy, but the total inefficiency of the business department, which had had nothing whatever to do with it.

After Levick came Arthur Samuels, out of an advertising agency, with previous experience as a newspaper reporter and a magazine promotion man. Art Samuels, who had been a member of the Cottage Club and the Triangle Club in his Princeton days, was a close friend and idol of Raoul Fleischmann, and any friend and idol of Fleischmann was a target for Ross's slings and arrows, and doomed from the start. Raoul once told me, "Art is one of the funniest men in the world on two Martinis." When I mentioned this praise to Ross, he said, "I guess I always got to parties when he was on his third, or left before he finished his first."

Samuels had taken over one of the largest *New Yorker* offices and furnished it with rugs, large handsome bridge lamps, and other fancy appointments that must have brought Ross's disapproving tongue out of his mouth when he first beheld this change. He himself liked a plain newspaper-type office—"I don't want to look like the editor of *Vanity Fair*." Samuels lasted until just after he came back from a six-week leave in Europe. I learned later that Ross had intended to fire him while he was abroad, but he put it off until Art's ship was back in the harbor of New York. Then, just before Samuels disembarked, he got a telegram from Ross telling him he was through. Late that afternoon the editor called me into his office. He was sitting with his head in his hands, and he said, "Samuels was just in here bawling the holy hell out of me. No white man would have fired him the way I did, I guess." I could tell he had taken quite a verbal lashing, and he was to get others.

Later, hell and high voices broke loose in his office when Geoffrey Hellman gave him a verbal going over, which no doubt Ross had coming to him. Some weeks after that, Ross held up a Hellman piece so long that Katharine White said to him at a Talk meeting, "Why haven't you put the Hellman piece through? We all think it's very good." Ross turned this over in his mind for ten seconds and then said, "He called me a liar," picking one of the least provocative of Geoffrey's descriptions of him. (He bought the Hellman piece that day.)

It was a basic fact of Ross's nature that he really respected no man who didn't, at one time or another, fight back and yell him down. I had many a yelling bout with him in his office, but we always ended up on good, even affectionate terms. One day ten years ago he and William Shawn were trying to explain to me what they thought was the matter with a couple of pieces I had written in a series on soap operas, and Ross snapped, not out of his heart, but out of his ulcers, "If you could see, you would know what we mean." That sent me rocketing into the higher reaches of lurid damnation of all editors. He said he was sorry, and he was, but he never immediately got over the effects of one of our yelling spells. That noon I was having lunch at the Algonquin with my wife and daughter (then sixteen), when Ross came over to our table. We talked amiably for a while and then he spurted, "Something happens to Jim once a month that makes him carry on like a woman." This indelicate allusion was remarkable in a man as self-conscious as a choir boy in the presence of women, and embarrassed to death if anyone then made a reference to the functional. My daughter had met him first when she was only nine and he was in one of his most blustery moods. I asked her afterward what she thought of him, and she said, "He's gruff, but I'm not afraid of him." She might have been speaking for her sex in general.

Thorne Smith doesn't properly belong in any *New Yorker* or, for that matter, any other category, but he underwent a stretch of torture, both give and take, as a member of the staff during the winter of 1929–1930. I had brought him in and

introduced him to Ross, saying that he had given up an advertising job to write a book—it must have been *A Stray Lamb*—and found himself unable to get work. Thorne Smith, straight out of Wonderland, looked like a cousin of the White Rabbit, and completely befuddled Ross. The editor took him on, though—mainly, I am sure, because he had edited a service magazine during World War I, a Navy publication called *Broadside*. The two men, disparate if there ever was disparity, talked about the *Stars and Stripes* and a mutual acquaintance who had been on the wartime Army *Gas Attack*. Everything went wrong between Ross and Thorne, who once didn't show up for a week. "You ought to know where he is," Ross told me. "He's your responsibility." I said that Smith was God's responsibility, not mine or any man's. When he finally did appear, Ross said, "Why didn't you telephone and *say* you were sick?" Thorne had a lovely answer to that: "The telephone was in the hall and there was a draft."

The *New Yorker* had in a special file at that time a stack of profiles that needed editing before they could be used, and Smith had been given an office and told to try his hand at fixing them up. It didn't work out. "He can't use a typewriter, or if he can, he won't," Ross told me, and then, with dramatic voice and gestures, "He sits out there writing on foolscap with a quill pen."

"By candlelight?" I asked.

"You have me there," said Ross. "Where the hell did you find him, anyway?"

"I didn't find him," I said. "God sent him to you." Smith departed soon after that, to join the other poor little lambs who had gone astray. It was only the other day that I found out he had once written, on foolscap, but with a modern fountain pen, an entire Talk department which was never used. Ross must have put him up to that secretly. I count it among my sorrows, and literature's losses, that his Talk department is nowhere to be found.

James M. Cain was a puzzle to Ross, too. All men puzzled him to some degree, but Thorne Smith and Jim Cain were much too much for his understanding. "We called him Dizzy Jim," an old-timer told me recently. "You were Daffy Jim." It seems that Cain liked to work on the floor, where there was a lot of room, and used to put the Talk department together down there. He once lifted high the hearts of Andy and Katharine White, at a Thanksgiving Day dinner at his apartment, by putting the turkey, platter and all, on the floor and carving it, blandly going on with the story he was telling, and he told stories exceedingly well.

Jim wasn't at the *New Yorker* long, only a few months, but the memory of him has not dwindled there. When he got the hell out, he didn't want to see Ross or the *New Yorker* again, and I don't blame him for leaving any mention of it out of the piece about him in *Who's Who*. He had been on the Baltimore *American*, the Baltimore *Sun*, and the New York *World*, and he was at one time a professor of journalism at St. John's College in Annapolis, where he had been born. Cain must have known Ross in France when he was editor of the 79th Division's *Lorraine Cross*. Jim is a big man, and Ross was always a little wary of big men. Once when he got into a hassle with Joel Sayre over a projected profile on Ross's detective friend, Raymond Schindler, the wary editor said to me, "Geezus, your friend Sayre is a *big* guy." My researches and reflections have turned up the interesting truth that all of the Miracle Men were of short physical stature except Cain and Ralph Ingersoll, and maybe one or two others out of the more than thirty. I am over six feet myself, but when Ross and I tangled, I weighed only 150. (I have reached 186 now, a weight, alas, I'll never be able to throw around in Ross's office during a monthly yelling spell.)

In 1931 my daughter had about seven months to go before she was born when her mother and I bought a house a mile outside Sandy Hook, Connecticut, and Ross pretended to be frightened when he heard about my plans to live in the country. Timid, as usual, about taking up personal matters with a man face to face, he assigned Cain the task of trying to dissuade me from moving out of the city. Jim had approached the subject gingerly in my office, with only a couple of sentences that I recognized at once as bearing the stamp of a Ross panic, when he suddenly stood up and said, "This is none of my business, or Ross's, either. I'm sorry I mentioned it. Live where you want to and the way you want to."

One day Jim had sent on to Ross some manuscript of which the editor could make neither head nor tail. He sent it back to Cain with a memo attached that is still in existence. It read, "What is the signifigance of it all?" Anyway, that is the misspelling of "significance" as I had remembered it for twenty-five years, but, as you will see, I was wrong. Just before Jim left he had the memo framed in leather and presented it to his successor, Bernard A. Bergman, who still has it. I wrote him to check the spelling of the big word and got this reply: "signigifance (sic)." Harold Ross's spelling was often grotesque. He was always looking up words he questioned in copy he was reading, but he never seemed to doubt his own accuracy. In all the years I knew him he never got "prodigal" right. He spelled it "progidal" and pronounced it as if it were spelled "prodgidal."

It was in 1934, to get back to Jim Cain, that he brought out *The Postman Always Rings Twice.* I once asked Ross if he had read it, and he said, "It wouldn't be my kind of stuff." I have no doubt that, if he had started reading it, he would have put it down, thus becoming the only reader in the country able to do that. He didn't even try to read *A Farewell to Arms,* and dismissed that novel with "I understand the hero keeps getting in bed with women, and the war wasn't fought that way."

I have a recent letter from Bernard Bergman about Ross that ends: "He was a great man. I wish I could have been close to him, but I never was." Bergman lasted almost two years, beginning in 1931. He quit because Francis Bellamy had appeared on the scene, and Bergie was wise enough to realize the newcomer was to become the new Genius; the old ritual of firing and hiring was about to begin once more. After Bellamy disappeared, in his time and turn ("He smoked cigars," was Ross's epitaph for this victim), the editor phoned Bergman, who had just left the Philadelphia *Record,* and tried to get him to come back. He rambled on, in his loud voice, about the job of "editorial publishing," whatever that meant, and the rebirth of his conviction that Bergman could handle "certain tough problems in the office." Bergman said, "That's just what I *was* doing," and he laughed, and Ross laughed, too, and they both hung up, laughing.

Bergman, like me, went to Ohio State, helped edit the *Daily Lantern,* and was a reporter on the Columbus *Dispatch.* We had been friends since 1915, and I persuaded Ross to hire him to supervise "Talk of the Town." Ross had finally found out, after years of hit and miss, what manner of man and writer I was, but I don't think he ever knew anything about Bergman. A man's past dropped away, and his life began anew, when he went to work for the *New Yorker*. Bergie had been a regimental sergeant major in World War I, a newspaper reporter and editor, and a New York press agent. In high school, in Chillicothe, Ohio, nearly fifty years ago, Bergman organized a four-piece orchestra to play for Saturday night dances at the Knights of Pythias Club. His clarinetist (Bergman played the violin, and played it well) was a youngster named Theodore Friedman, whom Bergman paid two dollars and a half a night until he let him go because he jazzed up everything, did funny things with a plug hat, and disconcerted the other boys. A decade later Theodore Friedman, alias Ted Lewis, was earning ten thousand dollars a week (the Palace, the *Ziegfeld Follies,* the Ziegfeld Roof), and Bergman was his press agent. For a long time, starting about 1928, Bergie had contributed to "Talk of the Town" the best items and suggestions of any outsider, and when Ross asked me, after the vanishing of Ingersoll, Raymond Holden, Ogden Nash, and several others, if I knew a good man for Talk, I brought Bergman in and he was hired.

I had asked Ross to promise me that he wouldn't elevate Bergman to the Genius chair, and he said he wouldn't, but he did. "I'm going to give Bergman a crack at that job," he told me. "I think he can run the magazine. Don't say anything about it, though, because I haven't told him yet." I left the room, giving the door a good slam. I hated to lose the man who had brought to Talk facts and anecdotes about a dozen New Yorkers whose careers fascinated Harold Ross, the Gee Whiz Guy. They included Jake Volk, the building wrecker; Louis Marshall, an eccentric millionaire lawyer who rode to work on the El and back home on the subway; George and Ira Gershwin; and George Grosz, the German artist, with whom Bergman and I once had dinner. Grosz, I told Ross, wanted to meet the *New Yorker* artist "whose work began where the other cartoonists' left off."

"Well, did he?" Ross asked.

"He meant me," I said shyly.

"Hogwash," said Ross, who didn't believe a word of it. The day that Ross promoted Bergman, I sat outside his office and eavesdropped. Bergman got the works, the whole rigmarole, from "You got to hold the artists' hands" through "I'm, by God, going to keep sex out of this office" to "I want to run this place like any other business office." I got up in disgust, went to the men's room, and put up the window because it was a hot day. I heard the door open and close behind me, but I didn't see who it was. Then I went out and met Bergman coming down the hall. "Ross's secretary just came in and said you were going to kill yourself in the men's room," he told me. "Ross turned to me and said, 'That's my life! Do something about it.'"

Bergman had one great failure and at least one great triumph at the *New Yorker*. His failure lay in his inability to build a "fake partition" by means of which Ross could get to the men's room unseen and ungreeted in the halls. Nobody else could have designed such a crazy partition, either, and the dilemma wasn't solved until someone suggested he have a lavatory built just off his office. "Well, I'll be damned," Ross must have said, when this simple way out of embarrassment was presented to his astonished mind. The lavatory was installed, and it not only saved Ross the torture of being spoken to by employees, but it eliminated uncomfortable dialogue with writers and editors in the men's room. Once, standing trough to trough with John Mosher, he grumbled, "Why aren't you writing any more casuals?" "Because I have lost the slight fancy that sustained me," Mosher explained. It was the kind of Mosher retort that left Ross flabbergasted, and he was miserable when he had nothing to say.

Bergman's great triumph was the hiring of Alva Johnston, and I'll let him tell that story himself:

"When I first took over the M.E. job, Ross said he had been trying to get Alva Johnston to come full time to the *New Yorker* for a long while. But Alva always refused. Said he was too old to change his field. He was a reporter and he didn't want to take a chance on magazines. Ross said to me that if I could get Alva to come to the *New Yorker,* that's all I'd ever have to do.

" 'How much did you offer him?' I asked.

" 'Oh, we never discussed salary,' Ross said.

" 'Well, let's offer him three hundred dollars a week,' I said. 'That's double what he's getting on the *Herald Tribune.* And if we offer him a lot of money, he just won't be able to turn it down.'

" 'Bergman, you're a genius,' Ross said. 'I never thought of offering him money.'

"So I made a date with Alva. I told him we'd guarantee him three hundred dollars a week. I can still see Alva turning pale, standing up, and saying, 'Gee, I'll have to think that over.'

"I went back to Ross and told him we got Alva. We had, too."

This incident, certainly important in the history of the *New Yorker,* "showed Ross's occasionally naïve and charming impracticality, although he was the world's greatest." The quoted words are Bergman's.

Harold Ross's loss of Bergman was William Randolph Hearst's gain, for the former *New Yorker* editor was hired to build up the New York *American*'s daily "March of Events" page, known to the printers as "the highbrow page," and build it up he did. A few months later Ross ran into him somewhere and said, "You're causing a lot of excitement at the *New Yorker*—and worry, too, I guess. But keep it up, I like it." I don't see how he could have liked it, because Bergman had signed up, among others, for one or two columns a week, Bob

Benchley, Frank Sullivan, Clarence Day, Ogden Nash, and Jim Cain. He also got stuff from Mencken and Oliver Herford which Ross would have liked for the *New Yorker*. I did some columns for the highbrow page, and quite a lot of drawings. The appearance of my drawings there caused Ross to pass the buck to Someone, who passed it to Someone Else, who passed it to Katharine White, who wrote me a note asking me if I hadn't broken my *New Yorker* contract by not first letting the art meeting see my drawings for the *American*. The *New Yorker* had seen them all and turned them down. I passed this fact to Katharine, who passed it to Someone Else, who passed it to Someone, who passed it to Ross.

My drawings ceased appearing in the *American* when Bergman got a note from old Hearst himself, which read: "Stop running those dogs on your page. I wouldn't have them peeing on my cheapest rug." In 1934 the Old Man stopped Cain's columns, too, over Bergman's protest that Jim was one of the best and most popular *American* writers. Hearst's final note on this matter read: "Get rid of Cain. I thought Abel had done it. Sorry he failed."

8

Onward and Upward and Outward

By 1933 the first decade of the magazine was running out, and the period might have been called, in Sir Winston's phrase, the end of the beginning. It was also the beginning of the end of the *New Yorker* as I had first known it—an irreverent, understaffed, comic weekly, with little on its mind, going nowhere in particular.

The 1933 scroll was charged with all kinds of things for H. W. Ross. The Depression, which had been aimed directly at him, was still holding on, though getting better (1934 was to be one of the *New Yorker*'s best financial years). Hitler had risen to power, the banks had closed, Prohibition was soon to become a sorry memory, and the Roosevelt family had come to Washington, thus supplying "Talk of the Town" with dozens of anecdotes and the art department with dozens of idea drawings. In 1933 Ring Lardner died, and the morning *World* came to an end—major sorrows that saddened Ross and all of us.

Then there was the bright side of the year. A young man named William Shawn came to work for the magazine as a Talk reporter, and St. Clair McKelway, a former *Herald Tribune* reporter, back from a long trip to the Far East where he had edited a paper in Bangkok, Siam, began writing Reporter pieces and profiles; Clifton Fadiman set to work on his ten years of reviewing books, and book publishers' ads flowed in as never before. The drawing pen of Charles Addams began haunting houses, and Clarence Day's reminiscences of his New York boyhood appeared. The Day stories were about New York and, after all, Ross's magazine was called the *New Yorker*. He gave up slowly and reluctantly his old original belief that the weekly ought to be confined to the scenes and people and goings on in that city. My own reminiscences of my youth in Columbus, Ohio, also appeared in 1933, but they were about a foreign country, a million literary miles from New York, and that bothered Ross at first. He had begun with a fixed idea that the *New Yorker* should have an exclusive metropolitan circulation and appeal, and carry only advertisements of the smartest local shops and products, but he adapted himself to the changing scope and the widening scene. He gladly printed Sally Benson's memories of her childhood in St. Louis.

Ross, true to his stature as an editor, learned to change his mind and his magazine with the changing of the world and the temper of the times. At first he had called anything that was serious "grim," but then he convinced himself that most of it was important, and he wanted his magazine to be important. In the first two years of his weekly, he had gleefully hung a total of twenty-one Talk anecdotes on David Wallace, a man known only to Broadway, the Round Table, and the Thanatopsis Literary and Inside Straight Club, but in 1933 Ross did not like to be reminded of these little old intramural gags, printed to amuse a comparative handful of people.

One thing that the *New Yorker* editor never failed to do was to come to his writers and tell them any praise he'd heard about their work, although he sometimes did it scoffingly, punctuating the recital of what he had heard with his well-known "Hogwash" or "Don't give it a second thought." One day, again in 1933, he lurched into my office and blurted, "Dorothy Parker says Hemingway told her that your *My Life and Hard Times* is the best writing coming out of America now."

"I am a remarkable fellow," I told him, "whose quality is detected by all critical intelligences, with the single exception, of course, of yours."

"Nuts!" said Ross.

A few weeks later he banged into my office again to say, in high glee, "It now turns out that Hemingway said that about your writing just to get Faulkner down. Left-handed compliment. Don't take it seriously, don't give it a second thought. If he did mean what he said, why the hell doesn't he give you a blurb for your book when it comes out this fall?" I told him that Hemingway did not write blurbs for anybody's books, but when *My Life and Hard Times* was published, its dust jacket contained a quote from a letter Hemingway had written me from Madrid, which began: "Even when Thurber was writing under the name of Alice B. Toklas, we knew he had it in him if he could only get it out." Ross had a lot of fun with that. He knew, for a wonder, who Miss Toklas was, and a little about the feud between Hemingway and Gertrude Stein. What he didn't remember was that the only piece Hemingway ever wrote for the *New Yorker*, his 1927 parody of the auto-biography of Frank Harris, had a section called "How I Broke with Gertrude Stein."

Things continued to go well for Ross and his true love, the *New Yorker*, in 1934, and one of them was the beginning of a real sense of order—at least, physical order around the offices. Ebba Jonsson came in as librarian, to find the files in much the same shape as a house in which only men had been living for years. In one small dusty room there was an old couch loaded down with carbons of letters, documents, and papers of all kinds. It must have taken her a year to get the files in order. Ross had hoped, in moving from the old building to the new, that "sofas" would somehow be left behind. A few were actually got rid of, including one that had been in the hallway outside White's old office. One of the women employees had offered to take it, and it was given to her gladly. Knowing something about furniture, she had recognized it as an old piece of Americana, and office legend has it that she sold it for twelve hundred dollars. But sofas remained as part of the furnishings of the *New Yorker* offices. "It's like a goddam rest home, or sun porch, or something," Ross used to bellow. "It's what I get for having to employ women."

He later had to have a couch put in his own office, for his doctors had ordered him to rest after lunch, and whenever he could, between tasks. Andy White, who has always had a couch, still preserves a note from Ross which he found one day in his typewriter when he woke up from a nap. It read: "Drop in on me when you wake up. I never disturb a sleeping man." Ross never disturbed a man if he was typing, either, or if there was, God forbid, a woman in his office.

When the magazine moved to West 43rd Street, offices proliferated, and there were now two editorial floors, the nineteenth and the twentieth. "Those guys upstairs," became "those guys downstairs," as the business department took over a lower floor. Instead of tearing down walls, Ross had fun having two staircases put in between the nineteenth and twentieth floors. Reporters from everywhere joined the staff, all of them top flight, most of them well known, some of them famous. Ross, newspaperman and ex-editor of the *Stars and Stripes,* was back in his original element. Stanley Walker, who had won national acclaim as the city editor of the *Herald Tribune* and the author of *City Editor,* was hired, in August, 1936, as the new Sense Maker.

Ross had known and admired Walker, as reporter and city editor, long before he met most of the rest of us, and he had been trying to get him on the *New Yorker* for years. As city editor of the *Herald Tribune,* Stanley was known to newspapermen from coast to coast, and everybody wanted to work for him, and almost everybody did at one time or another. In 1928 he had stolen Alva Johnston from the *Times,* where he had been getting a hundred and seventy-five dollars a week but no by-lines. Stanley got him for less money, to begin with, and then lost him when Bernard Bergman offered him three hundred dollars a week to come to the *New Yorker.* The *Herald Tribune,* in Walker's years, had perhaps the most notable array of city room talent of any paper in the country. Once, about 1926, Mencken wrote Walker to find out the name of the man who had written three pieces for the *Trib* that had caught Mencken's attention. They were the work of Nunnally Johnson. Even before Walker, the *Herald Tribune* had had such men as Herbert Asbury, authority on the old gangs of New York, and Forrest Davis, who became celebrated for his covering of the Scopes trial in Tennessee. (Later, Johnson, Davis, and I were all on the staff of the *Evening Post* for a time. Nunnally had been brought in to do the paper's daily column "Around the Town," which I had wanted, but the city editor had said, "We need a man with a name to write that column," and so I left, later to run "Talk of the Town.")

Walker's loss of Alva to the *New Yorker* was the first of a series of Ross raids on the *Herald Tribune* which finally persuaded Walker to leave that paper, too. Among the men who had worked under him and were later to continue their outstanding writing for Ross were Joseph Mitchell, whom Stanley had brought up from darkest Carolina; John O'Hara, who came to the *Trib* from Pottsville, Pennsylvania, at the suggestion of F.P.A.; Joel Sayre, and John and David Lardner, Richard O. Boyer, Sanderson Vanderbilt, Don Wharton, and McKelway. Walker had also wanted to hire A. J. Liebling and Jack Alexander, but his paper was already overstaffed. Liebling was on the *New Yorker* when Stanley arrived there, and Jack Alexander began his *New Yorker* work with a two-part profile on James J. Hines. (This profile, Walker has written me, "was really the beginning of the downfall of Hines, as I had meant it to be, and Tom Dewey carried the ball from there.")

Ross, at the start, had hired only one reporter (not counting Talk men)—Morris Markey; he now found it hard to keep all the new identities straight in his mind, often confused Mitchell with Liebling, or popped his head into Alexander's office to say, "How are things going, Boyer?" and then looked in on Boyer to say, "How are things going, Alexander?"

The problem of how to pay "all these guys" overwhelmed Ross. They were put on drawing accounts, of varying amounts, but since their separate output differed in quantity, Ross was up against one of his great monetary quandaries. "Markey was glib," he used to say, "and he turned out a hell of a lot of stuff, too damn fast. Sayre and Mitchell are great, but they're the slowest damned writers in the world." He worried intensely about differences in speed of production. "McNulty goes out on an assignment, and comes back the same day, by God, and hammers out his piece, as if he were on a newspaper deadline. Sayre is working in August on something he started in April." Ross's most remarkable worry about output was expressed to me like this: "Hersey took only ten days to write that Hiroshima stuff, but it's an office secret, so don't go telling it around town." Not long ago I asked Hersey about this. He took it in his quiet stride, and said, "I'm afraid it took a little longer than ten days."

Walker was an old city desk man, trained to make quick decisions and to get things done fast, and while Ross loved efficiency, he was also alarmed by any speeding-up process, for he had got away from daily deadlines to the more leisurely pace of a weekly. He was often trapped, in Walker's time and later, between the Scylla of celerity and the Charybdis of care. Walker thinks that Ross was conditioned by his army experience to feel comfortable only in a maze of rigmaroles, channels, memos, buck-passing and news meetings, but it is hard to pin Ross down with any label. After the Talk meetings had been abandoned in the early thirties, News meetings were set up and at one of these, after the war, Weekes said to Ross, "You want to run this like an army message center." Ross dismissed that with a hand wave and said, "Hell, no, it's more like a board of directors' meeting." Whatever it was like to Ross, it stultified Walker. "My experience on the *New Yorker*," Stanley says, "was, I suppose, something like trying to swim in a vat of blackstrap molasses while handcuffed. Or, maybe better, it was like fighting a revolving door in a blizzard. You can't win, but anger doesn't get you anywhere either.

"One day while I was on the payroll, I encountered an old newspaperman on the street and he said he wanted to do something for the magazine. I knew he couldn't do much, but I gave him a vague suggestion anyhow—a possible story over in New Jersey. The man, to my surprise, turned up with a pretty good story, and with a little reworking, it made the magazine and Ross liked it fine. Then it occurred to him that the suggestion and the assignment had not gone through the regular channels—that is, it had not been cleared and approved in conference, etc. He brooded about this for days. It meant that the military system had been flouted and that something was wrong somehow.

"Toward the end of my captivity, Ik Shuman came in one day, having been parted from Paul Block. I assigned him to a Reporter idea on an old motorman or something of the sort. Ik went out and got the story that afternoon and evening and wrote it the next morning. It required virtually no rewriting, or even editing, and Ross was so pleased with it that he gave Shuman a job. But, after some time, Ross began to worry about the story of the old motorman. How long had Shuman worked on it? Shuman told him the truth, and Ross was shocked and hurt. He thought such a story should have required at least a week's work and painful lucubration. Then, following this confusing line of thought, he wondered if he were not being cheated by the writers who took too much time. This way, of course, lies madness."

Ik Shuman, who held out for eight rough years, was placed, for a time, on Ross's highest pedestal. Ik had helped him work out "a philosophy on payment to contributors." Ik told me in a letter, "The more we spent on the magazine, the longer we held contributors, the greater grew the circulation and the higher grew the advertising rate. We raised every contributor, feeling out our way, and I once figured that for every dollar we spent then, we got back three dollars in revenue." This, to Ross, was one of the miracles of money, one of the wonders of free enterprise. I used to hear him bawling over the phone in his office, "I'll bring Shuman. I want you to meet him. He's finally making some sense out of this place."

Ik's greatest achievement, in Ross's admiring eyes, was a deal he made, in September 1936, with *Reader's Digest*, which had been paying only eighteen hundred dollars a year for the right to reprint Talk items. Ik not only got fifteen thousand dollars, retroactively, for what the *Digest* had run in previous years, but he got DeWitt Wallace to agree to pay twenty-five thousand dollars a year in the future. The *Digest* connection soon became one of Ross's major headaches, and he finally decided to break off the relationship and to refuse to let the other magazine reprint any *New Yorker* material whatever. "The *Digest* is a competitor of ours," Ross decided, "and I'll be damned if we're not helping them be just that." He called a conference, the only one in his life, of a group of writers to discuss the situation. They included Sally Benson, Robert Coates, S. J. Perelman, and me, and perhaps a few others. What really had him down, he said, was the *Digest*'s offer to pay *New Yorker* writers directly—that is, to relieve Ross's weekly of the financial burden of compensating for such pieces as the *Digest* wanted to condense and reprint. We all agreed, or at least Ross said we did, with his determination to end the *Digest* reprint system. I dissented, because, as I told him, I could get five times as much for a *Digest* reprint as I was paid by the *New Yorker* for first serial rights. The sputtering of letters between Ross and me about that went on for years. This odd correspondence baffles me now, on going over it, as much as it must have baffled Ross at the time. I came around in the end to his point of view. ("Thurber's crazy. You never know one day where he's going to stand the next.") I'm glad that I ended this exchange of blows with a bouquet: "The *New Yorker* is the only magazine for which a man can write with dignity and tranquillity." Tranquillity? I must have been in a rare mood indeed that day, but I'm glad that I wrote the letter, anyway.

The thirties were crowded with Miracle Men who came and went. One of these was Philip D. Hoyt, and for a time Ross was positive he had found a real organizational genius. Hoyt, who had not only been the youngest American major in the First World War, but, as Deputy Police Commissioner of New York in charge of traffic, had made new sense out of the city's traffic problems, was also a man with journalistic experience on the *New York Times*. Ross brought him in as secretary-treasurer, and he promptly became overwhelmed with paperwork that bored him. He was put in charge of reprints and copyright matters and also acted as liaison officer between the office and the printing plant. I think he lasted about a year.

Then Ross finally got what he had hoped for from the start, a team of Miracle Men—Ik Shuman, who was in charge of order, systems, and financial matters, and St. Clair McKelway, who became managing editor in charge of the editorial contents of the magazine. Here, then, were two geniuses, one with a wonderful lamp to rub when organizational difficulties arose, and the other with a magic wand to wave at writers and artists and such. In 1937 McKelway signed a three-year contract at an annual salary of fifteen thousand dollars—everything was going to run smoothly from then on, and the only trouble was that it didn't.

Suddenly the Second World War happened to H. W. Ross. God, how he pitied him! McKelway and Charles Cooke accepted commissions in the Air Corps; Hobart Weekes, the Comma King, became a captain; and almost everybody else seemed to blossom out in uniform. As the boys went off to war, Ross paced and worried. He muttered that the leaving of his key men for the war was "by God, disloyal," and tried to hold McKelway and Weekes on the ground that they were indispensable, but they wouldn't be held. He finally saw, as he always did, that they were right. Then God sent him William Shawn. Ross's successor as editor of the *New Yorker* had, to be sure, been around for eight years, but Ross had scarcely noticed him, and when Shuman suggested that Bill should replace McKelway, Ross spluttered, "What the hell makes you think he could handle the job? Dismiss it from your mind." He soon found out, however, that Shawn could handle the Big Job. Without Shawn's hard work and constant counsel, Ross would never have made the distinguished record he did as editor during the war.

On the Sunday of Pearl Harbor a flustered Ross showed up at the office, to find Shawn already there. They spent that day, and the next, putting the magazine on what Ross called a war basis, making over "Talk of the Town," ripping out civilian ornaments and replacing them with spots of cannon and of

flags, sending reporters scurrying all over for war features, profile ideas and Reporter pieces. Ross and his lieutenant, Shawn,
manned a central desk, assigned Liebling and Sayre and others
to cover various theaters of the war, and speeded up production as never before. Rea Irvin drew a war cover, and it was
put through and used in the unbelievable *New Yorker* time of
two weeks.

The devil-may-care magazine of the 1920's reached its
serious highwater mark with the publication in 1946 of John
Hersey's famous long article on the bombing of Hiroshima.
Ross, always the conservative, cautious in the face of radical
change, went along with Shawn's belief that one whole issue
of the magazine should be occupied solely by the Hersey
account of the bombing. A few irate subscribers canceled their
subscriptions, a few letters of denunciation came in, but there
was far more praise than attack, and before long a copy of that
issue, if you could find one, cost twenty-five dollars.

The *New Yorker*'s advertising rates, circulation, and stature
increased, to the gratification of Ross, but the increase in size
dejected him. "Goddam it, we'll soon be running two hundred
pages," he moaned. It meant increased work for him, Shawn,
Katharine White, Lobrano, and their assistants. Ross arrived
earlier than ever before, and worked later into the night, but
with the same meticulous care. He tossed restlessly in bed for
hours one night because Hersey had written, of a tangle of
bicycles in Tokyo after the bombing, that they had become
"lopsided." The next day—the story was then still in proof—he
argued that "Bicycles are not of the dimension of things that
become lopsided." The word was changed to "crumpled," and
Ross was satisfied.

One of the distinguished fiction writers who had gone to
war, to add to Ross's gloom, was Edward Newhouse. In May,
1958, he wrote me a letter, and what he reports in it seems to
me an important part of the history of Ross, the *New Yorker*,
the U.S. of that troubled era, and the U.S. Army:

Late in the War, the *Chicago Tribune* ran a series of articles which started things rolling. They said I'd published some fiction in *The New Masses* and other Communist or Communist-run publications, and what was I doing as an Air Force major engaged in highly confidential work on General Arnold's staff? I forget whether they mentioned that I'd been in my teens when I wrote for *The New Masses*, but I remember with great clarity that they said I had been decorated by Marshal Stalin at Teheran "for undisclosed services." I was at Teheran, all right, during the Big Three conference, but the American officers who received the Orders of Suvorov and Kutuzov there were Admirals Leahy and King, and Generals Marshall, Arnold, and Somervell. Anyway, Congressman Rankin (remember him?) made some speeches and demanded that I appear before some sub-committee or other. I was foolhardy enough to want to do just that, but thank God, John McCloy, who was Assistant Secretary of War at the time, wouldn't let me. Instead, Mr. Stimson sent General Bissell, then head of G-2, with a letter saying that the Army was satisfied as to my loyalty. Then Rankin asked for Stimson's resignation, no less, and everybody took the floor to say what a splendid fellow Mr. Stimson was, so I got lost in the shuffle. I don't think the *New Yorker* or Ross came into it, unless it was in the course of conversations with McCloy or Arnold or some other War Dept. people.

I saw a lot more of Ross during the War than I did in the years before or after. I was writing some stories about people in the Air Force, and not clearing with Intelligence or Public Relations or anybody else. Ross ran the stories but never without muttering that I'd be court-martialed and the magazine suppressed. He thought we were being very brave and reckless, and I could not convince him that this was not the case at all. True, there was one timid colonel who once called some of the stories to General Arnold's attention, but the old man shrugged him off.

I thought that Ross was being somewhat timid, too,

that no one in authority was even reading the stories, but in one instance at least he came closer than I to being right. In that story there was some stuff about the foolishness that went on at the Air Force Officer Candidate School in Miami Beach, and Ross was positive I'd lose my commission and the magazine would be banned or suppressed. I didn't find out until after the War that I would have been in for some trouble if I hadn't chanced to be on Arnold's staff. A commission was appointed to look into the practices at OCS; it made some recommendations, which were adopted for a time, but then the school reverted to all the old nonsense, or so I'm told.

Ross was ambivalent as hell about the military. One day "they" were going to ban the magazine or "they" were going to run it out of business by drafting everyone on the staff; the next day he would be unabashedly nostalgic about the old outfit on the *Stars and Stripes*. He groaned every time McKelway or Weekes or I got a promotion; the Air Force must be in godawful shape to have to dig that deeply into the barrel. He got hold of a photograph of General Arnold pinning the Legion of Merit on me, and he had it framed; it hung in his office until the place was dismantled after his death, and then Tom Gorman mailed it to me. Maybe Ross thought it was a funny picture; it was.

He made me promise I'd do everything to keep Gus Lobrano from getting a commission—threatened to close up shop if Gus left. "They" had drafted practically everybody else; *Time, Inc.* was getting thousands of people deferred or exempted, even ad men, and you will remember what contempt he could pack into those two words—ad men. He kept track of all the staff people in the service, and he succeeded, mostly through me, sometimes through John Winterich, in getting many of them transferred to more congenial posts. After the war, he did a lot to find us apartments or houses to live in—things like that.

What made Ross important was his editing, of

course. On a short casual of mine, a couple of years after the war, he came up with thirty queries. Gus and I between us ignored twenty-eight of them, but the remaining two made the difference between a good story and a poor one.

The boys had put on their battle dress and left Ross, but there were consolations and compensations. One evening in 1942, to settle an argument with my wife, I looked up a few letters a friend of ours named Mary Mian had written us from France. Helen read them aloud, looking for the name in France that had started the mild dispute, and it came to both of us at the same time that we were dealing with a born writer. I didn't get Ross out of bed, but I called him the next day and told him I had found another writer for the *New Yorker*. "You can't tell anything about letters," he said, "but tell her to get it on paper." She got it on paper, Ross knew it was good, and began printing the first of the series about France by Mary Mian that was later published in the book called *My Country-in-Law*. The last letter I got from her had this wreath for Ross: "Once he wrote on a story of mine, 'This is a good job,' and I'll never forget that as long as I live."

As the *New Yorker* came of age, Ross realized the futility of his original determination to keep all casuals casual, under two thousand words if possible, light of tone, with nothing particular to say. There had been a time when he actually toyed with the notion of "identifying" stories—that is, using some kind of symbolic decoration next to the title to indicate whether what followed was humorous or serious. "We could use a spirit lamp for serious pieces, and maybe the comic mask or something for humor, if we get any," he told me.

I think I had seen the coming era of the long short story, and the long long article, even before Ross did. I had once sent him a kidding note saying that it would be a good thing to get away from short aimless casuals that began "Mr. Pinwither picked up the begonia," and ended "Mr. Pinwither put the begonia down." Ross surrendered to the coming of length, though never unconditionally. His first important white flag was raised when he bought Mary McCarthy's "The Weeds," which ran to almost ten thousand words. He was quick to recognize the quality of such fiction writers as Newhouse, Irwin Shaw, J. D. Salinger, Jean Stafford, and John Cheever, to name only a few. There was more than one day, though, when he invaded my office, or White's, or Gibbs's, to lament the dwindling of humorous pieces with the growth of what he always called "grim stuff." When William Attwood turned in a brief parody of *PM* the young newspaperman was wined and dined and encouraged to submit more humor. Legend has it that Attwood's next piece was "grim." Ross said to me, in one of his darkest moods, "You find a guy that can write humor, and the first thing you know he turns in a piece about a man stumbling over the body of his wife on the floor, or something like that." He wondered what he could do to restimulate the inflow of humorous pieces, and I asked him if he had thought of changing the nature of the modern world and the grim course of the century.

A distinguished woman psychiatrist I once met attributed the decline of humor in the forties to the effect of the Depression on talented youngsters. Her argument went something like this: "Boys have a kind of inherited adjustment to the sight of their fathers or older brothers in uniform, but it was not so easy for them to adjust to the vague or meaningless tragedies that followed the stock market crash. If a husband, in civilian clothes, returned from work, say in Wall Street, pale and shaken, and said to his wife, 'We are ruined,' their growing children were likely to suffer a new kind of psychic trauma, and some of them did not get over it easily, if at all. Thus a burgeoning writer or artist might find his creative talent turning to what your Mr. Ross called 'grim stuff.'" Ross would say, "If a man in these goddam grim stories doesn't shoot his wife, he shoots himself. Everybody gets in bed with everybody else. It's a hell of a thing, but I guess there's nothing to do about it."

Harold Ross, inherently cautious, fundamentally conservative, stuck resolutely to his original belief that the *New Yorker* was not a magazine designed to stem tides, join crusades, or take political stands. He was not going to print a lot of "social-conscious stuff," because his intuition told him that, if he did, he would be overwhelmed by it. He has been accused of timidity—and he had a lot of that—of evasion of responsibility, and of the loss of his chance to turn his magazine into a voice of protest and rebellion. The *New Yorker,* he staunchly contended, was not the *New Republic* or the *Nation;* it wanted superior prose, funny drawings, and sound journalism, without propaganda. He didn't encourage, he even discouraged, pieces on McCarthyism, and in a letter to Frank Sullivan, who had suggested writing a piece about his cliché expert and McCarthyism, he wrote, "I don't think so. I'd think twice about it. I can't see it myself, and if I can't see a thing, I'm usually right."

By the time Ross died, the shelves of the *New Yorker* library were filled with four hundred books made up of stories and articles and drawings that had appeared in his magazine. His writers had won many literary awards, degrees from colleges and universities and other honors, and Ross, who took a quiet pride in being a kind of patriarch of a literary family, was gratified by every one. Andy White had got the honorary degree of Doctor of Letters from Yale, and that pleased Ross no end. He had a special, though inarticulate, respect for Yale. Back in the twenties, he had offered to send Carmen Peppe, then a youngster in the make-up department, and now one of its indispensable figures, to Yale—just why nobody exactly knows. Peppe did not want to go to Yale and so Ross gave up the project.

He lived to see his magazine expand from a tight and hard provincialism to take in fact and fiction and humor about practically the entire world, to have an army of contributors of a score of different nationalities writing about every nook and corner of the planet. The weekly still holds on to such vestigial standing departments as "Our Far-Flung Correspondents" and "Our Footloose Correspondents," old original apologies for pieces about far and foreign places. There were years when Ross was perturbed when "Talk of the Town" ranged as far afield as Connecticut or New Jersey, and he once asked me, "How the hell are we going to hang this Philadelphia anecdote?" After a few tries, I finally hung it, to his satisfaction, this way: "A horseman has just arrived in town from Philadelphia with the news that . . ." Nowadays a Talk item may begin "There is an odd sign in the window of a restaurant in Copenhagen," and the department could well be called the Talk of the World. When, two years ago, it reported the closing down of the last livery stable in Manhattan, the piece sounded quaint and comic, almost like a parody of a parody of the old "Talk of the Town," a dimming echo, a shadow out of the past.

Nothing pleased Ross more than the increasing sales of *New Yorker* casuals and articles to the movies, and the various successful Broadway plays that were based on *New Yorker* stuff, from *Walter Mitty* to the greatest *New Yorker* success of all, *Life with Father,* the Crouse-Lindsay comedy based on Clarence Day's *New Yorker* pieces, that ran for 3424 performances, or a little more than eight years. When Ross told Frank Sullivan that if he had never printed anything except Clarence Day's stuff, it would have been enough, he probably didn't know—at any rate, I hope he didn't—that the central theme of the play, the baptism of Father Day, was based on two stories that had appeared in *Harper*'s and later in a book called *God and My Father.* Oh well, no man can have everything, but Harold Ross had as much as the next man, and surely more than any other editor of his time and nation.

The old Tuesday afternoon art conferences did not long survive the death of Harold Ross. According to one staff member, they soon degenerated into long silences broken by polite murmurings. No longer was there a Ross to stare at a cover, lean forward, lean back, then stand up and look, and finally say, "Where am *I* supposed to be? In a building across the street from that house, or up in an airplane or where?" Perspective, foreshortening, and point of observation often gave him pause, or made him rant, or dictate some sharpshooting note to Miss Terry to send to the artist: "Get this damn building drawn so that I'm not looking at it while suspended in the air."

The *New Yorker* now has at least seventy-five artists who draw regularly for the magazine, and a file of thousands of captions that have been used, against which newly submitted captions are checked, so that only once in a long while is there a duplication. There was a dark day a long time ago when somebody recognized a drawing that had been printed in the *New Yorker* as one that had appeared many years before in *Punch,* with only a few slight differences, and there was a cover which, somebody told Ross, had been heavily influenced by a famous Daumier, and so he had a brand-new problem to worry about. The present editors take the drawings in their stride, and if the contrived gag sometimes seems to have

replaced the recognizable comic American scene, it has to be remembered that the changes have been rung on almost every conceivable humorous idea, and that, as James Geraghty, the art editor, says, "Seventy per cent of the drawings we were getting showed a husband and wife yelling at each other."

The department runs smoothly enough nowadays, but I still miss on Tuesday afternoons the old art meetings and the occasional sound of Ross's voice baying the moon of despair, rising like a trumpet solo out of a long silence that will never again be broken by the harried old perfectionist who so often wanted to know, "Do women wear hats like that today?" or, "That guy is not a major—he's a goddam doorman."

9

"Sex Is an Incident"

*One lovely day in October, 1933, Harold Ross, the unimperturb-*able editor of the *New Yorker,* went running to Katharine White, his office confidante in times of emotional crises, with a new and wild alarm: "Now Thurber's playing with dolls!" What had scared him could have been figured out quickly and calmly by a lesser man, a man untrained in the difficult art of how to approach everything the hard way. My daughter's second birthday was coming up, and I had bought her a big, beautifully dressed French doll. One of the girls at the office had taken it out of its box to show to the others, and had then set it up on my desk with its arms extended toward the door. Ross, banging into the office, deeply worried by the state of the world, or a comma, or something, had come face to face with what he regarded as new evidence that I was getting curiouser and curiouser, and likely to stop writing for his magazine any minute.

Mrs. White had a much easier time allaying his fears about me that day than she had had four years before when Ross lurched into her office one morning wailing, "Now Thurber's going with actresses!" My private life, like that of everybody else on the magazine, was a constant concern and puzzle to

Ross. Married in 1922, separated in 1929, later reunited, and then divorced, and married again to a second wife, I was too much for Ross to keep track of, and my status at any moment disturbed him. The night before he plopped his new worry into Katharine's lap, he had seen me at Tony's with an actress, but only one actress, and had sat down at our table. My companion, who didn't like to drink, had a glass of lemonade on the table in front of her, but Ross, gesticulating recklessly, knocked that over, too. This is not exaggeration, but simply the cold, damp facts.

Sex, in or near the office, in any guise or context, frightened Ross. Sex was, to him, an ominous and omnibus word that could mean anything from the first meeting of a man and a woman, through marriage and the rearing of children, to extramarital relations, divorce, and alimony. When he swore, as he often did, that he was going to "keep sex, by God, out of this office," and then added, "Sex is an incident," he meant handholding, goo-goo eyes, fornication, adultery, the consummation of marriage, and legal sexual intercourse. Whether or not Ross knew it, there was a wistful and comic military-headquarters quality in his oft-repeated directive about sex. He brusquely ordered it confined to quarters, or assigned it to KP duty to keep its mind off itself, or simply declared all the offices and personnel of the *New Yorker* magazine off-bounds for the biological urge. Sex, normal and abnormal, legal and illicit, paid little attention to Ross and his imperious commands. It hid from him, and went on about its affairs as it had been doing for thousands of years.

There were many office marriages during Ross's lifetime, among them the unions of Peter Arno and Lois Long, Andy White and Katharine Angell, Bernard Bergman and Frances Dellar, who had been Lois Long's assistant. Lois, whom Ross had been lucky enough to steal from *Vanity Fair* at the very start of the *New Yorker,* had once been an actress. She knew just how to embarrass the girl-shy editor, and loved to do it.

The first time I ever saw her, the day after I went to work on the magazine, she came into his office with the devil in her eye. Ross said hastily, "Don't kiss me, Long. This is Thurber. He's going to make some sense out of this place." Lois Long, alias Lipstick, alias L.L., who could tell more about a man in two minutes than Ross sometimes found out in two years, plainly doubted it. Arno was not the only New Yorker who fell in love with Lois Long. A middle-aged gentleman, who was in his twenties at the time, has written me that after Lois became Mrs. Arno, he was heartbroken and for several days and nights did little except play a record of "Who?" over and over on his Victrola. This lovelorn fellow, by the way, was the man who first suggested that Arno should turn the Whoops Sisters into a series. (It ran with great success until Ross decided the uninhibited sisters were becoming too drunken and bawdy for his family magazine.)

There had been a large reception room, with easy chairs, a couch or two, and screens, in the old offices in West 45th Street, but Ross had once had a shattering experience there, and he ruled out a reception room when he moved to the present quarters of the magazine. Men and women now meet in a widening of the hall, sparsely furnished, just as you step off the elevator on the nineteenth floor. It's as open as a goldfish bowl.

Ross's shattering experience, his first dismaying brush with sex in the office, occurred during the first summer of the magazine's existence. A young woman, one year out of Vassar, called on Ross with a letter of introduction from an old friend of his. He read the letter in his office and then ventured out into the reception room to interview the fair applicant for a job. She might have gotten it if she hadn't said, in conclusion, "Of course, I realize what would be expected of a girl in a place like this—I mean in addition to her regular work." Ross blenched, I have no doubt, mumbled something, turned tail, and fled from the room. Then he called a meeting of all the male members of the staff, of whom there must have been at least seven or eight at the time, and blamed them for what had just been said to him. "You're giving this magazine a bad name around town," he roared. "People are getting the wrong idea about it and about me." Nobody knew what he was talking about, but they were all used to that.

One of the chill traditions of the *New Yorker,* and I think it grew out of Ross's determination to dehumanize or at least de-emotionalize the place, was soon sensed by all of us when we went to work there. Almost nobody was ever introduced to anybody else, and there was never a general assembly of the staff to talk things over, for propinquity must have seemed to Ross a danger outweighing any benefits of staff cooperation. St. Clair McKelway had been working on the magazine for three months before we met. Lillian Ross had been there a couple of years before I met her on the stairs with someone who introduced us. Nobody has caught this cool state of unfamiliarity among co-workers better than Edmund Wilson, who became the magazine's literary critic in 1944. This is from a letter he wrote me recently:

> It was only after Russell Maloney's death that I realized that the person I had been thinking was Maloney must actually be somebody else. Since I was seeing him still in the corridors, I knew that it could not be Maloney. I thought that Geraghty was Lobrano for years. That girl with the built-in tape-recorder who did those articles on Hemingway and the Stephen Crane movie—about whom I had a certain curiosity—I have never been able to identify or get anyone to introduce me to.
>
> I must have been working in the office for years before Ruth Flint identified me correctly, and I should undoubtedly never have known her if she had not been a friend of my wife's. At about the time I started in, a new messenger to the printer's appeared. He was old-fashioned-looking and shabby genteel, carried a briefcase, wore a black derby and an old dark overcoat; his face was

pallid and faded, and he walked with averted eyes; his features were rather refined. He looked, as Ruth said, like someone who might have absconded from an English bank and come to the United States. She thought that this man was me. When she told me this, I became rather curious about him and found, on inquiry, that she was so far right that he was actually a disbarred Virginia lawyer. At one time I played with the idea of hiring him to impersonate me and deliver the lectures and after-dinner speeches for which I am sometimes asked.

Wilson was used to the office luncheons of the *New Republic* staff, and to even more intimate fraternization on the old *Vanity Fair,* where, on certain rainy days, charades were actually played by men and women of the staff. The game was instituted by the editor, Frank Crowninshield. Games at the *New Yorker,* or the merest suggestion of games, would have given Ross the jumps or an even worse seizure. Furthermore, the *New Yorker* people were not gregarious. White was a solitary luncher, for example, and I had been on the *New Yorker* a year before I had lunch with him. Most of us played our own versions of Post Office and Pillow here and there about town, but there was nothing doing in this area at the *New Yorker.* Oh, I could tell you a few stories, but I won't. There was another cause for the ungregariousness of the people. The first of a series of three or four *New Yorker* parties was held in the offices, in the American tradition, but there was so much spooning and goo-goo eyes, and drinking and worse, that Ross issued an edict saying that all office parties would be held elsewhere after that.

H. W. Ross was married three times to women, and once, and for keeps, to the *New Yorker* magazine. He differed from most men in that his office, not his home, was his castle. His inviolable, and formidable, selfness had no permanent fusion point with any woman. The only entity he ever fused with was the *New Yorker.* It was the deadly and victorious rival of each of his three wives. Neither I nor any other man ever heard Ross tell a dirty story, but when he became what he called "clinical" he could take your breath away with his forthrightness about the sexual nature, exploits, and disabilities of friends and acquaintances, true or just guessed at. I heard him only once in my life talk about a conquest of his own, and that time he was what Mencken used to call "spifflicated."

Ross, as I have said, divided women into good and bad, but there was a subdivision of the bad, which, while not exactly good, was somehow privileged. These were the women of great talent, especially in the theater, whose deviations from convention and morality in their private lives were, by the very nature and demands of talent, excusable—"*I guess*" he might well have added.

One night in the 1920's Ross persuaded a country bumpkin to go with him to Texas Guinan's night club—he never took me there, perhaps because he was afraid I would lose my innocence and the winsome, childlike quality of my prose. Between marriages, and not yet permanently "off the sauce," as O'Hara puts it, he was in a merry mood, and all of a sudden, to his companion's dismay, jumped up from his chair and crossed to a table where two couples were drinking and talking and watching the show, whatever it was. The charm of one of the ladies had caught Ross's fancy and he made a gallant, though misguided, effort to bend over and kiss the back of her hand. The kiss ended up on the nape of her neck. Chairs were pushed back and the two men at the table stood up. They did not enter into the spirit of Ross's merriment. An experienced bouncer appeared. The experienced Miss Guinan disappeared. The bouncer, stiff and firm, helped Ross and his friend into their overcoats and gave them their hats. Fifteen seconds after the editor's kiss, he and his companion were out on the sidewalk. Ross was bewildered and hurt. "I thought it was gay," he said dejectedly.

A few years after that, during a hiatus in both Ross's mar-

ried life and mine, we made the rounds of a few night spots in
the company of Burgess Meredith and Franchot Tone. Some
time after midnight, in one of the gathering places of café society, I told Ross I would demonstrate how gentlemen manage
a proper approach to the Strange Lady at the Next Table. She
happened to be one of the more famous post-debutantes of her
day, and Tone and I, arm in arm, went over to her table,
bowed, and presented ourselves. We were not thrown out of
the place, but we did get a cold and wordless rejection, becoming in a lady of quality. Her breeding and her hauteur were
untouched by both my dark sinister Latin charm and Tone's
boyish demeanor and frank open countenance. The next day I
found Ross stalking the corridors of the *New Yorker,* his shoulders sagging, his mood depressed. To my "What's the matter
now?" he replied, "Goddam it, I have a certain reputation to
keep up in this town, and I spend one whole night helping you
and Franchot Tone chase *girls* around night clubs." Once again
the Great Multiplier of Menace had turned one girl into girls
and was worrying about the bad effect of all women on all
men.

About this same era he came upon me one evening in the
Oak Room of the Algonquin having drinks with three or four
other persons, including Lilyan Tashman, whom I had never
met before and never saw again, and Humphrey Bogart, a
drinking companion of mine since well before he played Duke
Mantee in *The Petrified Forest* and went on to Hollywood and
fame. Ross wouldn't sit down with us, and I detected all the
signs of his discomfiture. The next day he said to me, "What
the hell are you going around with *Tashman* for? She's way out
of your league, Thurber." I explained that I was not going
around with Miss Tashman, and that my woman companion
the evening before was a housewife and homebody and the
mother of four children. "A likely story," said Ross, and then,
"Well, the hell with it. Now in this casual of yours here, you
use a colon where anybody else would use a dash. I'm not

saying you can't do it. I'm just bringing it up." After an argument, he agreed to let the colon stand, for he was, as I have
said and now say again, at once the most obdurate and reasonable of editors.

The first time I met Ross's mother, she suddenly said,
"Harold was always bashful with the girls, even as a little boy."
Harold was embarrassed and shushed her instantly with
"Don't tell Thurber things like that. He blabs everything.
Besides, it isn't true." It was true, though. Harold Ross
employed the technique I once called the "Get-Right-at-It
Move" in a series of drawings I did for the *New Yorker,* "The
Masculine Approach." He printed all of the drawings except
that one, which showed an impassioned male wrestling with a
girl on a sofa, the gleam of Pan in his eye. The troubled gamin
from Aspen, Colorado, had no subtleties of approach to the
female, no routine of sweet nothings, no romantic build-up.
Before marriage, and between marriages, he was, various
lovely and desirable ladies have told many of us, inclined to
make a sudden and unexpected dive at them, which usually
ended in chaos and the laughter of the love object. He seemed
to believe that "sweep her off her feet" was to be taken literally,
in the physical sense. Once, to a laughing lady he had brought
down with a veritable Catfish Smith football tackle, he moaned,

"What did I do wrong?" This Lochinvar, American Western style, was not alone in his shock tactics; they were practiced on ambushed damsels by a poet I know, a young publisher I used to know, and an English novelist I once met who has written of "tumbling lassies in the bracken," which puts him one up on Ross, for bracken is rougher than carpet.

It doesn't take a psychiatrist to realize that the sudden pounce, similar to what was known in the old six-day bicycle races as a "jam," is the natural reverse of the coin of masculine shyness, especially in the virile Western type, unlettered in the literature of love. There is desperation and high impatience in it, as well as desire, a restless determination to get it all over with in a smoke screen of blustery action. Ross was ever afraid that sex would forget it was an incident and become an episode, and then an interlude, and, before long, the whole story, God help us all, of a man's life.

The psychic trauma of Ross's experience with the Vassar girl in 1925 stayed with him to the end. He jittered at the sight of an unfamiliar female face in any of the offices, and told Katharine White, as the *New Yorker* increased in size and more and more women typists and secretaries were employed, that he had to find a woman of strong character and firm hand to ride shotgun on the goddam girls on the editorial floor. He found what he was looking for in Daise Terry, in 1929, and she is still there, her hand as firm as ever, though she has ten times as many girls to control as there were thirty years ago. The editor carried a lot of his "problems of a personal nature" to her. When my daughter was born, spang in the middle of the afternoon of Wednesday, October 7, 1931, Ross turned to Miss Terry with a nervous monologue that must have gone like this: "I hear Thurber has just had a daughter. I hope somebody's looking after him. Send Mrs. Thurber some flowers and say on the card they're from the *New Yorker*. I thought babies were born early in the morning or late at night. I'm surrounded by women and children. I have to look after everybody's personal life. Sometimes I wonder how the hell I ever get out a magazine. I hear the baby only weighs seven pounds—is that *enough*? I know damn well *I* weighed nine pounds. It has something to do with diet now, and is probably a fad of the doctors." Then he must have stared about him morosely and harped on a theme he never left unharped on long. "This place isn't a business office, it's a sitting room, and it's becoming a, by God, nursery."

Ross didn't like it at all when he found out, bumbling into what we called the Goings On room, that the girls there brewed both tea and coffee every afternoon, and he was appalled when he bumped into a Coca-Cola machine that had been installed while he was away. "If we have a *candy* counter, I don't want to know where it is," he bawled. "I heard somebody's daughter running up and down the hall yesterday, as if this were a goddam playpen. I understand she fell and hurt herself. I hope they found the arnica—oh, we *must* have a medicine chest somewhere in this *house!*"

At about that time a series of my drawings called "The War Between Men and Women" was running in the *New Yorker,* and I got a telegram one day from Dr. Logan Clendenning in St. Louis that read, "Help. I'm surrounded by women." I showed it to Ross, and he was off on his well-worn lecture again. "Doctors don't know what it is to be surrounded by women. They can turn women patients over to nurses, or psychiatrists, or something. What we need here is a registered nurse and a trained psychiatrist. It's the only office in the world where paste and scissors are kept in desk drawers. The women do that. And if they don't show up for work, you can't ask why. I wish the hell I was back on the *Stars and Stripes*—it's the only place I ever really enjoyed working."

It takes two or more women to surround the average man, but Harold Ross could look as beleaguered as Custer in the presence of only one. He let an editor go in the early years because the man brought his wife into Ross's office to meet

him. Ross looked up and there she stood, seeming to be closing in on him from all sides. Very few women, even among
those employed there, could enter the inner sanctum of old
Surrounded. Of the privileged females, my second wife, Helen,
was one. We walked into his office one day unannounced, and
he didn't start or turn pale. He had known her for quite a while
by then, liked her personally, relaxed in her company, and
admired her because she had been a magazine editor and once
got out two monthlies all by herself, from cover to cover. More
than once he grumbled, "I got *fifty* men and women I don't
even know walking around here with pieces of paper in their
hands, getting in each other's way, and Helen Thurber used to
get out *five* magazines a month all by herself." It was on that
day in his office that Ross, discussing some guilty pair, said,
"I'm sure he's s-l-e-e-p-i-n-g with her." He was the only man
I've ever known who spelled out euphemisms in front of
adults.

Ross had not liked the idea of my getting married again
when he first heard about it, and he asked Bob Benchley to
"talk to Thurber. See if you can't do something about it."
Benchley did talk to me one evening, over cocktails, in his suite
at the Royalton. He was repeating, I knew at once, Ross's concern: that if I became happily married, something bad would
happen to my drawings and stories. Benchley was married only
once and told me he didn't believe in second marriages. A man
had his wife, whatever their relationship might be, and that
was that. The rest was his own business. A woman friend of
Bob's once gave him a drawing of mine for Christmas. It
showed a man hiding in a tree while a woman on the ground
is calling for him, and the donor of this Christmas gift said,
"The man is poor Bob, and the woman is all those women
who keep after him all the time." Later Bob met Helen, liked
her, and said to me in an aside, "Why don't you marry the girl?
What are you waiting for—Ross's permission?"

All that Ross ever said to me about Helen, before he met

her, was, "Is she quiet?" Afterwards, I suppose, he was sorry, in his fashion, that he had told Benchley to see what he could do about changing my mind. It must have gratified him no end when the people in my drawings suffered no noticeable beatification except in one spot I did deliberately to scare him, which showed a man and a woman and a dog drifting dreamily among the stars; and he was further reassured when a piece called "A Couple of Hamburgers" indicated no lessening of tensions in my prose war between men and women.

We were often at Ross's apartment, especially during his second marriage—to the former Frances Clark, mother of his only child—the marriage in which he was still young enough and well enough to seem comfortable at home, if I can use such big words as comfortable and home about him. Slowly he turned every apartment into an annex of his office and a gathering place for his men friends. "I got too many personal possessions," he would say. There were only a few he wouldn't have got rid of, out of a sense of escape, and among these was a collection of Gideon Bibles sent to him, from time to time and from most American cities, by his great friend Joe Cook when he was on tour. Ross kept his possessions, including his house near Stamford, but toward the end he lived in a suite at the Algonquin, looked after by a male nurse. He kept rejecting his third wife's efforts to take care of him, partly because he wanted to be let alone when he was sick. Being looked after, or cared for, at such times only fretted him. He didn't want any woman around. When, toward the end, we called on him in his Algonquin rooms, he complained about being "fussed over" and said, "I usually get rid of women callers by saying I have to lie down. One woman didn't go, even then. Two hours later when I got up, she was still sitting out here." After his death, it is said, an envelope containing a considerable amount of cash was found in a safety deposit vault marked "Getaway money." It meant, I think, get-away-from-the-world-of-women money.

He didn't want to get away from work, and kept at it until his final visit to the hospital in Boston where he died. One of his last projects, and one of his keenest interests, was the five-part profile on Duveen by S. N. Behrman. He had one of the galley proofs in his suite on our last visit there. He had put it aside momentarily to eat what he called supper. Its nature shocked Helen a little, as it would have any woman. He was eating sardines right out of the can. "It's practically the only thing I can taste," he said. I still keep thinking, against my will, of that brief visit, and of the tired, cloyed, but dogged efforts of Ross to fight against the disease that was killing him, and I like to turn from it to brighter thoughts of him.

I remember his panic the evening he got home from work and was told that he was going to be a father. He leaped to the phone, called a woman friend who gave him the name of an obstetrician, and then called the doctor, who came running. After a brief examination, the doctor came out of the bedroom, as annoyed as Ross was distraught. "It is possible that your wife is pregnant," he said, "but it's too early to tell for certain. As it happens, this is not an emergency, as your call indicated. I could actually have taken time to eat my dinner."

"Judas, I didn't know," Ross told me the next day. "I thought you had to act fast."

Ross's daughter, Patricia, was one of the great things in his life, and the only female who could handle him with ease. When she was only seven he brought her to the Algonquin at lunchtime to show her off to his friends. She had a good time and didn't want to leave. "I have to get back to the office," he told her as she lingered in the lobby talking to people. "Just wait," she told him, and he sat back in a big chair, with a deep sigh of restive resignation, and waited. Like any other father of a first daughter, he was sure that a girl in her infancy was a fragile object. "Can she *breathe*, lying on her stomach like that?" he asked her nurse when the baby was not yet one year old, and again, "Is it all right for them to sleep with their hands above their head? I think my mother said it's bad for them, but I forget why." I remember the day he tiptoed into Patricia's room to show her to my mother. She quieted his fears about the baby's fragility. "They usually outlive their husbands," she told him, "and they always outlive their fathers, so I wouldn't worry about her."

The Gee Whiz Guy became utterly enthralled by the miraculous phenomena of conception, gestation, and parturition, and was always lecturing to one or more of us on the subject. This was his "being clinical," that attitude of mind toward the functional which was privileged—in conversation, that is, not in type. When he had been a father for less than a year he went to a party one night at the home of Charles Mac-Arthur and Helen Hayes in Nyack. "I had gone out into the kitchen to shake up some fresh drinks," MacArthur told me, "and when I came back I stood there in the doorway listening to Ross. He was haranguing our guests, most of them fathers and mothers, and some of them grandparents, about the goddam miraculous cycle of menstruation. 'Nature is wonderful,' Ross was saying. 'The damn thing stops at the right time and then resumes without any interference or help.'" The MacArthur guests were, I gathered, mostly men and women of the world of literature and the theater, and far from being shocked or bored, they listened in fascination to this lecture by the editor of the *New Yorker*. Charlie ended his description of the scene this way, "Ross has the charm of gaucherie."

At about the same time, the spell of the miracle of birth still being upon him, he came over to me during a party at the apartment of Elliott and Norma Nugent. "I understand there's an obstetrician here, a friend of yours and Nugent's," he said. "Can we get him in a corner for a minute? I want to ask him a clinical question." The obstetrician, one of America's most distinguished, had been a fraternity brother of Elliott's and mine at Ohio State. I got him and Ross together in a corner. The clinical question he asked him was a hypothetical one, it turned out, and it had been troubling Ross's waking hours. He wanted to know how many women could be impregnated, theoretically, all things being equal and all women being nubile and willing, by a single seminal ejaculation. The doctor told him 300,000,000. I had never seen Ross look more profoundly thoughtful. "Geezus, nature is prodgidal," he said, "nature is prodgidal."

One morning, circa then, I found Ross, worried and stoop-shouldered, pacing a corridor, jingling those pocket coins. He came right out with his current anxiety. "Goddam it, I can't think of any *man* that has a daughter. I think of men as having boys, and women as having girls."

"I have a daughter," I said, "and I wanted a daughter."

"That's not natural, is it?" he demanded. "I never heard of a man that didn't want a son. Can you name any, well, you know, goddam it—terribly masculine men with daughters?" After protesting that I could outmasculine him the best night he ever saw, I said that Morris Markey, a masculine Virginian, had a daughter, and so did Joel Sayre, once described by Stanley Walker as "the wandering behemoth . . . a great man." Ross brightened, but the sun and moon of reassurance shone in his face when I came up with, "Jack Dempsey has two children, both girls." His day was saved from the wreckage of despair, but he still had one final depressed word. "Goddam it, I hate the idea of going around with female hormones in me."

Ross kept going to Boston during his last few years, first to see a specialist about his ulcers, and then to endure the torment of the bronchoscope and other ordeals after tests had shown that he had a minimal cancer. On one of these visits the man who knew almost every actress of his time called on one of his favorites backstage at a theater in which she was starring in a play translated from the French. Ross said to her, "Is the author of the play in love with you?" She turned away from her dressing-room mirror, her pretty eyes wide and her pretty lips parted, and said, "He's sixty!" Ross was fifty-eight then, with less than a year to live, and it hurt him deeply to have his age group so tactlessly brushed aside as men in whom love has turned to ashes. I was fifty-six at the time, and not crazy about what the lady said myself. I told him she never would have said it if she had realized he was nearing sixty. "She thinks you're still in your prime, as young as you look and as boyish as you talk."

Ross ran a big hand slowly over his face. "The hell with it," he said, and put, or tried to put, his mind on something else.

10

Who Was Harold, What Was He?

Franklin Pierce Adams took Ross tobogganing one wintry afternoon
in the twenties, somewhere in Connecticut. A few days after
that, at the Algonquin Round Table, someone asked, "What
does Ross look like tobogganing?"

"Well," Frank said, "you know what he looks like *not*
tobogganing."

Ross looked like various things to various people. To Margaret Case Harriman he had "a clown face," and it isn't hard
to visualize the vivid portrait Rouault could have done of him
as Pagliacci. To Ben Hecht, his old friend, Ross was "burglar-
faced." When the Algonquin circle put on a theatrical benefit,
back in the twenties, Ross was cast as a taxi driver. Stanley
Walker has never got over a notion, thirty years old, that the
rugged *New Yorker* editor, whose ancestry was Scotch-Irish,
was an American Indian, probably Ute or Shoshone. Here is
ethnologist Walker on Ross, the Amerind: "Did you ever
notice the way Ross walked? It was an Indian walk, slow,
shambling, head bent forward, oddly like a camel's swaying
motion. Only the little Indians from below the Rio Grande
were any good on their feet, graceful runners, rhythmic boxers.
Of course Jim Thorpe could run, but when he walked he

walked like Ross." I never saw Ross run, but something tells me he didn't run like Thorpe.

Ross was always figuratively on the run in the office, but in his outdoor activities he was ambulatory. He was an ardent fisherman and a fair croquet player (once he drove his ball into the rough and when he came back to the lawn a few minutes later, he not only had the ball, but a case of poison ivy). Vivid tales of Ross as fisherman are still heard in the land. Once, in New Brunswick, he went out in a canoe with an Indian guide and let the guide do most of the fishing for him. Ross was absorbed in reading a book he had brought along. He used to say that if you wanted to read a book you had to get away from New York, or at least away from home and office. One of his favorite Talk stories was about a businessman whom a friend was astonished to behold coming out of a house in Greenwich Village, far from his usual haunts. To the friend's "What are you doing down here?" the businessman said, "I'm finishing a book." The friend said, "I didn't know you were writing a book," and the man said, grimly, "I'm not writing a book, I'm reading one."

Ross did most of his fishing in Colorado and Nevada, usually with Dave Chasen, Frank Capra, and the social historian Nunnally Johnson, who wrote this report of one of their fishing expeditions: "If you think Ross was sartorially a man of undistinction in the fashionable world of smart New York, you should have seen what he looked like on a fishing trip, I can't even imagine where he got such garments, unless they'd been discarded by Joe Jackson, the tramp bicyclist. He looked so villainous that he attracted worried attention in a truck drivers' diner where we stopped for breakfast on the way to Nevada."

I have no data at all on Ross as a swimmer, but ever fresh in Johnson's memory is a story of Ross at a moonlit swimming pool in Hollywood. During an evening party, twenty years ago, a lovely young blonde suddenly "shucked," as Nunnally

She's all I know about Bryn Mawr and she's all I have to know."

puts it, and ran out to the pool, naked as a Renoir nymph, only slenderer. One of the gentlemen also shucked and tore after the lady, and they were disporting like porpoises in the water when the male porpoise looked up and saw Dave Chasen viewing the antics with interest. Ross was there, too, but with his back squarely to the pool. He was trying to divert Dave's attention. The male swimmer heard him say, in his loud voice, "Where do you get your asparagus, Dave?" The swimmers dressed, all ardor spent, and the party was resumed in the living room, the embarrassed Ross nervously turning the conversation to a midnight probe of the parsley situation.

Since these are glimpses of Ross away from home and office, they should contain a glance or two at the editor as a party guest. He rarely went to a party, in the twenties and thirties anyway, without playing some prank on another guest. At Howard Dietz's one night in 1934 he sought me out from a hundred others there, and said he wanted to play a joke on David Selznick, who had been bragging about the enormous success of his movie *Dinner at Eight*. "I'll bring him over here and tell him you're the *New Yorker* treasurer, Elmer Jenkins," he said. "Tell him we grossed ten million dollars last year, or some number like that." We went through with the little charade, but later on Selznick found out that I was not Elmer Jenkins, but just a dime-a-dozen *New Yorker* writer. He decided that the incident called for single combat with Ross or with me. Needless to say, Ross disappeared, probably by way of the back door, and I was left to do battle with Selznick, a welterweight against a heavyweight. Our tactful host quietly persuaded us that it was a night for gaiety, not for fisticuffs. There was only one blow struck that evening, a slap across my cheek, lightly, by the great Beatrice Lillie. I had asked her who were her favorite men friends in New York, and she said, "Aleck Woollcott and Harold Ross," and I said, "You are meeting the wrong class of people." That ended amicably, with her singing, by request, " 'Don't Stand There on the Coconut Mat.' " As one orderly guest said to me at the end, "It's always a pleasure to say good night to you and Harold Ross."

No picture of Ross outdoors, where, like Bob Benchley, he could identify only the robin and the rose, would be complete without a peek at him and that ominous monster of our disturbed era, the gas engine. First, though, it should be said that Ross approached all things mechanical, to reach for a simile, like Henry James approaching Brigitte Bardot. There was awe in it, and embarrassment, and helplessness. "Why can't we get better paper clips?" he kept asking Miss Terry. "These damn things don't work." His big fingers were not made for paper clips, or stapling machines, or almost anything else that had to be manipulated. Jane Grant insists that he was good with a saw and hammer and nails, and once made a workmanlike bookshelf and a sound end table, but when he put down these tools and tackled any device or contraption, he was either baffled or thrown. Many years ago, when Ross was interested in the paint-spraying machine I mentioned back in Chapter 1, he asked his friend Gummo Marx to let him demonstrate the thing for him and some others. Gummo took him to a room in a newly built office building, not yet occupied, and Ross began squirting the walls. "The paint is not discernible at first," he told the others, "but it will appear." It didn't, though, and Ross turned to Gummo in perplexity. "He didn't know it, but he was covered from head to foot with green paint," Gummo told me. This heroic green knight reminds me of another rugged American, the female cousin of my mother's who, after struggling for half an hour with a cream separator on her farm, shouted, "Why doesn't somebody take this goddam thing away from me?" Nobody had to take the sprayer away from Ross. He gave it up.

It was Andy White who taught, or tried to teach, the editor of the *New Yorker* to drive a car, and he has written an account of that ordeal, the story of Ross at the wheel:

"Ross soon learned that I could drive a car, and it was one of those isolated facts he used to store away in his mind. 'White can drive a car.' I owned at that time a Model A Ford roadster, and when Ross asked me one day if I would take him out and teach him to drive I said sure. The minute this offer escaped my mouth, I felt sharp pangs of misgiving. I had taught plenty of children to ride bicycles, and I had taught a couple of applicants to drive a car, but I realized that when it came to Ross I was on new ground. I suspected that his approach to the automobile would be like his approach to almost everything else: he would assume that there was some simple key that would unlock the whole mystery. Just a matter of discovering this key.

"Anyway, I decided that if I was going to put Ross at the controls of a car, and stay in it myself, I would pick a highway that offered unbroken stretches of clear track. I told Ross we would go out on Long Island for our lesson and he agreed readily. We not only went out on the Island, but we went way the hell out. Just how far I can't seem to remember, but the name Smithtown comes to me. The road was concrete, and the traffic was extremely thin. (In the twenties, there were such things as empty highways—you couldn't, of course, find anything like that today.)

"At a likely looking spot, I drew up to the side of the road, put Ross in the driver's seat, and told him to sit still for a minute while I explained things. I gave a short speech covering the function of clutch, brake, accelerator, etc., and then described the process of shifting from one gear to another. I also told him that for a beginner, the mere matter of steering the car was challenging, and that when we got under way he must devote himself quite largely to learning to steer properly before fooling around too much with anything else.

"Ross listened to all this with the greatest impatience. As always, he wanted action, and we soon got it. He put the clutch out and felt around for first, and then, with me talking him into the take-off in a tense monotone, we racketed forward in a series of incredible lurches and were soon in orbit. It was clear to me from the first that Ross's steering was not only inadequate but that it was touched with playfulness. I had to grab hold of the wheel every few seconds to get us back on course.

"He was delighted with the feeling of being in motion, and he was crazy about the horn button, which he pushed with great frequency and for no reason. 'Just flirting, White,' he kept saying. 'Just flirting.' His idea of steering a car was to keep experimenting with the wheel, to test the full range of its possibilities. This, of course, put us all over the road. Ross's natural noisiness and buoyancy were transmitted to the car to a very high degree. In those days I was used to living dangerously and didn't usually give it a second thought, but there were moments during my ride with Ross when I wondered what I was doing in a fix like that. I recall sitting in a half-turned position, to give me a view both ahead and behind, in case any car should make the unthinkable mistake of trying to pass us.

"At the end of the lesson, Ross was cheerful, grateful, and seemed perfectly satisfied that he had mastered the art of driving and was ready for the road. I, too, felt grateful. He was a real wild man at the controls, and I was extremely thankful that I had taken him a long way out of town. Only a wilderness road, such as the one I picked, would have accommodated his flirtation with the automobile.

"Years later I learned that Ross had bought himself a big car. Whether he took a refresher course I don't know. But I always felt uneasy when I thought about him at the wheel. He did not have a mechanical bone in his body, and if anybody needed God for his co-pilot, Ross did."

I had driven various cars since 1913, with only a few minor accidents, but Ross would have none of Thurber at the wheel. He would as soon have stayed in a room where I was cleaning a shotgun. In May, 1937, I had taken my Ford sedan with me to Europe, and I was in Paris in the summer of 1938 when Ross showed up there. "I'll show you my Paris, Thurber," he said one day, "and then you can show me yours. We'll take taxis. I'm not going to drive with you."

Ross's Paris turned out to be only two places, and the first of these was the building, near the center of the city, that had housed the *Stars and Stripes* in 1918 and part of 1919. After twenty years, the *Stars and Stripes* had been forgotten, at least by the French. The four thousand members of Post Number One of the American Legion, in Paris, could tell you all about it, but the little old nervous French *concierge* we encountered in the building clearly thought we were two crazy Americans who had lost our way. Ross boomed into the place, loud of voice and high of confidence, and began gesticulating and jabbering to the little man, who lit a cigarette and began puffing nervously and edging away from us. I had the distinct feeling that he had always suspected something like Ross would happen to him, and now here it was. *"Comprends pas, comprends pas,"* the man kept repeating, backing up like a wary lightweight boxer. "What's he say?" Ross demanded, and I told him the man did not understand English. This annoyed Ross. "Goddam it, I'm talking slowly and clearly enough!" he yelled. I tried my own creaky French on the old man, but it only got us in deeper and deeper. When I told him, or tried to, that my friend had been editor of an American newspaper in that building during *la Grande Guerre*, which I have a way of pronouncing *la grande gare*, I think now he must have thought I was saying, "My friend was editor of an American newspaper when this building was a great railway station." The *concierge* muttered something and disappeared through a door. "He's probably gone for the police," I told Ross. Ross was disconsolate. "You're a great help, Thurber," he said, as we left there for the other place in the Paris of H. W. Ross.

The second place was a bistro on, I think, the Rue Lafayette, with half a dozen iron tables and wicker chairs out front. "I'll take it from here," Ross said. "I know this place." A waiter appeared who did not know Ross. "They say nothing changes in Paris," Ross said, "but everything changes. I had a beer right at this very table with Raoul Lufbery two weeks before he was killed in action." He said, "Beer," to the waiter, and I knew what he would get, and he got it—two small glasses of the drink the French called *Byrrh*. Ross stared at them unhappily and said, "Okay, Thurber, you try it. God knows what we'll get—a couple of dames maybe." I said, *"Deux demis,"* and that's what we got.

When it came my turn to show Ross my Paris, he said, "I don't want to go to Sainte Chapelle, I've been there," and he added something that comes back to me now as "Stained glass is damned embarrassing." He wouldn't get out of the taxi when we stopped in front of Notre Dame, but he opened the cab door and stared at it. "That cathedral has never been sandblasted," he told me, and we drove on and stopped to look at the Louvre. "I've never been in there, either," he said, "but there are only three things to see, and I've seen color reproductions of all of them." He meant, as any other ex-doughboy would have meant, the Venus de Milo, the Mona Lisa, and the Winged Victory. We had dinner that night at the Ritz, where he was staying with his wife, and where the waiters spoke English and were not, by God, too stubborn to admit it.

Later that summer, in London, the Rosses stayed at the Dorchester. The news that the editor of the *New Yorker* was in town got around among newspapermen and the literary gentry, and everybody wanted to meet him. One of those I brought over for cocktails was John Duncan Miller, later *The Times* of London man in Washington, and now on the staff of the World Bank. "During the first half hour," Miller told me later, "I felt that Ross was the last man in the world who could edit the *New Yorker*. I left there realizing that nobody else in the world could."

11

Up Popped the Devil

*If it wasn't one thing it was another, at the New Yorker, and some-*times both. There was the day, twenty-five years ago, when two New York detectives called on Ross. They wanted to ask questions about, and then of, one E. B. White, a writer and, the dicks half suspected, the brain guy behind the daring robbery of a bank in Ardsley, New York, not far from Tarrytown. Andy at that time owned a Buick sedan, which he kept in a garage in Turtle Bay, on New York's upper East Side; it had been stolen from the garage one night and used in the robbery by a group of bandits. After a wild chase by state cops the robbers had abandoned the automobile with a few bullet holes in it. The car was then taken to the state police barracks at Hawthorne. They wouldn't let White have it for almost a month.

Ross, who was always at ease with cops, in uniform or in plain clothes, had a wonderful time about it all. He said to the detectives on their first visit, "I think you're on the right track all right. White has been silent and brooding—he's definitely got something on his mind that's worrying the hell out of him." He took the men to White's office, grinning widely, made a big gesture with his right hand and said, "There's your man, officers."

"The detectives paid two or three visits to my office, which pleased Ross greatly," White wrote me. "They would sit around on my couch and just study me, occasionally asking a question when they could think of one. The question I loved was when one of them said: 'Say, how did you get into writing, anyway?' I replied that I had just drifted into it."

The walls of Andy's office interested the detectives a lot. They contained some cockeyed drawings of mine, and the back jacket of Max Eastman's book, *The Enjoyment of Laughter,* which had a photograph of the handsome author laughing. I had taken a pencil and blacked out two of his fine even white teeth, drawn a lock of hair over his forehead, and given his eyes and eyebrows a demented look, the whole thing lending a tone of loony abandon to the office. Also, on one wall, Andy had written down the day and hour of an appointment with his dentist, and above the date I had scrawled *"Der Tag"* and above the hour *"l'heure."* I don't know what the cops made of this piece of cryptic trilingualism, but they must have wondered and worried about it. Andy got his car back finally, and the detectives were smart enough in the end to realize that the man who had just drifted into writing had not drifted into bank robbery, too.

The first major legal crisis, I remember, developed in 1927 when the magazine's Skyline department said that a new Fifth Avenue office building had the grace of a freight elevator and rashly went on to say that architects who walked past the building became sick. The *New Yorker* was promptly sued for half a million dollars by the architect of the new building. Ross sent me down to talk to one of the magazine's lawyers—we then had a firm in Wall Street—and I came back with a report that made him gloomy. The lawyers thought that it would be advisable to settle for a retraction, out of court, on the ground that a jury might decide the plaintiff's reputation had been inexcusably injured by a young smart-aleck magazine. Ross had planned a veritable Roman holiday in court. He was going to call to the witness stand some well-known critics of the theater and of books, Heywood Broun, Bob Benchley, Laurence Stallings, Woollcott, and at least half a dozen others. They would all testify that public buildings should be just as subject to criticism as plays or novels. My report took the wind out of that sail and the light out of the Ross face. I told him the lawyer had said that such testimony would be barred as immaterial, irrelevant, and irreverything else. There was another point, too. The lawyer felt that the *New Yorker*'s crack about other architects getting attacks of nausea when they gazed upon the building would be regarded as malicious and far outside the bounds of privileged criticism. The case never came to court.

Ross's approach to the law was that of the plunging fullback, hitting the line with his eyes closed. When the Sherry Netherland was opened and the *New Yorker* wrote about it, another crisis was in the making. The new hotel didn't get mad, because it had been praised to the skies in a rave notice that said the place was so elegant even the floor maids wore a certain famous and expensive perfume. The *parfumeur,* one of the most celebrated in the world, did get mad, though, about the implication that his aristocratic product was worn by menials, and another lawsuit was threatened. "Goddam it, I'll send every one of those dames a quart of the stuff!" Ross yelled. When somebody told him what this particular perfume cost, he cut down the boastful size of his containers. "Well, what's the smallest goddam bottle there is? I'll send each one of them the smallest bottle." I think he would have, too, although his lawyers were scarcely enthusiastic about such a tactical move. In the end, the whole thing quietly died out like the fragrance of white clover at summer's end.

Ross disturbed his legal advisers by his rough and tumble approach to everything in the field of jurisprudence, and also by his old newspaperman's idea of "getting something on" the plaintiff. "I know damn well they're digging up all they can about me," he would say. "That always happens in lawsuits. So I'm going to send out a couple of guys to dig up facts on them." His favorite reporter for such work was Eugene Kinkead, whom he admiringly called "the best gumshoe in the business."

When Pearl White, the illustrious heroine of the silent movie serial, *The Perils of Pauline,* died in Paris in 1938, Wolcott Gibbs wrote a nostalgic Comment about her and quoted the chorus of a song, "Poor Pauline," which came out about 1912. The *New Yorker* was promptly sued for having reprinted copyrighted material without permission. The case was decided in favor of the *New Yorker,* and it established the rule that copyrighted song lyrics could be lawfully used without permission in fiction and nonfiction for the purpose of establishing mood and background, provided the use was reasonable and not excessive.

I had my own legal troubles, too. The late Charles Yale Harrison jumped or flew to the conclusion that "The Secret Life of Walter Mitty" had been inspired by a novel of his, *Meet Me on the Barricades,* and he wrote me a polite letter saying he felt I had been the victim of what he called "a psychological deep freeze"; that is, I had read his novel, stored it in my unconscious, and used it unbeknownst to myself. Nobody can be so implacable as an author who thinks he has been plagiarized, and it did no good for the *New Yorker* lawyers to tell Harrison that I had been in Europe when his novel appeared, had not read it or any reviews of it, and had written daydreamer stories for Ross long before *The Barricades* appeared,

one of them, "Mr. Pendley and the Poindexter," having given me the idea for "Mitty." Mr. Harrison wrote a long comparison of his novel and my short story, in which he tried to establish similarity between a drumbeat in his book and my own "ta pocketa pocketa," which had been as close as I could come to the sound of the idling of a gas engine. Ross was jocund about all this and, after his fashion, both shared my indignation and was entertained by it. I refused to submit the case to an arbitration board made up of five writers, and Harrison did not bring a legal action against me and the *New Yorker*.

When I was in London in 1938, I had written a casual called "The Macbeth Murder Mystery," and the authors of a parody mystery novel based on Shakespeare's *Macbeth* figured I must have been inspired by their book. Ross was gleeful, as always in triumph, when it was established that my piece had been written and submitted to the *New Yorker* before their book had appeared on the stands. Then, in one of a series of pieces I wrote on soap opera, I inadvertently left out the conclusion of some litigation in Chicago, which had been settled out of court. Lawyers for the aggrieved soap opera writer wired Ross that he would be hearing from them further in apt season. This was all amicably smoothed out when, in a subsequent piece, I apologized for my oversight and explained what had taken place out of court. But Ross continued to have a lot of fun with me about these cases. Every now and then he would break in on me, grin, and say, "How's the defendant?" or "You haven't got a leg to stand on, Thurber."

Far and away the most important legal case in the history of the magazine, and the only one that ever reached the United States Supreme Court, resulted from an article in the *New Yorker* of August 14, 1937, entitled "April Fool." It was one of the "Where Are They Now?" series, for which I did the rewrite. The series naturally dealt with once famous front-page figures who had been lost to public view for considerable lengths of time. One of these was William James Sidis, son of a psychotherapist named Boris Sidis. The article, which was to become forever celebrated in legal and publishing circles everywhere because of the important precedent established by the courts, affecting all so-called "right-of-privacy" cases, began like this:

> One snowy January evening in 1910 about a hundred professors and advanced students of mathematics from Harvard University gathered in a lecture hall in Cambridge, Massachusetts, to listen to a speaker by the name of William James Sidis. He had never addressed an audience before, and he was abashed and a little awkward at the start. His listeners had to attend closely, for he spoke in a small voice that did not carry well, and he punctuated his talk with nervous, shrill laughter. A thatch of fair hair fell far over his forehead, and keen blue eyes peered out from what one of those present later described as a "pixielike" face. The speaker wore black velvet knickers. He was eleven years old . . .

The astonishingly brilliant boy could have passed the entrance examinations for Harvard when he was only nine, but he was not permitted to matriculate there until he was twelve. There was a precedent for that. It was the same age at which Cotton Mather had entered Harvard. In July, 1938, the lawyers for Sidis filed suit in the Federal Court on two counts of breach of the right of privacy and on one count for libel. (The libel charge, at first held in abeyance, was decided as late as 1944, in favor of Sidis. The judgment was small, for the libel, whatever it was, had been a minor slip and not intentional denigration.) Judge Goddard in the lower court and three judges of the Circuit Court of Appeals decided in favor of the *New Yorker,* sustaining the argument of Alexander Lindey that a decision in favor of Sidis would, to summarize it briefly, result in continual and multitudinous cases of public figures suing the authors and publishers of newspapers, magazines, books, and encyclopedias. The opinion of the judges could be condensed into eight words: "Once a public figure, always a public figure." More than three years after the suit was instituted, it reached the United States Supreme Court, which refused to review it, and so the long legal saga ended in favor of the *New Yorker*.

The Circuit Court had agreed with the *New Yorker* counsel on the point of law, but the three judges sympathized with Sidis. In the course of the opinion, written by Judge Clark, it was not contended that "the manner of the author" was unfriendly, but the piece as a whole was described as a merciless and ruthless exposure of a once public character who had sought privacy, or, as one lawyer expressed it to me recently, "espoused obscurity." The general tenor of the article was called "amusing and instructive" but nowhere was there any indication whatever of what I thought had stood out all through my story, implicit though it was—my sincere feeling that the piece would help to curb the great American thrusting of talented children into the glare of fame or notoriety, a procedure in so many cases disastrous to the later career and happiness of the exploited youngsters.

The great importance of the Sidis case lies in its having become the principal authority in all similar cases in which the right of privacy is claimed by a person who is, or once was, a notable public figure. It was to save the *New Yorker* from a similar suit which came about following the publication, in August, 1953, of St. Clair McKelway's "The Perils of Pearl and Olga," one of the magazine's "Annals of Crime" series. This was McKelway's lead:

> On the morning of December 31, 1946, two young women, among many other people, got on a subway train separately at the Fifty-fifth Street B.M.T. station in Brooklyn, and sat down across from each other in a car as the train moved off toward Manhattan. They had never met, had never spoken, but their lives had been drawn together and the entwinement was a sinister one. They were both

working girls and more than ordinarily attractive. One of them was tall, with pale, clear skin and large, dark eyes and shining black hair; she was twenty-eight years old, and her face, besides being beautiful, had an interesting, troubled look about it. She had noticed that the other girl was carrying a gift-wrapped package about the size of a large shoe box. It had an aperture at one end, from which protruded what looked like the lens of a camera. Without thinking much about it, she wondered idly what kind of gift was inside the package. The other girl was barely nineteen and was small and blond . . .

The young woman with the gift-wrapped box had been duped into believing that it contained an X-ray camera that might reveal stolen jewels under the clothing of the other woman. This situation had been carefully plotted by the dark lady's husband, who called himself Allen La Rue. What the box actually contained was not a camera but a sawed-off shotgun, and when it was set off on the subway platform, one of the most terrible scenes in New York police annals occurred. The dark woman lost most of one leg, later sued the city, charging negligence on the part of the police, but lost that suit. Then, when the *New Yorker* revived the story, she sued for violation of her right to privacy. The judge, personally sympathetic to the plaintiff, had to abide by the precedent established in the Sidis case.

The *New Yorker* had one permanent, or built-in, crisis—Ross's personal war on Raoul Fleischmann, owner of the controlling stock of the magazine. The business department has recently called this war "a balance of terror," but it wasn't balanced. Ross was an invading Hannibal, Fleischmann a beleaguered Rome. Ross put up barbed-wire entanglements, and the off-shore fire of his cannon could be heard on even days and odd. John McNulty used to get off the elevator on the editorial floor with his hands above his head, shouting, in mock terror, "Editorial department! Don't shoot!" He was far more amusing than the war, which became a bore to all of us, like a persistent holiday drizzle of rain. It would take a new kind of investigator, a psycho-financier, to unravel the *casus belli*. "I don't know whether Harold resented my having the money, or my putting it in the magazine," Fleischmann once told me. Ik Shuman put it this way: "Ross seemed to enjoy being both constructionist and conflagrationist." And another aging editor has said, "Ross built with one hand and tore down with both."

Naturally some strange things happened during the intramural war, and one of them still remains a major mystery. In the summer of 1934, while Fleischmann was in Europe, Ross sold most of his *New Yorker* stock, two thousand, one hundred and ninety shares, to Time, Inc., for about one hundred and four thousand dollars. Officers of the Fleischmann high command who have survived the war believe that Ross sold his holdings to the Luce enterprises simply to spite Fleischmann. Nobody at the *New Yorker* seemed to know much about the remarkable transaction, and so in the summer of 1958 I wrote directly to Henry Luce and asked him about it. In a prompt reply he told me that the simple truth was he had forgotten all about it, but he would ask his colleague, William Furth, "to look up that bit of history and tell you what he can about it." A few days later, Furth sent me the details. In October, 1934, the shares were split two-for-one, which made *Time*'s holdings four thousand, three hundred and eighty shares at a cost of $23.75 per share. In 1936 and 1937 all the shares were sold by *Time* for a profit of sixty-one thousand, three hundred and fifteen dollars, indicating that the average sale price was about $37.50. I now turn the strange story over to Furth:

"The purchase had been made for Time, Inc. by Charles Stillman, now Vice President (then Treasurer). To the best of his recollection he had heard from a Wall Street acquaintance that Ross wished to dispose of some of his stock. Since the *New Yorker* appeared to be a promising investment, Stillman arranged to meet Ross at '21' (this he recalls clearly), and over the luncheon table they made the deal. As for Ross's motive for selling to Time, Inc., Stillman was puzzled at the time, and still does not know the answer. He does recall that Ross said to him that he felt it improper for an editor to own stock in his own magazine—but Stillman wasn't much impressed.

"The record then shows that in 1935 Ralph Ingersoll heard from a broker named Philip Boyer, then of 67 Wall Street, that Ross considered disposing of the remainder of his F-R stock (not indicating what this amounted to); but Time, Inc. was not in the market for it. In fact, Stillman had begun to think that if he could fetch forty dollars per share, he would favor selling for the profit that had been his only motive all along.

"In the next several months Time, Inc.'s directors decided as a matter of policy that the company should not own shares in another publishing enterprise. (It also had some stock in *Look.*) And so, in 1936, the F-R shares were sold through White, Weld & Co. to Hartley Rogers & Co., an investment house at 14 Wall Street.

"All of the dealings appear to have been highly impersonal. The only occurrence of Luce's voice in the surviving correspondence is a scribbled note from him to Ingersoll, just before the 1936 sale, inquiring what was the price paid by Time, Inc. for the F-R shares on the basis of the 2–1 split. While this recital may tell you the 'how' of the Ross-Time, Inc. transaction, and the 'why' so far as this Company is concerned, I fear it sheds little light upon your main subject."

The *New Yorker* and *Time,* founded within a couple of years of each other in the crazy twenties, engaged for ten years, off and on, in an intramural feud, sometimes collegiate, occasionally merely childish. When T. S. Matthews became editor of *Time*—and a better man neither *Time* nor time has known— the relationship of the two weeklies became normal and sane. In 1951 *Time* printed a cover story about me, written by my long-time friend Joel Sayre, who has worked for both the *New Yorker* and the Luce magazines. The friendly overtures of Tom Matthews began when he asked Andy White, and then Alva Johnston, to write the cover story. Each of them felt that he was not the man for it, but that Sayre was. At one time, in the summer of 1950, I had offered to do the profile myself if he couldn't find anyone else, but to this Matthews had said, in all seriousness, "We don't want an unfavorable story." The old feud was indeed drawing to a close. The cover story was printed four months before Ross's death, and I don't even know whether he read it or not, but I am sure the idea pleased him. For the cover of *Time* that week I had done, in white crayon on black paper, the last drawings I was ever able to make.

The big trouble, and it seems pretty small in retrospect, followed the publication in *Fortune,* in 1934, of a careful, comprehensive, and well-illustrated profile of the *New Yorker* written by Ralph Ingersoll. Reread today, it seems more like a bouquet of roses than anything else, with only here and there the buzzing of a bee among the blossoms. But it annoyed some *New Yorker* editors, because it printed, under photographs of them, an estimate of their annual *New Yorker* income which, if anything, was somewhat magnified, like the eleven thousand dollars a year that I was said to make at the time. Ross did not read the article (he always maintained that he never read anything about himself, and I believe it, because publicity made him self-conscious). When he was told that his salary had been set down in *Fortune* as forty thousand dollars, he put up a note on the *New Yorker* bulletin board that read: "It is not true that I get $40,000 a year." Then Andy wrote, for the Comment page, this single sentence: "The editor of *Fortune* gets thirty dollars a week and carfare." That cryptic intramural jibe brought in a flood of phone calls and a small flow of letters, some of them asking what was the big idea, others correcting the *New Yorker* figures. The little stab on page one was gener-

ally considered by outsiders merely a curious typo. The tiny
hassle might have ended there, but one of our editors suggested retaliation for the *Fortune* profile in the form of a parody
of that magazine which should take up one entire issue of the
New Yorker. This was promptly voted down by Ross, but he
and McKelway and others—my own opinion was never
sought—hit on the idea of a profile of Luce and his magazines.
I think it was McKelway that suggested that this should be
done by Wolcott Gibbs, and that expert parodist did it in the
form of parody. "Time . . . Fortune . . . Life . . . Luce" was to
become one of the most famous, and most often reprinted,
articles the *New Yorker* has ever run. When Gibbs died, it was
mentioned in most of his obituaries, and its most famous single sentence was variously misquoted, even by the Associated
Press. The sentence is, in imitation of *Time*'s style, at that
period: "Backward ran sentences until reeled the mind." In the
last letter I ever got from Gibbs, he thanked me for a blurb I
had written for a collection of his pieces then in production at
Henry Holt, and this paragraph of his letter ended: "I told
Holt that I wanted to change 'the fabulous profile on Luce' to
'the ill-advised etc.' and they are still trying to figure out what
to make of that."

It was said that Gibbs and his helpers could not obtain
from anyone at *Time* the exact financial statistics they wanted,
and so Gibbs invented them. "I just began hitting the number
keys of the typewriter at random," he once told me. Preliminary proofs of his profile were sent to *Time*, where they came
first to the attention of Ingersoll. That editor, trained in temper
under Ross, telephoned the *New Yorker* and accused its editors
of "Hearst tactics." At this Ross said, "Then let Luce give us
the real figures," and efforts were made to arrange a meeting
between them. The tale tells that Luce's secretary and Ross's
secretary got each other on the phone, but that Ross didn't
take up his receiver until he was assured that Luce was on the
other end. When his secretary finally told him that Luce was

on, Ross, who had been leaning against the wall of his office, took a couple of slow inhales of a cigarette, stamped it out on the floor, then sauntered to the phone and said into the transmitter, "Hi, Luce." The publisher of *Time* wanted to get together with Ross, but the *New Yorker* editor insisted the meeting had to be at his own office or in his own apartment. Since Ross was in the catbird seat, he had his way, and the two men met at Ross's apartment one night after dinner. Ingersoll was there, too, and so was McKelway.

When Wolcott Gibbs set out to do "a job" on a profile subject, he brought out a fine array of surgical instruments, a rapier and a pearl-handled blackjack. (*Time* once called the Gibbs profile of Thomas Dewey "one long catscratch.") As parody, the Luce profile was excellent, and often superb, but it seems to me that Luce and Ingersoll were justified in resenting the tone of the piece, here and there, and some of its statements. The meeting ended well after midnight, with certain concessions to fact and fairness on the part of Ross and Mc-Kelway, but the temper of the piece, of course, remained unchanged. When, at one point during that nocturnal conference, Luce protested that there wasn't a single favorable line about him in the whole profile, Ross snapped, "That's what you get for being a baby tycoon." Luce and Ingersoll had made several objections to various inaccuracies in the profile, and to these Ross finally said, "The inaccuracies are a part of the parody of *Time*."

After the Luce profile had been published, Ross sat down at his typewriter one day and wrote the publisher of *Time* a remarkable five-page single-spaced letter, covering all the ground that had already been covered at the conference, and in the profile itself. The present editors of the *New Yorker* have no copy of this letter and none of them, so far as I can find out, has ever seen it. George Frasier, when he was writing his book about the Luce weekly called *It's About Time,* tried, like me, to find a copy, but without success. Then one day in Paris, in

October, 1958, a young woman I do not know sent me a copy of it. In her accompanying letter she wrote, "As you probably know, Mr. Ross's letter to Mr. Luce has been used, for twenty years, in journalism courses in various colleges and universities around the country."

That's my life.

12

The Dough and the System

Money, which Ross almost always called dough when he talked about it, and he talked about it a lot and worried about it even more, had been invented, we all knew, for the singular and dastardly purpose of driving him out of his mind and into the bughouse. I like to think that among his most fervent prayers there must have been one that went: "O Lord, please give all our contributors a million bucks and don't let them bother me about dough again. Keep them productive, Lord, and lead them not into laziness, but deliver them from booze and dames and such. Amen. P.S. Please let Thurber get the system through his head; he doesn't know what goes on around here. And send me a man to make some sense out of this place. Done and done, Lord."

The financial life and career of H. W. Ross of Aspen, Colorado, New York City, and Stamford, Connecticut, was an amazing compound of fairy tale, case history, double talk, and melodrama. I could begin almost anywhere, but what I call the Curious Case of the Forty Bucks of Harpo Marx makes as good a starting place as any. I was, then, on my way to Grand Central Station one afternoon in May a long time ago, to take a train back to my home in the country, when I suddenly realized that the next day was a family anniversary, the banks were closed, and I didn't have enough to buy my wife anything presentable. The gods of chance, having nothing better to do, took it from there. At the corner of 43rd Street and Fifth Avenue I ran into Frank Sullivan, who was politely but firmly waving away two twenty-dollar bills another man was trying to press upon him. The other man was Harpo Marx. He turned to me and said, "Will you give this money to Ross? He won it the other night playing cribbage, but I can't locate him and I have to go back West today." I grabbed the money, said I would give it to Ross, stopped in at Abercrombie & Fitch and spent most of it on a gift. The following Monday I gave Ross two new twenty-dollar bills and told him what had happened. He was in an affable mood and said. "An unlikely story if I ever heard one, but I did win forty bucks from Harpo the other night," and he stuck his winnings in his pocket.

I already knew a couple of incredible stories about Ross and his gambling, and it seemed improbable to me that he could win anything at any time from any of the Marx brothers. In the spring of 1958 I wrote to Groucho, the Marx brother I know best, and he began rounding up letters for me from the rest of the clan. One of them, a few weeks later, was this, from Harpo:

> I loved Ross, he was wonderful company and his friendship was warm and personal. It was always a wonder to me that such an unworldly man could originate and edit the sophisticated *New Yorker*. He was great fun to gamble with, violent and noisy whether winning or not. We played constantly at backgammon, at which I invariably won, or cribbage, at which he murdered me.

A few days later Harpo remembered another anecdote about Ross's gambling:

> I was living at the Garden of Allah as a merry bachelor when Ross arrived from the East. I was awakened at a very

early hour by the sound of his shaking a dice box outside my window. He was all ready to play, with a backgammon board tucked under his arm. We had quite a long session, and every hour or so he would bellow, "Where are all those Hollywood beauties I've heard so much about?" Unbeknownst to him, I finally arranged with the local Madam to send over three of her more presentables. But when they arrived, he furiously handed each girl twenty bucks and said, "Go home, girls, I'm on a triple blitz!"

Ross began as a dice shooter in the AEF, and ended up with a gambling compulsion. Nobody knows how many thousands of dollars he lost in his time at poker, backgammon and gin rummy, but it ran way up into five figures. He finally gave up sky's-the-limit poker, but would often play all night in Reno or Colorado, on his trips West, in games where the stakes were only a dollar or so. He must have won at poker sometimes, but I don't think he ever really got the hang of the game; certainly he didn't bring to it the intuitive sense he brought to proofs and manuscripts. He once told me about what he called the two goddamdest poker hands he had ever seen laid down on a table. "One guy held a royal flush, and the other had four aces," he said. When I asked, "Who got shot?," he looked puzzled for a moment and then said, "All right, all right, then, it was a straight flush, king high, but I've been telling it the other way for ten years." His greatest gambling loss occurred in New York, in 1926, when he plunged into a poker game with a tableful of wealthy men. He got off to a lucky start, and was two thousand dollars ahead and going to drop out when one of the players said, "Winners quitters, eh?" Ross, who was drinking in those days, stayed in the game, kept on drinking, and lost thirty thousand dollars. I have talked to several men who witnessed the great debacle, including Raoul Fleischmann and the late Heywood Brown and Gerald Brooks. Broun told me, "I don't think Ross finally knew what cards he was holding. It was murder, but nobody could get him to stop." The big winner that night was the late Herbert Bayard Swope, who, like Brooks, Fleischmann, and some others of Ross's poker-playing friends in the old days, was a wealthy man, and Ross didn't have any dough to speak of then.

Herman Mankiewicz, also an incurable compulsive gambler, once went to a psychiatrist to see if anything could be done about it. "I can't cure you of gambling," the analyst told him on his last visit, "but I can tell you why you do it." I don't know why Mank did it, but I think Ross's compulsion grew out of the strictures of a hyper-thrifty boyhood in Salt Lake City. The letters he wrote me about money though the years— some twenty in all—explain his fiscal perplexities better than I could describe them. Here is one, written a couple of years before he died:

> I've just read the story on Aunt Wilma and Mr. Hance, and thought it fine. You speak of that revolving telephone as saving a few dollars a month. I didn't query that on the proof at all, but I was reminded that in Salt Lake City we never paid anything like that for service. Our first telephone cost one dollar a month, by God, and my mother considered that so high that we didn't have one for three years, and when we did get it it was a partnership proposition with a next-door neighbor . . .

I know almost nothing about Ross's infancy and boyhood in Aspen. When he mentioned his youthful years in letters, it was always about Salt Lake City. It was there that he went to high school, and also, for a year anyway, to some military school, working as an office boy for a morning newspaper after hours, and before long being sent out on stories as a cub reporter.

His father, George Ross, is a dim figure in the background of his son's life. As in the case of my own family, it was the mother and not the father that dominated the scene. The elder Ross has been variously described as voluble, jovial, likable, and difficult. Harold seems to have had trouble with his father during his boyhood, in the American tradition, and to have threatened to run away from home once in a while. George Ross was one of a family of four sons and four daughters, all born in County Monaghan, Ireland. Except for two of the girls, the children emigrated to America when they were young, George arriving in 1881 at the age of twenty. In 1890, he met and married Ida Martin, and they had two sons; the second died in infancy. George was variously a street and road contractor, a mining technician, and a house wrecker. In any case, the family lived on a small budget, and Ida Martin Ross was obviously a stern keeper of the budget. Born in Salina, Kansas, she had been a schoolteacher in the Indian territory, later Oklahoma. This somewhat surprising fact was revealed to me by a first cousin of Ross's. He himself never told me that his mother had been one of those women schoolteachers that he so often damned as the chief cause of what was the matter with so many men. Perhaps he excluded her from the category. I just don't know. His father died in August, 1925, when his son's magazine was only six months old.

Ross's mother visited him several times in New York, when he was between marriages. To Mrs. Ross, her son Harold was still a growing young man who needed all the rest he could get, and she would reproach him if he stayed out later than eleven o'clock at night. The wayward son, however, often stayed out until after midnight and once came home at two o'clock in the morning, to find his mother waiting up for him. He told her a cock-and-bull story he had made up on the way home from the gay party he had attended. "We were all going to leave at ten-thirty," he told her, "when suddenly our host locked all the doors and windows and said, 'Nobody is going to leave this house until one-thirty.'"

"Why, I never heard of such a thing in all my born days!" his mother cried. "What kind of a man is he, anyway?"

"Very strange," said Ross, "very strange."

Then, one day, Ross called my wife in the country and wanted to know if she could dig up a doily around our house that looked as if it had been made by a man. It turned out he had called several other women friends, too. It seems he had once explained his late hours by telling his mother that he belonged to a men's sewing class that had to meet at night because all its members worked during the day. Mrs. Ross had fallen for this one, too, and that not only bewildered but shocked my own mother when I told her about it. "I'd just like to see *your* father come home from a party late at night and say he had been at his embroidery class," she said. Ross laughed about that; he laughed about the whole thing, but in it all, it is easy to see now, there lingered the effect of what must have been a truly severe Momism.

I first met Ross's super-thrifty mother in the early thirties when she came on from the West. She was shaken by New York prices in every area and on every scale. Ross had to tell her that hotel rooms cost only a dollar a night, and he would arrange with the waiters at the Algonquin and in various restaurants he took her to, not to let her see the menu. She believed that lunch cost only fifty cents and dinner less than a dollar. When he took her to an optician to have her lenses changed, and she found out that her new spectacles would cost fourteen dollars, she stalked out of the shop saying, "Mercy, I never heard of such a thing in all my life!" Ross had to buy the spectacles secretly, and then arrange with one of his friends to drop in at his apartment with them, and pretend to have found them on the street. The same thing happened in the case of a round-trip ticket Ross wanted to buy her so that she could visit some relative in a town upstate. "Why, I wouldn't think of paying that much!" she protested. Again a rehearsal friend turned up at the apartment and said he had found an envelope on the sidewalk with a round-trip ticket in it to Hartsville (or whatever town it was).

Mrs. Ross's notions and fears about money were, of course, not uncommon in women of her generation. To her, as to my own mother and other old ladies, the *New Yorker* was a small upstart weekly without much chance of lasting. After Ross had shown his mother about the offices, he said to her, "Well, Mama, what do you think of the *New Yorker?*" The old lady sighed and said, "Well, Harold, all I can say is I hope some day you become connected with the *Saturday Evening Post.*" My own mother once wrote me reproachfully that someone had told her I had bought the *New Yorker,* and she couldn't understand why I didn't offer my brothers jobs on my magazine. My mother apparently thought the *New Yorker* was about as expensive as a Packard limousine. Also, there was a dowager in Columbus, Ohio, who once told my wife, "Oh, I never read the *New Yorker*. I just take it to help Jim." A fourth old lady, living in Litchfield, Connecticut, from whom I once rented a house for the winter, was not satisfied with the *New Yorker* as a reference, and I had to substitute for it my publishing firm, Harper & Bros. (founded 1827, and nearly a hundred years older than Ross's insecure little weekly). None of these ladies—except, of course, Mary Fisher Thurber—amused Ross's friends as much as his own interesting mother. Russel Crouse remembers how she used to hurry to a mirror and fluff up her hair before answering the telephone in Ross's apartment; she had become so used to the idea that when a bell rang, it was not the telephone, but the doorbell.

Ross and I used to go through a slow and tortured ritual

once a week, in 1927, which he called "Talk pricing." I would open a rough copy of the magazine at the Talk department, read off the names of those who had sent in the anecdotes and the ideas for visit and personality pieces, and he would pace up and down, frowning, sighing, often seeming miserable, and tell me how much to pay each contributor. One good anecdote had been sent in by Ring Lardner, and it took Ross a good thirty seconds to make up his mind what to pay him. Then he turned to me quickly and said, "Give him six dollars." A few years later, Lardner's health broke and he was confined to bed in Doctors' Hospital, where Ross visited him frequently. The editor urged him to write a weekly column about radio for the New Yorker, for he had discovered that Lardner did little but listen to a portable radio in his room. He did write a radio column for us, called "Over the Waves," and he got the usual pittance pay for it. When he was asked why he continued to write it for so little money, Lardner said, "I would rather write for the New Yorker at five cents a word than for Cosmopolitan at a dollar a word."

Ring Lardner's feeling for the New Yorker was typical of the attitude of Ross's contributors. Ross got our primary allegiance and our best work, and then rewarded us with secondary recompense, continually defending his position with a ramble of justification: "Goddam it, I want writers to get paid well. It isn't my dough, it's Fleischmann's. But if you pay a writer too well, he loses the incentive to work."

One day Ross came into my office when I wasn't there, and saw on my desk a few pages of a play I was trying to write. Later he expostulated about this in a great bluster of words. "All of you are writing for the theater or the movies, or some other magazine. You even write for Luce. I know we don't pay as well as some other magazines, but we haven't got that kind of dough. This isn't the Curtis Publishing Company, or Crowell. We've got to have a system of pay that works fairly for everybody, some kind of universal contract."

When Ross talked about the System, or wrote about it, he sounded like a man who believed that somewhere in the world he would come upon an equation, or talisman, or incantation that would make all writers equal in quantity and quality of output and worthy of the same recompense. From the beginning to the end, Ross worked at setting up the System with all the ardor that he gave to tearing down walls. What came out of it all was one of the most complicated patterns of pay ever set up by any publication in the history of the world.

The *New Yorker* did not begin paying its contributors real dough until it was nearly twenty years old. It was three years old before it began making a net profit, to be sure, and this had a traumatic effect upon Ross, and, I think, upon Fleischmann, too. Raoul used to say, "The *New Yorker* will never pay a thousand dollars for any story." He was wrong about that. It often pays a lot more than a thousand dollars now, and if it didn't, its great big glittering ads couldn't save it, for writers no longer write for the *New Yorker* out of sheer loyalty the way some of us used to. "The *New Yorker* is a showcase for writers," Fleischmann told me once. It certainly was, and other magazines, out shopping for writers, began buying *New Yorker* contributors for from three to five times as much money as the *New Yorker* thought it could pay. It became a great relief to receive a check from another magazine without a complicated voucher attached to it. The System, to make a dull story short, required a writer to sign a contract in which he agreed to show everything he wrote to the *New Yorker* first. If he turned in four or more stories a year, he was paid, retroactively, a twenty-five per cent "quantity bonus" based on his word rate. ("All word rates were equal, but some were more equal than others," to twist a piece of pertinent double talk from George Orwell.) I was occasionally paid, during the lifetime of Ross and Lobrano, a quality or just-because-we-love-you bonus, arrived at God only knows how. A percentage was taken off every check for a retirement pension fund, and there were semiannual additional payments for what Ross called Cola or Cost of Living Adjustment. If you had borrowed money from the magazine, a certain percentage was taken off each check. The System finally became so complicated that it annoyed and even baffled our tax advisers. Out of it all Ross got a strange sense of security, the security of a worried woman alone in a burglar-proof house.

One day, before I gave up my desk job in 1935, he sent me a nervous memo that read: "I've just been advised that you owe Talk three thousand words." I had been getting a hundred dollars a week for rewriting a thousand words of Talk. I was instantly mad, and sent him a brisk note asking if he would like to have me tear three thousand words out of the Oxford English Dictionary or out of some children's book the auditing department could understand. He came into my office to say, "I know how you feel, but goddam it, how are they going to get it off the books?" I told him they could just cross it off. I guess they did. Anyway, I never heard of the matter again. I know that Ross several times crossed old loans and advances off the books, for one reason or another, canceling old debts of writers when they were down.

It was in the late thirties that I ran into Ross one day at the water cooler in the hall, which he visited from time to time to take doses of sodium bicarbonate. I told him I had spent the evening before with Sid Perelman and Frank Sullivan and that all three of us had groused about *New Yorker* pay. "You wonder why we write for the theater and the movies and for other magazines," I told him. "Well, if each of your humorists turned in ten good pieces a year, he would make an annual income of about thirty-five hundred dollars." Ross darned near dropped his Lily cup. "I never thought of it that way," he said. "Why, that's a ribbon clerk's salary."

On March 23, 1945, he wrote this to me: "What I can't do is say to publishers that they are robbing authors, because I am not an author, and they can come right back at me and say

I am robbing authors, too, or am a party to robbing them. It is true, at least, that I have been a party to robbing them, or I unquestionably sat around this joint for years and didn't see that authors were done right by." He began seeing that they were done right by from then on, and bonus money flowed like water. There was no system to these bursts of generosity, and some old-timers were inadvertently left out of it.

Harold Ross's letters to me about the dough and the system tell more about him than I, or anybody else, could possibly hope to encompass, in prose or poetry. I'll lead in to one of them with a letter I wrote to Gus Lobrano on July 8, 1949:

DEAR GUS,

I object strenuously and indignantly to the cut of sixty dollars from "Daguerreotype of a Lady" by the auditing department, and I demand that a check for sixty dollars be sent to me. I don't know who is paid to recount corrected proofs, but I think he or she should be fired. I resent the assumption and insinuation that I am trying to get away with something and would turn in stories longer than I intend to make them in the end. This piece may be added to, since it is one of my favorites, and I have worked on it for months, even years. I have both added to proofs and cut them, and I do not want to be paid for additions or taxed for cuts. Going over a proof takes time and work, and improvements may lie either in shortening or lengthening. In any case, it is hard work. I have added whole paragraphs to stories and taken some out since 1927. Whatever I do to a proof in the future is no business of the overstaffed auditing department. I think it should be investigated before I come down and take it apart some day. The cheap and insulting sixty-dollar cut upset me for three days and I ought to charge for this loss of time.

I have made several small cuts in "The Literary Scene." This would amount to $2.85, but nobody should be paid for such recounts.

In the future, no re-examination must be made of my

proofs by any auditor, after the check has been mailed. Cuts and additions balance out in the end and save you at least one hundred dollars a week on the salary of whoever was hired for this unnecessary and degrading work.

See you Monday.

Love and kisses.

Ten days later, Ross wrote me:

DEAR JIM,

This is an answer, head on, to your letter to Lobrano about the sixty-dollar overpayment, so called, on "Daguerreotype of a Lady."

To begin with, Lobrano was in so wise responsible for that, nor was the accounting department. I am the boy, throughout, entirely, and in toto.

I can understand an author's dismay at being thus docked, especially on a piece he has put in years on, and is especially fond of, but at the same time I have sympathy with myself, for the financial side of such an undertaking as this is a most brutal thing to be up against. It damned near killed both me and the magazine in the early days and why I remained and still remain up against it, I don't know. I must be crazy to go on in the spot I am in. The only editing job I ever had that I have really liked was on the *Stars and Stripes* in the Army, where nobody got paid anything, and no financial factor came in at all; this misled me into the financial hell-hole I got myself into thirty years ago, and still am in.

I say as follows in my behalf: we worked out a payment system which, I think, is magnificent in its adaptability to a very peculiar situation. Having worked it out, it must be administered, and administered fairly. One thing the system calls for is prompt payment. God knows, we get checks through quick—quicker, I believe, than any other magazine ever did or ever does. This means that all pieces go through on a somewhat tentative basis and are paid for on that basis. Almost certainly the piece isn't going to end up the exact length it was when it was set.

You say "cuts and additions balance out in the end."
For the office to take this viewpoint would be unfair to the
authors, for experience shows that the tendency of stories
is to grow between the time of use—the author thinks of
something he wants to get in, or we want explanations of
things, and the wordage goes up. It was early found that it
would be unfair to the author to assume that cuts and additions balance. They do in the case of you, within a reasonable limit, I admit, for there is no record of an adjustment
of pay on a piece of yours in the last several years, at least.

The system of rechecking the length of a proof when
it reaches the final proof stage has been in effect for many
years. We rarely find, as I indicated, an overpayment. At
the moment, I recall only one other, a long piece by Cheever, which he cut a couple of galleys out of. But all the time
we find underpayments, and make good. We do not make
adjustments for $2.85, or other small sums. The amount
has to be considerable, usually fifty dollars, although I
think in some cases we have made smaller payments than
that when we thought it was right to send an author (with
a somewhat lower rate than yours, say) an amount that
would matter to him.

You say the elimination of the rechecking would "save
at least a hundred dollars a week on the salary of whoever
does this unnecessary and degrading work." You have the
wrong picture. No actual word counting is done. Our stuff
is set in galleys 12 inches long. The girl who does the
check-count multiplies the number of full galleys by 12 (in
her head, my daughter could do it); adds to that the inches
of type on the last galley, thereby getting the total number
of inches the piece runs. She then multiplies the number of
inches by the word-bogey per inch (forty-three, as I recall
it) and that's that, except that doubtless she doesn't actually
perform the last multiplication because she has a chart with
the total right before her. Total time elapsed in the whole
calculation: fifty-four seconds. Total time spent per week
at this work (we run an average of 3.6 non-department

pieces per week): 3 minutes, 14 seconds. Cost: a trace. (Don't think the girl gets anything like $100 per week.)

I am willing to put you on a give and take basis—everything comes out even in the course of a lifetime—and I am having a check sent you, but want to improve any impression that I am a damned fool—although I am one, or I wouldn't be mixed up in this kind of goings on when I might be out in the open air or cultivating my mind with a good book. I'm crazy, all right, but you can't say that most of my mad acts haven't been in behalf of writers.

The check will be along later.

As ever,

H. W. ROSS

In November, 1944, while at the Homestead in Hot Springs, Virginia, I came down with a ruptured appendix, and underwent an emergency operation at a railroad hospital at Clifton Forge late one night. Obviously, Helen and I were going to need money, and so she wrote directly to Ross himself. She remembered that I had turned in some drawings that had not yet been bought and paid for, and she wanted an advance against these. Ross's letter to her surprises me in only one detail—his self-reassurance that the peritonitis I had contracted, and which the doctors thought would finish me off, had not actually developed at all. I have no idea what Dr. Ross was talking about in that passage of his letter, which follows here:

DEAR HELEN,

I got your note, but since Miss Terry called up last evening, I scooped you on its contents, I guess. I was slightly worried by the peritonitis version carried in the newspapers (I think by the A.P.). The word from you was a great relief although, as I said, my worry was only slight, for as I understand it, peritonitis develops in twenty-four hours or not at all.

As to dough, under our peculiar system we can't figure up finally the amount coming Jim on the Natural History series. The system works fine, except in such a case as this, where it seems foolish, but I am having a check for $750 deposited to your account, and you can count on that being in the bank Friday morning. This is written late Wednesday and in a hurry, and the banks won't be open till Friday. Our check will be deposited by the time any check you write gets to the bank, though. If that isn't enough dough—and it very well may not be—let me know and I will have the business office deposit any amount you can think of. Just get me a word.

  Yours in some haste (it's a short week),

Sincerely,

H.. W. ROSS

Whenever I reread, or just think about, Ross's correspondence with me on the subject of money, I am reminded of the little girl's criticism of a book her teacher had made her read about penguins: "This book told me more about penguins than I wanted to know." I hope that these two concluding letters are not more than my readers want to know about Ross and dough.

DEAR JIM,

  I'm undertaking to get the agreement worked the way you want it. Meantime, a couple of points that are on my mind: You are already given a two-year period to make the quantity bonus, and have been for years; and whereas you suspect Truax of having a business-office mind when he requires firsts from you, he is blameless in this respect. It is we, the editorial department, who want the first clause. Christ, if we hadn't had that we would have missed the Mrs. Forrester story, which you only showed to us because you were obliged to, and at that you ran it down with talk of having written it only with the *Saturday Review* in mind, that Maxwell gave it back to you, evidently considering the act as perfunctory. It would have been a hell of a note if we'd lost that, which we would have if Lobrano

hadn't just happened to get back from vacation then, or
sickness, or something.

I hope you are having a good time. I am now.

As ever,

H. W. ROSS

The second system letter, and the longest of many I got,
was written on March 1, 1945.

DEAR MR. AND MRS. THURBER,

The money is rolling in. A third check has appeared
on my desk since I talked to you two hours ago. I therefore
enclose three checks. I will explain them according to their
chronology and their size, which happens to be the same.
The largest check, for $1,009.43, is in settlement of the
bonuses which it has been decided you were entitled to.
This pays you up to date on bonuses for pieces and pictures. I think I explained all that over the telephone, in
general. The details are contained in a statement from the
business office so complicated that I am not sending it to
you. I will hold it around for reference during an oral
explanation that I will make after your return. The second
check, $143.00, pays off the balance on the ten Natural
History Series drawings put through make-up so far. (It
does not count the drawings which haven't been sent to
the engravers yet.) The third check (and, incidentally, I
trust you will notice now that these checks are not all of
the same color, for some reason which even I am unable to
explain) is for $100 and is a binder for signing the agree-
ment for first look at your writings. This is the check I
forgot to tell you about. The lawyer says it is necessary to
make the agreement legal, and since $100 is $100 I didn't
say anything about it further than to comment briefly on
the wonders of the law.

One of the two other enclosures here is the aforemen-
tioned contract, which I explained over the telephone
clearly and eloquently and which also explains itself. It
doesn't commit you to doing any particular amount of

work. It merely provides that *if* you do a piece we get first chance at it. This is being made standard now for all the writers who want to go in for it, which seems to be practically everyone. For signing this contract, you get the $100 check enclosed and 25% more on all writings of yours that we buy.

The fifth enclosure is an explanation of how our bonus-for-quantity-production works. The last paragraph of this says the bonus period is twelve months, but in your case it is to be for twenty-four months on the grounds that you are entitled to this since you are both an artist and writer, a unique person generally, and a very fine fellow. The same goes for your bonus period on drawings—twenty-four months. I should have written you a separate letter about this, but that would have meant a sixth enclosure and I make it a rule never to send out a letter with more than five enclosures. Moreover, it is late in the day. I subsequently will write you a neat, succinct letter setting forth this quantity-bonus understanding and deliver it to you.

You probably will gather that, from your standpoint, the gain in making the settlement on your quantity bonuses at this time is that you henceforth get the bonus for first reading. That is, providing you sign the contract. Please sign this at once and mail it in to me.

I told you over the telephone that we have raised rates, too. That is true, but the rate set forth in the contract is the rate you have been getting to date. That is because we are setting the rates lower than we intend to pay. You will note that the contract says explicitly, "minimum rate." The main reason for that is that if there is a general raise the contract still stands. The intention is to pay you a rate four cents above the contract rate, unless there is something peculiar about your stuff.

If you figure the thing out, the rates are to hell and gone up, what with the two bonuses: you get twenty-five per cent for giving us firsts and you can readily make another twenty-five per cent of the base price, plus twenty-five per cent of the first reading bonus, which means that you can more than double your base price and make real dough if you take the matter seriously.

Please get the contract back to me. On second thought, I am enclosing an envelope for the purpose, although that makes six enclosures.

I trust you will have a good vacation.

God bless you,

H. W. ROSS

13

The Secret Life of Harold Winney

Harold Winney, who seemed to me, and still does, as unreal as the look and sound of his name, was Ross's private secretary from 1935 until the middle of August, 1941. In his years with Ross, the pallid, silent young man steadily swindled the editor out of a total of seventy-one thousand dollars. His multiple forgeries, his raids and inroads upon Ross's bank account, expense account, salary, and securities, belong in McKelway's "Of Crime and Rascality," somewhere between the magnificently complicated defalcations of the Wily Wilby and the fantastic dollar bill counterfeiting of Old 880. Bankers, tax men, and accountants still shake their heads in wonder and disbelief over the case history of Harold Winney, which has become a part of the folklore and curiosa of American capitalism.

Nobody at the *New Yorker* offices knew, or cared, very much about Harold Winney, who had been born about 1910 in or near Albany, New York, the only child of a man who died when his son was very young, and of a mother who fortunately did not live long enough to know about her son's crimes. I remember Winney mainly for his cold small voice, his pale nimble fingers, and his way of moving about the corridors and offices like a shadow. I do not believe that Harold Ross ever looked at the man closely enough to have been able to describe him accurately. He was what Ross once irritably described as a "worm"—that is, an unimportant cog in the *New Yorker* wheel, a noncreative person. As a secretary, Winney was competent and quiet.

He took dictation speedily, and transcribed his notes the same way. I would be sitting in my office, and suddenly his voice would surprise me, for I never heard him enter the room. "Mr. Ross would like your opinion on this," he would say, and hand me a typewritten query about something or other; this was in the days when I could see to read. He would stand there absolutely motionless, without a word, and wait for me to tell him what I thought, or to type my reply on a piece of paper; then he would silently vanish. He was master of the art of protective immobility. I remember that he was neat to the point of being immaculate, but the clothes he wore were as unobtrusive as his manner. When investigators examined his apartment, they found, among other things, a hundred and three suits of clothes which he had bought with the money stolen from Ross. They also found, in a private correspondence file, a long exchange of letters with a real estate firm in Tahiti. Winney had planned, a little vaguely, to flee when he had piled up enough of his employer's money, but the embezzler never does get enough, and when, in the summer of 1941, his crimes were discovered, the war was on and he could not obtain a passport.

Discovery, in the end, was inevitable. The miracle is that it didn't come years sooner. If Winney drank or smoked, it was usually in moderation, and there was only one subject in the world that could light up his cold eyes and his impassive face. That was horse racing. He was a horse player, completely addicted to it, and a steady loser. Nobody will ever know how much he lost in gambling on the horses, or what exactly became of the seventy-one thousand dollars he stole. Copies of his private letters to men friends revealed that he spent his money lavishly upon some of them, buying one an expensive sports car, outfitting another with complete skiing equipment, and giving them money for their vacations and holidays. Investigators were baffled at every turn in trying to trace what happened to Ross's money. There was, however, a record of a big champagne party Winney gave in a suite at the Astor Hotel on the night in November, 1940, when Roosevelt was elected President for the third time. "I walked past the Astor several times that night with friends," Ross told me gloomily, "and I guess I was hit on the head by my own champagne corks." He gestured toward the room just outside his own office where Winney had had his desk and typewriter. "He sat out there and fed me cake," Ross moaned.

Winney was, by a familiar caprice of nature, incapable of emotional interest in females, and this was as apparent to all of us, except Ross, as the simple fact that Mary Pickford is a woman. To Ross, however, who never scrutinized his secretary or gave him any real thought, he was nothing more than a chair in his office or the ash tray on his desk. "Did you know he was *that* kind of a man?" Ross asked me and the rest of us, and we all just stared at him and said, "Yes, didn't you?" Ross would brush this aside and say, "Then it explains the whole business. That kind of guy always wants to ruin the normal man."

Ross was by no means, of course, financially ruined by

Winney, for he still had plenty of money of his own after the loss of the seventy-one thousand dollars.

During the almost seven years that Winney robbed Ross, day after day, the editor was at the peak of his work and his worries in every field. In 1935, the year Winney came to work for him, Ross's daughter was born, and the magazine was developing rapidly in every way. In the midst of all this, Ross recognized the necessity of "delegating" some of his duties and some of his worries. He made the big mistake of delegating to Harold Winney complete control, without any safeguard whatever, of his bank accounts and securities—he had two separate accounts in one bank. The bank tellers and vice-presidents became familiar with the quiet, well-behaved, efficient young man who was Ross's private secretary, and in whom, the editor had made it clear, he reposed every trust. Thus, when Winney showed up at a teller's cage with a check made out to cash, signed with the unmistakable signature of H. W. Ross, the check was not subjected to more than casual scrutiny. Even if it had been, Winney's forgery of Ross's name was so perfect that after the secretary's death, the few canceled checks that could be found baffled not only handwriting experts but even Ross himself, who could not swear whether a given signature was his own or Winney's. Winney's own initials were H. W. and all he had to imitate were the six letters of H. W. Ross. He became an expert at it.

As the years went on, he grew bolder and bolder, and in one week, the record shows, cashed three separate checks for a total of six thousand dollars. At that period, Ross's main financial interest was in his friend Dave Chasen's restaurant in Hollywood. About the time that Harold Winney began robbing Ross, the restaurant began to make money. Ross had originally lent Chasen three thousand dollars, a generous personal loan of the kind for which he was well known to his intimates. Sums of money like that did not bother Ross when it came to helping out one of the men to whom he was most devoted. Later he began investing in the restaurant and his profits increased, but he could never quite accommodate himself to the idea that he deserved the profits, which amounted finally to more than two hundred thousand dollars. "Goddam it, I never intended to make a lot of money out of Dave's place," he once told a lawyer. "It's hard for me to think he owes me anything, except on the basis of personal loans." The difference between a loan and an investment had to be explained to him patiently. "I know, I know all that," he would say, putting on his well-known expression of worry and wonder.

Winney began cautiously by forging six checks in 1935 for a total of about fourteen hundred dollars; the next year he forged seven checks for a total of nineteen hundred dollars. In 1937 there were nine checks, and the amount was twenty-nine hundred dollars, and in 1938, the year before he threw caution to the winds, he forged seven checks for twenty-seven hundred and thirty dollars. During all this time he was careful to fill out checkbook stubs and reconcile them precisely with Ross's monthly bank statements. He had soon discovered, but probably couldn't believe it, that Ross did not want to be bothered by studying his checkbooks or monthly statements. So Winney "summarized" them, as he explained it to Ross, and would simply lay a typed sheet of paper on Ross's desk when he was asked about the state of his account. If Ross spotted some familiar amount, such as $113.13, and said, "I thought that check went through last month," Winney would simply tell him quietly that he was wrong. The cake became easier and easier to feed to Ross, and Winney finally abandoned entirely the unnecessary work of justification. He would simply tear a check out of a checkbook, fill it out for whatever amount he wanted, sign Ross's name, and cash it at the bank. When he really began to splurge with Ross's money and visit the bank several times a week, he would hand in the check and wink slyly at the teller, as if to say, "The old boy's at it again." I don't know how many persons, outside the *New Yorker* and Ross's circle of friends, knew how often Ross gambled and how often he lost, but it was scarcely a state secret. Dozens of checks for gambling losses, averaging around five hundred dollars, were duplicated by Winney before he sent them, with Ross's genuine signature on them, to the lucky winners. During 1939 and 1940 and up until the end of July, 1941, Winney forged a hundred and sixty checks for a total of about sixty-two thousand dollars. By the end of July, 1941, he had withdrawn all of his employer's salary through December and, along with it, several thousand dollars of Ross's expense account money.

Winney was a well-implemented student of his employer. He was, however, at all times skating on ice that grew thinner and thinner, and he must have known that sooner or later it would break under him. It may be that he hoped to restore the money he had taken if he could only win a large amount on the horses or make some quick and profitable investment, but nobody knows about that, or if anybody does, nothing has ever been revealed. Winney's friends, or such of them as were found and talked to, claimed they knew nothing about his secret life, and this may well have been true. He was as tight-mouthed as he was thin-lipped.

The withdrawal in advance of Ross's salary and expense account money had to be accomplished through the *New Yorker*'s own business department, and, in spite of the tension between the editor and that department, it remained something of a miracle that nothing was said to Ross about these massive withdrawals until the middle of August, 1941. One man in the business department, who has been there for more than thirty years, told me what I already knew: that if the business department ever mentioned money to Ross, he yelled them down, or said they were crazy, or announced that he didn't want to talk about it and hung up the phone. There were years during which he would refuse to discuss anything at all with Fleischmann, and such communications as passed between them were carried on circuitously. Winney was also a close student of this situation.

In 1938 Ross and his second wife spent several months in France and England, and before he left he put his securities in Winney's hands, giving him power of attorney over them. In order to replenish this or that account, in a crisis, the secretary would sell some of Ross's securities. Ross both played into Winney's hands and made things a bit difficult for him by carrying loose checks in his pocket and making them out to this person or that or to this firm or that, sometimes remembering to tell Winney about them the next day, but often forgetting it. In this way, Winney could never be sure what situation would confront him at the end of any given month.

During the last year of Winney's peculations, he caused Ross to be overdrawn multiple times at the bank. When this situation occurred, Winney would either transfer some funds from the account in Jane Grant's name to Ross's own account, or cover up by selling some more of Ross's securities. The "mad, intelligent Ross," as Janet Flanner once called him, had simply forgotten to cancel Winney's power of attorney, after the editor got back from France. Ross expected to get loyalty from those around him the way he expected to get his mail, but he didn't always get that, either. All communications from the bank and several letters from a firm of tax experts, suggesting that they supervise Ross's financial interests, were simply torn up and thrown away by Ross's secretary.

When it comes to money, bank accounts, and everything else fiscal or financial, I am not one to throw stones, but a pot as black as the kettle. I once had a checking account in a famous old Fifth Avenue bank, through the recommendation of Ralph Ingersoll, but after I had been overdrawn three times, I was invited to talk it over with a vice-president of the bank. He was shocked almost beyond words when he discovered that I did not fill out my checkbook stubs. "Then how do you know how much money you have in the bank?" he asked me, and I told him, "I estimate it." He turned a little white and his hand trembled. "You—*estimate* it? he croaked. That bank was glad to get rid of me.

I have always had the good sense to let my wife handle my finances, but Ross would just have goggled at anyone who suggested that he put such a responsibility upon his own spouse. It was not only his strangeness about dough, but his erratic judgments of men, that put such a powerful temptation in the way of Harold Winney. One of those around him in the early years, a man he both liked and trusted, and rightly so, was Ralph Paladino. When he was young and single, Ralph took a course in public accounting at a night school, and Ross attended his graduation exercises. Ralph, it seemed to us in those days, kept track of everything for Ross. He was an expert on order, organization, dough, records, and everything else that Ross worried about. Then Ralph was married and after a while had children, and needed an increase of salary, and Ross would not okay this. I still get mad at him when I think about it, and I once bawled him out for it, after Ralph quit and took a better-paying job. "I haven't got time for little people," Ross snarled, and I told him that was a hell of a thing to say. He later apologized for it, murmured something about all the physical troubles that he had at the time, a jaw infection, his ulcers, and the spreading of the metatarsal bones of one foot. Ralph Paladino, by the way, is now head of the make-up department at *Newsweek*. Last year a man who works there told me, "He is our one most indispensable man."

Harold Ross had a lot of things to think about in 1941, including his approaching third marriage, three of my five eye operations, the war and all that it did to him, and a hundred other concerns. He himself had withdrawn some of his salary and expense account that year, and this gave Winney the idea of withdrawing the rest of it. Such transactions as this had to be okayed by the Miracle Man—during most of this period it was Ik Shuman. One day after Winney had withdrawn Ross's salary and expense money for October, November and December, Raoul Fleischmann sent for Shuman and said, "Did you know that Ross is hard up?" They discussed the matter, and Ik said he would look into it.

For a while Ross simply did not believe, or even listen to, what Shuman had to tell him about his withdrawn salary. Then he sent for Winney. That doomed young man knew that he had come to the end of the line, but he didn't turn white, or begin shaking, or break down and confess. He simply double-talked Ross into deeper and deeper confusion, until the editor said, "Oh, the hell with it—I'll stop in at the bank tomorrow and find out all about it myself." That sentence was Harold Winney's death sentence. After work he went home to his expensive and tidily furnished apartment in Brooklyn, turned on the gas in the kitchen and took his own life.

When the body of Harold Winney was discovered the next day in his Brooklyn apartment, Ross was greatly upset, and when the first batch of his manifold forgeries came to light, he expressed pity for him, and even compassion, according to Shuman and Gene Kinkead, Ross's great "gumshoe." Kinkead had been assigned to find out as much as he could about what Winney had done to Ross, and when the staggering total of the quiet young man's thefts became clear, Ross no longer said, as he had been saying, "The poor little guy." What mainly bothered Ross, however, was not the amount of his losses, but the feeling that his "friends at '21,'" as Shuman put it, would never get over kidding him about it all. So the actual total of the forgeries was not given out to the papers. They were told that it was somewhere between seventeen thousand and twenty thousand dollars. That's what Ross told me, too. I think that he was wrong about this. Any American can be taken for seventeen thousand or twenty thousand dollars, but it takes a really great eccentric to be robbed of seventy-one thousand dollars right under his busy nose.

I am told that Ross could not be reimbursed by the bank

for his losses, because he had made this legally impossible by
the way he ignored his monthly statements, and by his having
given power of attorney to Winney, which he never withdrew.
It seems that Ross did get five thousand dollars of Harold Winney's insurance money. What I remember mainly about the
wreckage of that tragic August was a strange threat Ross made.
He was going to get even with the bank, he said, by "hiring
Steve Hannagan." Just what he expected that late, famous public relations man, sometimes known as the "Discoverer of Flor-
ida," to do, I have no way of knowing. Ross soon realized, of
course, that publicity was precisely what he did not want.

Among those to whom Ross occasionally lost money at
backgammon or gin rummy was a well-known New York publisher, and whenever he won from two hundred dollars to five
hundred dollars from Ross, Winney would duplicate the
check, so that Ross really always lost twice as much as he
believed he had. Losing anything to a publisher was, to H. W.
Ross, something that there could be nothing more deplorable
than. He fought publishers, on behalf of writers, all his life,
and wrote literally hundreds of letters bawling them out. One
of these, to Marshall Best, runs to two thousand words. In a
letter to Ross, the publisher had accused him of obscurantism,
and Ross ended his reply, "Whee! Let's have oceans of obscurantism." Ross and the *New Yorker* never took any subsidiary
rights at all from writers and artists, but were satisfied with
first serial rights. When Ross found out that publishers often

got a percentage of their authors' sales of movie or theater rights, he banged away at them on his trusty typewriter, and you could hear it all the way down the hall. He also fought them for better royalties for writers and for a more equable arrangement on anthologies. He once got a letter from Christopher La Farge, then president of the Authors' League, thanking him, on behalf of the authors of the country, for what he had been doing and was still doing.

I don't know how to end this account of the short, unhappy life of Harold Winney, but I guess I'll just put down what two different admirers of Ross, who did not know the Winney story, said, in the same voice, after I had told the tale. "What a wonderful man!" said one of them. "What a crazy guy!" said the other.

14

Writers, Artists, Poets, and Such

Bob Benchley sat down at a table in Tony's one night, before the unlamented death of Prohibition, and found himself in the midst of a discussion about the comparative unendurability of writers and artists. Someone asked, "If two ships were sailing from New York tonight, one filled with writers and the other with artists, which would you get on?"

"Do I *have* to get on either one of them?" Benchley asked.

I told it to Ross the next day and he said, "You and Benchley don't know what you're talking about. You don't know how easy your life is. I have to get on both ships every goddam day." This was not the literal truth. Ross dealt directly with only a small percentage of both writers and artists. Some of the oldest and best-known contributors to his magazine he never encountered face to face in his life. Charles Addams had been sending in drawings for more than a decade before Ross ever laid eyes on him. He saw him first during the war years, when the editor felt sheepish about his aloofness and began taking some of the writers and artists to lunch. Direct contact with them had been delegated to James Geraghty, Katharine White, Gus Lobrano, William Shawn, William Maxwell, and other Ross lieutenants who met head on a great many of the persons and problems Ross was much too self-conscious to take on himself.

"I didn't meet Ross until the end of '42, just as I was about to be drafted," Charles Addams wrote me last year. "As you know, he made a point of not meeting the contributors, especially the artists, ever. What broke him down I don't know. Probably thought I'd fall in a German gas attack, and having nothing to lose, he would take a look anyway. I had been submitting stuff for eleven years without ever seeing him, though once I thought I saw him in the corridor, but it turned out to be one of those elderly messenger boys they still employ around the office. Ross took several of us to lunch at the Algonquin—Steinberg, Roberta MacDonald and me, of the artists. He was exactly as pictured. Everyone was tense, including Ross, who was voluble, too. I don't remember what he said, but he puréed his own peas, out of respect to his duodenals. The work of no one present was discussed. I can find only one letter from Ross which I'm enclosing.

"So I never saw much of him, though I was certainly not only fond of him but an enormous admirer—and we did have a very friendly if casual relationship, especially in his last two years. Most of my knowledge of Ross comes from Gibbs and McKelway . . ."

Ross had sent Addams a belated bonus check—whatever its amount, it wasn't enough—and the artist had thanked him, and then Ross wrote him this letter: "Don't give it a second thought. It's no more than fair, if that. We might have done better if it weren't for wartime regulations, but if it weren't for the war boom maybe we wouldn't have been able to do anything. God knows. I think the last drawing of your tasty little household looking at the home movie is probably a masterpiece. I suspect you ought to have more characters in that household. The dearth was borne in on me by this picture. Anyhow, it's a good humorous line, when you get ideas for it, which isn't easy."

It's too bad that Ross had not sat around with Addams, in the home of one or the other, or at Tim's or "21," for the Gee Whiz Guy would have had an enchanted evening listening to some of the artist's experiences. "I have gotten a lot of letters about my work, most of them from criminals and subhumans, who want to sell ideas," Addams told me. "I can rarely use them as they're in the worst possible taste, but sometimes funny in a grotesque sort of way. Some of the worst come from a minister in Georgia. Also people send me photographs of houses with mansard roofs, as if I'd invented them. A man in Boston sent a picture of a local shoe store, a very old one, with shoes for the club-footed, for shortened legs, etc.; underneath the window in gold-leaf on black it said, 'Shoes for the entire family.'

"A woman in Plainfield wrote in to say that my drawings had been revolting her for years. The last one she tore out and burned, and she was canceling her subscription at once. Later, I found out (I come from Westfield five miles away) that she keeps the ashes of her husband on the mantelpiece. I am enclosing a postcard from an admirer showing a rural bridge over a rocky stream. Among the rubbish are two baby carriages.

"Also, this letter from an eleven-year-old gag-writer: 'I thought up a joke which I think you will be interested in. It concerns the Horrible family that you created in the *New Yorker*. It shows the inside of the haunted house, on two nails are hanging two strait jackets. On one there is imbroidered his on the other hers.' "

The whims of the Ross personality were, like those of all the rest of us, elusive, and I would have no way of explaining why he was more at ease with Peter Arno and Helen Hokinson, among the artists, than with any of the others. Certainly those two had little in common except talent. Ross was often in Arno's evening company, especially in the first years of the magazine, and he loved to regale the rest of us with accounts

of their nocturnal adventures. Arno was one of the few contributors that Ross didn't mind confronting personally when
he had a bone to pick with him. He took Peter out for a couple
of drinks a few days after the appearance in the *New Yorker* of
that controversial full-page Arno of the couple and the cop in
the moonlight. One of the oldest and soundest of *New Yorker*
editors has quarreled with my statement, in the opening chapter of this book, that Ross had printed the drawing without
knowing what it meant. This drawing, in which the man is
shown with the rear seat of a car under his arm and is saying
to the cop, "We want to report a stolen car," was surely understood by everybody else between the ages of fifteen and
seventy-five. "On our second drink," Arno told me recently,
"Ross said to me, 'So you put something over on me.' " Arno
naturally wanted to know why Ross had printed the drawing
if he didn't understand what it meant. The remarkable editor's
remarkable explanation went like this: "Goddam it, I thought
it had a kind of Alice in Wonderland quality. It would have
had the same effect on me if the guy had been holding a steering wheel instead of the back seat." If Peter had anything to
say to that, and I can't imagine what it could have been, he
doesn't remember it.

Ross's unending cross-examination of meaning rarely
extended to poetry, whose very nature baffled him. Fadiman
wrote me: "Ross never understood a word of the occasional
poetry reviews that Louise Bogan wrote, and used to ask me
to explain why they should be printed. This didn't mean that
he thought they should *not* be printed; it was just his way of
expressing bewilderment." One of the last times I was ever in
the editor's office, he had the dictionary open, he wore his Sunday scowl, and his tongue was edging out. "Now what?" I
asked him, and he spluttered, "I've got a poem here that says
'the leaves bronzen.' Now 'bronzen' is not a verb but an adjective, just as I thought. I know, I know, it's poetic license—

White has told me all about that. But I don't think there should be a license, even in poetry, to get a thing wrong."

Ross's opinion sheets, which must have run into millions of words during his nearly twenty-seven years as editor, were regarded as just a part of the day's work, and almost all of them were thrown away after the pieces they referred to had been put through. This is a pity, for there was more of Ross in them than any biographer could cram into two volumes. My wife has preserved, fortunately for this record, a couple of the editor's opinion sheets on pieces of mine, and I can see clearly now that turning them out was not mere drudgery but a kind of sanctuary, in which he could forget, for the time being, all his personal woes and worries.

In 1948 I wrote a slight casual called "Six for the Road," which I came to like so little that I never included it in a book. When the piece reached the *New Yorker*, both Lobrano and Mrs. White were away, and Ross sent his opinions direct to me. I set down here most of what he had to say about "Six for the Road" because it is Ross, pure and unalloyed:

"1. It isn't a typical party you're talking about here— doesn't include the kind of mild parties you've enumerated in preceding paragraph, but a party typical of this particular circle, the Spencer-Thurber circle. Also, suggest that these people here be pegged as suburban, as I have marked, or some such, for later in the piece, much later, it turns out that they live in places with stairs, which means houses, not apartments. You start a story like this off without a suburban plant and a reader assumes you're talking about metropolitan apartment house life, and is unfairly surprised when he comes to a passage about someone going upstairs.

"2. You might, if you want, clinch the suburban atmosphere by putting in here the name of some town in the region—Rye, or a Connecticut town.

"3. Above you twice call this function an *evening*

party, in one instance saying it begins in afternoon. Here you say the Spencers were asked to dinner. Now, even in the Spencer circle the dinner guests can't be asked to come in the afternoon, certainly. This mixing up of a dinner party and an evening party that begins in the afternoon baffled me for quite a while, and I have come up with the suggestion that the party be made a cocktail party with buffet dinner. I think this is a brilliant suggestion. You never later have the people sitting down to dinner, nor do you take any notice whatever of dinner. If you make cocktails and buffet dinner, there is no question in readers' minds at all, and it seems to me the kind of a function the Spencers would give—as I did in my younger days. This the real reason I'm writing these notes direct. I think such a fix would help considerably.

"4. It seems to me that the *however* isn't right in this sentence, and that some such phrase as marked might be better. Please consider.

"5. This sentence won't parse as is. Needs insert such as marked, or *points out that* or some such.

"6. *June* will probably sound stale by time we get out. Can be changed later, I assume. (Am noting here so query will be carried.)

"7. There hasn't been more than one phase of this ailment, has there? (The second phase—itching knees—isn't mentioned until later.) Also, please give this point a thought: You tell the story of the party in the present tense, but you have this paragraph in the past tense. Shouldn't this paragraph be in the present tense? I suspect so, and with initial, to help with the switchover. Also, suggest that there might be more definite wording here to indicate this is the evening of the party. The transition here may not be quite right.

"8. If you don't make it a buffet dinner, or do *something,* it seems to me that these people are leaving awfully quick. I thought maybe all this happened before dinner, because you have *early in the evening* a paragraph and a half above (7) and you've accounted for very little time lapse; not much has happened.

"9. The sentence at (a) differs in nature from sentence at (b). In the (a) sentence you are writing from the viewpoint of the Bloodgoods, in the (b) sentence you're the omnipotent author, knowing all about it. Seems to me wrong.

"10. The *over their shoulders* phrase here give the right picture? Suggests to me *on their shoulders,* like a Greek maiden holding vase. (Small matter.)

"11. Very unexpected to learn at this late date that there's a bar in this place. Not mentioned before, and the definite pronoun has no antecedent.

"12. Is it consistent that Mrs. Bloodgood would be the respository for this confidence in view of the fact that she and her husband met the Spencers only two weeks before and have only seen them that once? And is it as clear as it should be *what* Dora whispered?

"13. And same question here. Remember, Mrs. Bloodgood has only met the Spencers that one time, when she asked them to the party. How could she know?

"14. A timid suggestion: Would phrase written in help point it, or would it over-diagram it?

"Pardon me for being fussy. Most of the foregoing not important, but I think that buffet dinner business is, and the locating of the story out of New York City. You'll see another proof of this, set in regular type. Some of the incidentals may be untimely by time this can be used. Can check on these later.

"P.S. The only other complication I can think of is that the very next story we bought after this one was titled 'One for the Road.' My tentative stand is that you have seniority around here and the junior man will have to get another title."

In December, 1948, a year in which Ross said, "The issues are getting bigger and bigger," he again sent me, directly, his opinion sheet on something of mine called "A Couple of Snapshots," and I reprint it here to fill out the picture of Ross poring over a casual. The reference to the "Java Jive" grew out of a strange small problem he had made for himself, and had mentioned in two previous notes to me. John McNulty had given me a recording of the song, and I had used this line from it: "I love the Java Java and it loves me." That simply threw Ross, who, I am certain, knew neither the melody nor any of the words of "Smiles" or "Hindustan," although he must have heard them, without listening, a hundred times. He had finally decided that what I was talking about was that old song, "Jada, Jada." I refused to get snarled up in all this anxious nonsense. Here, then, are his notes on "A Couple of Snapshots":

"1. You've made a fix here, and earlier in the paragraph to coincide. In the proof you sent back, there is a note in the margin, presumably written by Helen: 'Seems to us that the fact that Thurber's home is Columbus is implicit; also pretty well established by now.' True, but I point out that our pieces are signed at the end and a reader starts them cold, not knowing who wrote them. Also, the conditions have changed since you last wrote on Columbus (*Life and Hard Times*): your father has died and your mother has moved to an apartment to live. Old followers of Thurber are bound to wonder why you don't stay at the family home when in Columbus instead of going to a hotel. I wondered why, presuming that your mother was continuing to live in the old home, and was stumped. I thought it was cold-blooded of you that you didn't stay with your mother when you returned. It was only when you told me orally that your mother closed the home after your father died and went to an apartment that I got an explanation. Up to then I was stumped, and wondering. I think a lot of other people will do the same, even with the fix made, most Thurber followers probably not even knowing that your father is no longer living. I suggest, to clear my conscience, that the wording here might be along the line of '. . . where I have always stayed since my father died and

my mother moved into an apartment.' There is interest in you and your family, and no question about it, and I respectfully suggest they'd be interested in knowing how, and where, your mother is making out. But, as I said, up to you, clear without it and no argument. I'm merely a journalist shooting off, maybe.

"2. You've got *drawn up* and *made* up in this sentence, and you've got a *tidy* here and repeat of it at 2a, next galley.

"3. Nobody at all has got this Java Java business. The latest I've had is a note from a checker saying the song is 'Java, Jive,' indicating that he's recalled that combination in some song or other. Apparently Java is a popular word with lyric writers, which astonishes me.

"4. Repeat of *going to* here.

"5. 5a. Repeat of *turned*.

"6. Checking says this a church, not cathedral.

"7. You've got an *out* here and two others nearby, at 7a, 7b.

"8. And a *simple* here and at 8a, next galley.

"9. *Stood up* here and *clear up* second line following.

"10. See. . . . see.

"I'm listing the repeats because I thought you might like to know about them. None of them are pernicious, it seems to me.

"Merry Christmas."

No survey, however slight, of Ross's opinion sheets would be complete without the inclusion of one or two of his classic and deathless queries and comments. I think the two favorites of most of us are these: "What woman? Hasn't been previously mentioned," he wrote when he became puzzled by a reference, in a Perelman casual, to "the woman taken in adultery." The other indestructible Rossism was a comment on one of Arthur Kober's finely accurate stories about the Bronx family he knows so well and has made so well known to *New Yorker* readers. Kober's Bella had said that she had been "on tenderhooks all day." Ross's comment: "Think she would get this wrong. Think she would say tenterhooks."

Among the more famous stories the *New Yorker* has printed, there was one that, it seemed to me, must have been bought and used when Ross was out of town, or down in bed, or going through one of his infrequent spells of sulking in his tent. This was Shirley Jackson's controversial and widely discussed "The Lottery," published in that bigger and bigger year, 1948. It has been variously described as a parable, a modern fable, a piece of symbolism, and even a joke played on Ross and his editors. It has withstood both unintelligent attack and obtuse praise and, I expect, will appear in anthologies into the next century. Shawn told me that Ross's opinion sheet on this story, as on almost all other stories, has been lost, and so I wrote to Miss Jackson herself, to find out how she had thrown her fast ball past the cautious Harold Ross who had said, more than once, "I'll never print another story I don't understand." Here is Miss Jackson's reply to my letter:

I am sorry to have to tell you that I have almost no information regarding Mr. Ross's reaction to my story, "The

Lottery." I never met Mr. Ross, and all my dealings over the story were with Gus Lobrano; I do know that when Gus called me to say that they were buying the story he asked—"for our own information"—if I cared to take any stand on the meaning of the story. I was interested in what I naturally regarded as his only important remark—that they were buying the story—and while I was still fumbling for some happy phrase he asked if I thought the story meant that superstition was ignorant; if the story might be called an allegory which made its point by an ironic juxtaposition of ancient superstition and modern setting. I said yes, indeed, that would be fine, and he said, "Good; that's what Mr. Ross thought it meant." I do not believe that at that time anyone expected that the story would raise the kind of fuss it did, and I have always assumed that Mr. Ross and Gus were only checking to make sure that Mr. Ross was not printing something he didn't understand. This interpretation of the story was later the basis for Kip Orr's answers to the letters that came in asking what it meant.

There were several hundred letters, many of which were addressed or forwarded directly to me, and many more which came addressed to the magazine, some of them even addressed to Mr. Ross himself. Mr. Ross had all of them sent to me, including the ones addressed to him or to Dear Editor or Dear Ed. Because I am sentimental I put them into a scrapbook, and it is now almost impossible to get them out again. I find, however, that among them is the one note Mr. Ross wrote about the story, or a copy of it, since even that was not to me, but to a Mr. Forster, directing that the letters be given to my husband to give to me, as useful publicity for the book of stories of mine which was to be published the next spring, and which naturally featured "The Lottery." Since I cannot get Mr. Ross's note out of the scrapbook, I will copy it for you and enclose it. . . .

I wish I had more information to give you. Since we

were here in Vermont during the entire uproar, I knew nothing except what was written to me; perhaps I am just as well off, not having had a chance to hear what Mr. Ross had to say about it all.

This is Ross's memo to Louis Forster, on whom he depended for a hundred different kinds of things, and a note he sent at the same time to Stanley Hyman, Miss Jackson's husband, then on the staff of the *New Yorker:*

MR. FORSTER:

You asked me if I thought anything could be done in the way of exploitation in using the letters of applause that came in on the Shirley Jackson story, "The Lottery," and I said I didn't. It now occurs to me that one thing that might be done with these is turn them over to Miss Jackson's publisher for use when the book containing the story comes out. He could make one or more releases on them, I should think, and get up some statistics on the number of letters Miss Jackson received and that we received, what the letters said, etc. Also, this might make blurb material for the jacket, which would have value because I think a lot of reviewers get their cues and jump-off ideas from the blurbs on book-jackets.

I think this is a good idea, maybe, but have we got the letters? Don't bother to answer this question. I suppose they've gone to Miss Jackson, and come to think of it now, I'm sending a copy of this letter to Mr. Hyman with a suggestion that he advise Miss Jackson to damned well hold onto the letters for this possible use, and maybe other uses that may come to someone's mind. There is going to be discussion when the story comes out and fuel for the reviewers will help.

H. W. ROSS

MR. HYMAN:

Please see attached, especially the third sentence of the second paragraph. Maybe there's an idea here, and that you ought to tell your wife. And, while at it, tell her that

the story has certainly been a great success from our standpoint, as it was a certainty to be. Gluyas Williams said it is
the best American horror story. I don't know whether it's
that or not, or quite what it is, but it was a terrifically effective thing, and will become a classic in some category.

H. W. ROSS

I cannot let Kip Orr, mentioned above, pass and be forgotten without a further word. For one thing, he had a tank of
live fish in his office, and some potted plants which he tended
with great care. ("I don't want to see 'em. I don't want to
go in there," Ross said when he heard about it.) Upon Orr's
shoulders fell the tedious task of answering all mail directed to
the magazine or "To the Editors." At least one of his replies to
a testy male subscriber will be remembered forever. A colonel,
whom I shall call Comfort-Smothers, had written the *New
Yorker* from his club in the city to say: "Every time I pick up
your magazine I fall asleep trying to read it." Kip Orr answered
that as follows:

Colonel J. T. Comfort-Smothers,
The Oldsters Club,
New York City.

Dear Colonel Comfort-Smothers:
Pleasant dreams.

(It was into Kip Orr's office that one high-strung Miracle Man tiptoed one day and said, about a certain letter, "I
wouldn't send it airmail. It looks like rain.")

Ross sometimes read proofs so long at a stretch, dwelling
on every word and phrase, that he became confused when he
shifted to a piece of humor after spending hours on factual
stuff. I once wrote a short parody called "My Memoirs of
D. H. Lawrence." In it there was this passage: "I saw Lawrence for the first time pacing a platform of a railway station in
Milan. He had the look of a man who was waiting for something. In this case I think it was the train." On his opinion

sheet Ross wrote, "It was obviously the train." When that came to me from Lobrano, who would have cut it out before I could see it if I hadn't given him strict orders not to tamper with Ross's queries, I sat down and wrote the editor this note:

DEAR MR. ROSS:

One of us is obviously losing his touch. In this case I think it's you. If it's me, I'm going to give up humor and become a train dispatcher.

Ross came into my room laughing about that, and then he said, "I keep telling you I haven't got time to read for pleasure."

I didn't immediately hear anything from him after he had read and bought "Walter Mitty." Then, a week later, he sent me a note that began "Old Fellow" and ended "God bless you." He had read the story, one night, finally, in the magazine, for pleasure.

Through it all went the unending fuss and fret about commas. The *New Yorker*'s overuse of commas, originating in Ross's clarification complex, has become notorious the world over among literary people. In Paris, in 1955, an English journalist said to me one night, "The biography of Ross should be called *The Century of the Comma Man*." A professor of English somewhere in England wrote me ten years ago a long, itemized complaint about the *New Yorker* comma, objecting to, among other things, its use after "moreover" and "furthermore," in which, he said the comma is implicit. He picked out this sentence in a *New Yorker* casual of mine: "After dinner, the men went into the living room," and he wanted to know why I, or the editors, had put in the comma. I could explain that one all right. I wrote back that this particular comma was Ross's way of giving the men time to push back their chairs and stand up.

Now and then, the weedy growth of that punctuation mark, spreading through the magazine like dandelions, was

more than I could bear with Christian fortitude. I once sent
Ross a few typed lines of one of Wordsworth's Lucy poems,
repunctuated after his exasperating fashion:

> She lived, alone, and few could know
> When Lucy ceased to be,
> But, she is in her grave, and, oh,
> The difference, to me.

Ross accosted me in the corridors with a long harangue
on the subject. "You ought to lecture somewhere," I told him
irritably. I should like to be able to report that I also told him,
"This magazine is in a commatose condition," but it wasn't
until ten years later that I thought of it.

It was often nothing weightier than a comma that
brought a furrow to Ross's brow and a baffled look to his eye.
There was a day when he came to White's office—I happened
to be there, too—wondering what the *New Yorker*'s style
should be on "the red, white, and blue." That happens to be
the way he decided it should always be punctuated. What had
bothered him was a "red, white and blue" he had stumbled
over in some manuscript. I suggested, and still think I was
right, that the style should be "the red white and blue" and I
told Ross that. "All those commas make the flag seemed rained
on. They give it a furled look," I said. "Leave them out, and
Old Glory is flung to the breeze, as it should be." "Very funny.
Very pretty, too," Ross said. "Get it down on paper. Write a
piece about it, and I'll punctuate the flag any way you want
it—in that one piece." Ross often summoned Hobart Weekes
when a comma had popped up to worry him, and he would
ask Weekes, "What is the rule?" Then he would run into
Weekes later in the hall and say, "There isn't any rule." He had
the volatile gift of shifting from rule-bound to rule-free, and
once, in the same issue of the magazine, permitted Benchley to
use "oblivious to" and me to say "oblivious of," since each of
us was adamant about his preference. Ross wanted to know

why we disagreed and I told him that Bob believed in the dative following "ob" whereas I thought of "oblivious" as meaning "forgetful." He went away, shaking his head, to look it up in Fowler, I suppose.

Frank Sullivan has sent me Ross's opinion sheet on "The Cliché Expert Testifies on the Tabloids." I am glad Frank saved it, and here it is:

"1. Haven't the tabs got a better adjective than *pretty* here. That seems ordinary. On other hand, maybe it is their word, though.

"2. In view of fact that *Graphic* has been out of business many years, suggest tense changed marked, to take better cognizance of this fact. It's 20 years, I think; whole generation has grown up—and gone to war.

"3. Well, does Kinsey report mention rape? Surprises me that it does, for I've heard of no rape quotes from that book (which I haven't read).

"4. Here a peculiar point, and one that has long obsessed me. The tabs use *exotic* wrong, nearly always. *Exotic* means, merely, foreign. But they apply it to domestic ladies freely. A man who worked long on the *Daily News* told me that *News* rewrite men were given a list of ten or twelve words to use in stories and headlines that sounded snappy, would be thought by the readers to mean something more than they really mean, or something other than they really mean, something snappy—and wouldn't be

libelous. At head of list was *exotic*. Tab readers are supposed to think that *exotic* means *erotic*. It would be libel to
call a lady *erotic*. I guess. Sullivan might possibly go into
this with a question or two—on this unusual use of the
word, but doesn't matter. I'm just writing this to be interesting."

I'll always remember the day, a quarter of a century ago,
that I took John McNulty into Ross's office and introduced
them. McNulty was a man most men liked the moment they
saw him, and Ross was not an exception, but the pieces
McNulty tried to sell to the *New Yorker* for the next few years
were invariably rejected. Beginning about 1936, though, his stuff
was bought, and by the time he died in 1956 more than sixty
of his stories had appeared. One of the admirers of John's stuff
was Mencken, who once said, "This is writing. This is it."

In the years when John was unable to sell to the magazine,
Ross had spotted him as a writer of journalese. Once Ross got
that idea in his head, it was hard to dislodge, and I was afraid
that McNulty would never make it, in spite of his rich and
special talent, his knowledge of what Donald Ogden Stewart
has called "the little man in the corner," as well as the man in
the street and the men at the bar and the man in the lonely
rented room, and all sorts and conditions of men in Third Avenue, which McNulty, of course, called Third Avenya. For some
reason, in 1949, after McNulty had been to Hollywood and
back, I got the wind up about what I thought was happening
to him on the *New Yorker*. He had written a notable piece
about a trip to Ireland, called "Back Where I Had Never
Been," and I wrote Ross, sternly admonishing him and his
editors, to "Let McNulty stuff alone." I told him McNulty's
pieces were not journalese or noncreative, but imaginative literature. There had been, and still is, a great deal of critical
argument about the so-called *New Yorker* style, and while I
agree, in the main, with Fadiman and others that there is no
such thing and that most of the *New Yorker*'s outstanding con-

tributors have styles of their own, I was increasingly disturbed by Ross's insistence on super-clarity, overpunctuation, and strict rules of grammar and syntax and parsing. I knew that if McNulty became a prisoner of pattern, something warm and unique would go out of his writing. I have Ross's letter in reply to my admonitions and warnings, and reprint it here. The reference in the final paragraph is to a story of mine that had appeared in the *Saturday Evening Post* in 1940—a story about a midget baseball player entitled "You Could Look It Up."

As to McNulty's Irish story, you understand wrong throughout; you understand as wrong as a man can understand. Whoever told you that McNulty "had a terrible struggle for survival" is a liar or a spreader of outrageous slander. There was never a flicker of struggle. McNulty got some help, and seemed grateful for it, as he always does, and I'll bet you a hundred to one that he would tell you so. The help he got was considerable when you consider that, after he decided with Shawn to write a story on his Irish trip, he then backed out of it several times, declared his efforts a failure, and only wrote it because of Shawn's patient and persistent encouragement. The fact is that, beginning with a five-hundred-word nugget, he fed it to Shawn in fragments and shreds, which Shawn assembled. He never turned it in as the entity it became. He finally got it done, triumphantly, but Shawn was the obstetrician, the midwife, and the godfather of that piece, and it never would have been done without him. No one ever called his piece noncreative around here. I never heard anyone call it journalistic, either, although I don't know quite what the word means in this connection.

I will now change the subject. Grantland Rice took me to a World Series game, and for a couple of innings talked about your baseball story, going over with great rel-ish the scene of the midget at bat. He thinks the story would make a movie, and, by God, I do, too, although it has been a long time since I've read or thought of that story. Do you want me to start selling it? Remember I'd have made a better deal on the Mitty story if you had let my plan run its course. The thing to do is stir up interest and sit tight until the ferment gets well along. Give me a signal and I'll start.

The midget story was never made into a movie, but it was done on a half-hour radio program supervised by Grantland Rice. I have several letters from Ross, written in various years, telling me of his efforts to sell "The Secret Life of Walter Mitty" to Nunnally Johnson, Frank Capra, and even Richard Rodgers, in all of which he called himself "a fan of that story." One letter says, "I ran into Jack Benny the other night in front of the Stork Club and talked to him about the chances of his doing Walter Mitty. He had read the story, but he seemed a little vague about it all." I should have let Ross handle the movie sale, but it wasn't until I reread his letters that I became aware of all the effort he had put in on it with practically everybody he met who was associated with the movies or with Broadway musicals. I don't know where he found the time to do so much for so many people.

15

Dishonest Abe and the Grand Marshal

I was in Harold Ross's office one hot day in the middle of August, 1928, when the phone rang, and he turned to it impatiently and said, sourly, to the transmitter, "Yeah? Hi, Aleck. Just a second." He cupped the transmitter with his hand and said, "It's Woollcott. He wants to tell me about the wedding of Charlie MacArthur and Helen Hayes . . . O.K., Aleck, go ahead."

   Alexander Woollcott, American phenomenon, once called by Stanley Walker "the first citizen of New York," began talking in the fluent, practiced, almost compulsive way he had of telling a story. Ross promptly put the receiver down, gently, on the top of his desk, got up, walked across the room, and began alternately staring out the window and scowling at the jabbering receiver. An unintelligible babble came out of it, a little like the sound track of a Donald Duck animated cartoon. Against this dim and distant monologue, wasted on the office air, Ross set up a counterpoint of disdainful comment. "Listen to that glib son-of-a-bitch," he said. "He thinks he's holding me spellbound. He thinks he knows more about everything that happens than anybody else. He only knows a few things, and he tells them over and over, and sells them over and over to magazines." I was embarrassed by this charade, but couldn't do anything. Finally the gibbering came to an end and Ross leaped to the phone and said into it, "I'm sorry, Aleck. I suddenly had to go to the can." Woollcott hung up sharply, like a slap, without a further word.

I had seen Woollcott at the Algonquin Round Table and at the theater, but didn't meet him until late in August, 1927, when I was working on a Talk piece about the coming theatrical season. It was shaping up into one of the biggest seasons on record, with some three hundred and fifty different comedies, dramas, and musicals slated to be brought to Broadway. "You better go up and talk to Woollcott about it," Ross told me. "He doesn't know much, but he ought to know about what's coming in. There's a damn good piece in it, from what I hear."

I had already drafted a five-hundred-word piece, based on what I had got from producers, playwrights, and press agents, but Ross was afraid it might not be sound. I telephoned Woollcott and asked him if I could come to see him. "I won't read your copy," he snapped, "but I'll talk to you."

He met me at his apartment door that afternoon the way he met everybody, man or woman, clad in pajama bottoms

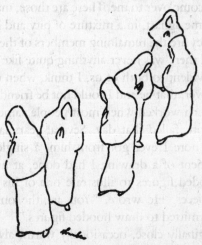

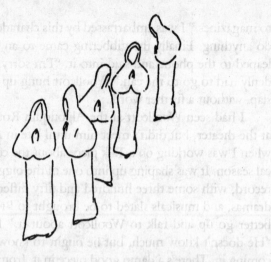

which were only partly covered by a dressing gown that he wore carelessly and whimsically. He began the audience with a long running attack on Harold Ross, a man who knew nothing, was mentally curious, like a child, without intellectual curiosity, however, and had a contempt for anything he didn't understand, which was practically everything. The legendary charm of Alexander Woollcott, the still talked-about spell he cast, did not come over to me. There are those, mainly women, who stare at me aghast, in a mixture of pity and horror, when I say this. They are the remaining members of the great Woollcott cult, and there was never anything quite like it.

It was evident to both of us, I think, when the two-hour session was over, that he and I could not be friends. Something chemical, which worked when most people came into contact with Woollcott, failed that day. Several years later he wrote me the only note I ever got from him, a single sentence in acknowledgment of a drawing I had done, at his request, of a line of hooded figures to illustrate one of his "Shouts and Murmurs" pieces. He wrote, "You are the only artist that should be permitted to draw hooded figures."

The originally close, occasionally warm, always ambivalent, and often sadistic friendship of Ross and Woollcott had begun years before I met either one of them. As a reporter on the New York *Times,* and later its dramatic critic, Woollcott had known and worked with Jane Grant, Ross's first wife, and it was Woollcott who introduced them to each other in Paris. As in the case of virtually every other woman in his life, Woollcott had been half in love with her himself and, as always, both approved and disapproved of the marriage. It was in Paris, during the *Stars and Stripes* era, that Ross played his first pranks on Woollcott. The one he talked about most gleefully was the time he saw General Pershing approaching and deliberately failed to remind Sergeant Aleck that he was wearing a stocking cap instead of his regulation uniform cap. A group of the Stars and Stripers had been clowning around outside the newspaper building, taking turns putting on the stocking cap. Pershing, according to Ross, reprimanded Woollcott for his unsoldierly appearance.

I suppose that the strangest edifice in Ross's life was the cooperative house, far over on West 47th Street, that he and Jane Grant shared with Woollcott and their great friend R. Hawley Truax from well before the *New Yorker* started until 1928, when the ménage broke up. How it lasted so long, and why it began in the first place, I leave to older friends and better psychologists than I am. The Rosses and Truax and Woollcott had separate living quarters and a communal dining room. Woollcott held forth at dinner almost every night, telling the stories that enchanted many visitors. He knew and was revered or feared, liked or avoided, by almost everybody of any consequence on Broadway and in the realms of gold round about. I was there for dinner once, in 1927, but time has drawn a veil over that evening, leaving me only a sense of having been self-conscious, nervous, and apprehensive all the way.

Russel Crouse remembers how Ross, after dinner, used to drag a cushion off a "sofa," as he called all couches and davenports, put it on the floor, lie down, and go to sleep, while

Woollcott talked and Rome burned. Ross resented his friend's easy command of narrative and his ability to hold most of his listeners. Ross was by no means the skillful talker, the wit, the master of repartee, that Woollcott and many another of their friends were. Ben Hecht has written that Ross was not capable of a bon mot, and it is clear that the *New Yorker* editor picked up a lot of hints and helps in the art of verbal give-and-take from such of his intimates and acquaintances as George Kaufman, Dorothy Parker, Marc Connelly, Charles MacArthur, Bob Benchley, and Herman Mankiewicz. Ross was better at parry than at thrust, and that is why he learned to use, so often, his familiar "You have me there" and "A likely story" and "*That* I'd have to see." Some of his Round Table cronies instigated and implemented the gags and waggeries and practical jokes that Ross loved to play on people. He never became easy or expert at the art of ribbing, but went about it with some of the dogged determination he brought to the task of fixing up manuscripts and proofs in the office. Perhaps he had learned, partly from Woollcott, the knack of writing single sentences of praise, or of persiflage, but it seems to me he gave his lines a bounce and sincerity of which the style-conscious and Thespian Aleck was not capable.

When the 47th Street house was given up by its occupants, partly because Ross and Jane Grant could never count on a night's sleep uninterrupted by the late entrance into their room of Woollcott, brimming over with tales and anecdotes of his evening, the battle lines were even more sharply drawn. Woollcott claimed that, in dividing up their separate personal properties, Ross had "stolen" a set of silverware that was a Woollcott family heirloom. It was then, I think, that he called Ross a "dishonest Abraham Lincoln." I asked Ross about this one day, but he went instantly into a high diatribe against his old friend. "He has the emotions of a fish. He'll do anything for two hundred dollars—I get tired of seeing his face in testimonial ads. Goddam it, the magazine once printed a photo of him lounging in the back seat of some make of automobile. I didn't catch it in time. Nobody ever tells me anything. Have you ever been to one of his *famous* Sunday morning breakfasts?"

I said I'd never been asked to Wit's End, as Dorothy Parker had named Woollcott's best-known apartment in New York. "You're lucky," Ross said. "He sits there like a fat duchess holding out her dirty rings to be kissed."

Through the years, relentlessly, Ross badgered Woollcott, laid traps for him, built up involved practical jokes to bedevil him. It is not easy, at my distance from it all, to figure why Woollcott was the perennial victim of so many gags and booby traps, invented by Ross, MacArthur, Connelly, and others, but I do have a theory. He was not so much a mere participant in his own daily life as he was the Grand Marshal of a perpetual pageant, pompous in demeanor, riding a high horse, wearing the medals of his own peculiar punctilio and perfectionism. His men friends loved to put banana peels in his portentous path to bring him down, high horse and all, while his women friends, whom he could slay in the subject of a sentence and eulogize in the predicate, loved to catch him before he could fall, or to pick up his outraged bulk. Gibbs thinks they tolerated his insults because he also called them, or most of them, geniuses.

In many of Ross's shenanigans he had a willing accomplice. Margaret Case Harriman, in her book *The Vicious Circle*, relates one of these cooperative pranks perfectly, and I reprint her version here with her permission. As often happened, Ross this time had the invaluable help of Marc Connelly.

"Some people, including Marc, think that the Ross-Woollcott feud which everlastingly waxed and waned between these two true friends stemmed, partly at least, from Ross's happy indifference to time in those days as contrasted with Aleck's almost violent punctuality. One broken appointment between them was clearly Ross's fault, and it led to a lively evening.

"Aleck had invited Ross to dinner at his apartment—this was after the 47th Street household broke up—and to a first night afterward. Woollcott had long made it plain to his friends that an invitation from him was a command, and most of them indulged this whim—partly because they preferred to obey his slightest wish whenever convenient rather than suffer the abuse that would follow if they didn't.

"Early in the evening Ross ran into Marc Connelly, who also asked him to dine, at the Algonquin.

" 'Can't do it,' said Ross. 'I'm having dinner with Aleck and he's taking me to an opening.'

"Marc can look horrified better than anybody else in the world, and he did it then. '*Tonight's* opening?' he exclaimed. 'But that's the worst play in history! Nothing like it has ever been seen for sheer *nothing*! Haven't you read the out-of-town notices? Look here, Ross, Aleck can't *do* that to you!'

"Ross stood still in his tracks. 'Why, that goddam son-of-a-bitch,' he said sincerely, 'this is the *second* time he's taken me to a lousy play. Lead on, Connelly.'

"Ross and Connelly were dining pleasantly when Woollcott, lacking his guest, bounced into the Algonquin in search of somebody to take to the play. 'He was wearing his opera cape and he looked just like a Sandeman Port ad, blown up for posters,' Marc remembers. After a tour of the lobby, Aleck glanced into the dining room and, naturally, the first thing his eye lit on was his expected guest, Ross, comfortably having dinner with Marc. Aleck marched up to the table and delivered himself of a six-word diatribe that Ross still cherishes.

" 'You,' he said to Ross, 'are *a fourth-rate person*.'

"After Aleck had bustled out, cape flowing and sparks flying, Ross worried a little. He *had* been rude in standing up his host, and the Round Tablers were never rude to

each other, except conversationally. They weren't even
rude to Woollcott, unless in self-defense. Ross was
unhappy about the whole thing until Marc solved it by
sending for a telegraph blank and wiring the following
message to Woollcott:

" 'DEAR ALECK,

I find myself in a bit of a jam. If anybody asks you
where I was tonight would you mind saying I was with
you?

Yours

ROSS' "

One of the better-known anti-Woollcott gags revolved
about a full-length portrait of him that had been done by Cyrus
Leroy Baldridge, the *Stars and Stripes* artist. The picture hung
on a wall in the 47th Street house. Ross told the tale many
times, building it up and ornamenting it as the seasons rolled.
He said that when Woollcott left town one time on a lecture
tour or something, he had Baldridge do an exact replica of the
portrait, with one slight difference: instead of looking straight
ahead, as in the original, Woollcott's gaze was turned slightly
in one direction. "When Aleck got back to the house," Ross
used to say, "I had a bunch of people over and seated them so
they couldn't help seeing the picture. I kept staring at it, and
finally Woollcott and the others did, too. 'That goddam picture's moving,' I said. Woollcott didn't say anything, but he
knew something was wrong with the thing. I hoped he would
think he was going nuts. It got to him, all right." When Woollcott left the house the next day, the fake portrait was withdrawn and the original looked out again directly upon the
room. The tale tells that Woollcott was never let in on the joke,
died without knowing about it. Cy Baldridge, in a letter to me,
dismisses the prank as having been overelaborated by Ross: "I
merely made a quick tracing out of focus (rather *à la* El Greco)
and substituted it in the frame. That's all. Never knew what
Aleck may have said when he probably discovered it later."

Every time Ross played one of his tricks on Woollcott he told me and everybody else about it. The year the dramatic critic won the *Variety* award of a silver-headed cane for having been the reviewer that had most accurately forecast the season's hits and flops, he brought it to a party attended by Ross and many others. The ornery conspirator from the Far West, with what confederates I do not know, swiped it and then joined in the search for it when the party was breaking up.

"I helped look for it, in closets and under sofas," Ross said, "and it wasn't easy bending over because I had the god-dam thing stuck down one pants leg." The next day—I think with the help of Charlie MacArthur, who described himself about that time as "a middle-aged pixie"—Ross found out from a mutual friend that a certain gentleman he didn't know was about to sail for Europe. This fellow was persuaded to send Woollcott, from the middle of the ocean, a radiogram to this effect: "I seen to have picked up by accident a silver-headed cane belonging to you. I shall be in Egypt for three years. What do you want me to do with it?" When Woollcott read that, he sensed in it the not too fine American hand of his great pal. "He threatened to call the police and have me arrested," Ross said, "if I didn't get it back to him at once. He was always going to have me arrested." As I remember it, the cane was returned to Woollcott wrapped in such a fashion it took an hour to get it loose.

When Ross let Woollcott begin writing his weekly page for the *New Yorker* called "Shouts and Murmurs," in 1929, all of us were sure hell would break loose constantly between the two men, and it did. It helped to wear their thinning friendship even thinner, for Ross complained about almost everything Woollcott wrote, and rejected all or parts of some of the columns. He brought one of them to me once and asked me if two of the jokes in it were familiar to me. They were, and I said so.

Ross killed both stories and Woollcott resigned, but we

all got used to that. He resigned the way other men went home to dinner. Some of the resignations lasted longer than others, and in a few the rancor ran deep. He even tried to get Ross's job once, sending for Katharine White, telling her it was urgent. He met her at the door clad as usual in pajama bottoms and dressing gown, and every now and then during his monologue that day his great bare belly would coyly appear and disappear, like a romping sea lion. "What would you think of me as editor of the *New Yorker*?" he threw at her to begin with. She indicated, just as quickly, that she wouldn't entertain the idea for a minute. Katharine does not think that Ross found out about this, but it may well have been the occasion that caused him to wire Raoul Fleischmann, "If you hire Woollcott, this telegram is my resignation. Ross."

Ross barged into my office one day, spluttering and swearing, to show me a story by Woollcott that had just appeared in the *New Yorker* and in *McCall's*. The writing was not identical, but the substance of both stories was the same. It served as the text for a long lecture on the sins of Woollcott-ism, which ended something like this: "Aleck only knows about nine words and phrases, and he uses them all the time. He writes about putting on his tippet, and going buckety buckety to the theater, and riding in his rickshaw, and he uses 'These old eyes' and 'At long last' in every third sentence." I had first heard this ancient denunciation early in 1927, but Ross went right on buying Woollcott profiles, some of them only a few pages long, on Harpo Marx, Charles MacArthur, the Lunts, George Kaufman, Marc Connelly, and three different *Times* men.

Ross the Wag rarely combined his waggeries and his work, but there was the classic episode involving Woollcott and the so-called Great Chalice of Antioch. This precious first-century object, dug up in 1910, was put on exhibition at the Brooklyn Museum, as one stop in a nationwide tour that had begun with its display in 1933 at the Chicago World's Fair. It was the kind of thing calculated to bring out Woollcott's fluent phrases in full flower, and he gave it the works in a "Shouts and Murmurs" department. The piece ended this way:

"I know not what others feel about it, but for my own part I believe that after seeing Mr. Ripley's exhibit of freaks in the Midway and watching the plausible antics of a life-size, synthetic dinosaur on view in a papier-mâché, prehistoric jungle, after drinking a beer at Pabst's and escaping from the touts who advise an inspection of the nude models in the Streets of Paris, I came along at sundown in my rickshaw to this white building, and, with my own eyes, beheld the Holy Grail."

That instantly gave Ross the inspiration for another elaborate joke. He arranged to have a man MacArthur knew in Chicago send Woollcott a telegram the Wednesday the *New Yorker* reached the stands with the chalice article in it. The wire went something like this: "If you plan to write anything about the Antioch Chalice you'll be interested to know that it is a hoax stop it was made by a man named Frank L. Schwartz in St. Louis in 1908." Woollcott got Ross on the phone at once and told him to withhold the "Shouts and Murmurs" piece and substitute something else. "Geezus, Aleck, the magazine's practically on the stands. I can't do anything about it," Ross told him, in mock concern, and then, "Goddam it, don't you know a phony when you see one?" This episode was finally forgotten, but not until Woollcott had been made to suffer for a day or two. The next year, 1934, Ross was married again, and things ran smoothly for a while between him and Woollcott.

The baptism of Harold Ross's daughter, Patricia, so named because she was born on St. Patrick's Day (in the year of our Lord 1935), had little of the anguish attending the memorable baptism of Clarence Day's father, but a lot more complications, and a sudden theatrical gesture supplied by that old critic of the drama, Alexander Woollcott himself. Ross's wife had told her husband she wanted the baby to be baptized in the Catholic faith.

"The trouble was," Ross's great friend Frank Sullivan has written me, "Frances did not know how to go about arranging the baptism, and of course Ross didn't. It was arranged from a rather unexpected source. One night, at the Rosses' Madison Avenue apartment, the matter came under discussion when Dr. Eddie Devol and his pal, Bishop Samuel Trexler of the Lutheran Church, were present. Sam said, 'Why, I can arrange it for you, Frances. I know some of the priests at the Cathedral.' And he did, and that was how Patricia came to be baptized in the cathedral of her name saint, through the good offices of a Lutheran bishop. That, however, did not end the complications. It seemed that Woollcott had been invited to be godfather, probably by Ross, but the fathers at the Cathedral told Frances and Ross that a Catholic baptism necessitated a Catholic godmother and a Catholic godfather. Was Mr. Woollcott a Catholic? No. Then he was out, as far as being godfather was concerned.

"I never learned how Ross broke the news to Aleck, but it must have been a moving scene. Aleck wasn't used to being dismissed like that. Anyhow, I was selected as second choice because I was a Catholic. . . . Patricia was baptized one pleasant June afternoon, and among those who showed up was Aleck. If he couldn't be godfather he was at least going to look on. Father Furlong, now Bishop Furlong, was to officiate, and when he arrived at the font and saw Aleck he came over to me, drew me aside, and said, 'Look here, you are to be the godfather, is that understood?' I said 'Yes, Father,' and the ceremony began. At one point a two-branched candle was used, shaped like a Y. Father Furlong asked the godmother and me each to place a hand on a branch of the candle while he said some prayers. As I reached to do so, a hand followed by an arm slid past me from the rear and the hand joined my hand on the candle. Need I say that the hand was Aleck's? I glanced at Father Furlong, but he said nothing and went on with the prayers. I may be mistaken, but I thought there were signs of suppressed mirth on his face. Anyhow, Aleck got in on the baptism in spite of the Church, and I don't suppose Patricia was any the less effectively baptized because of his alien touch."

Ross had paced and paced, and thought and thought about it, before he agreed to let Woollcott contribute a weekly page of any kind to the *New Yorker*. Their quarrels were instantaneous and interminable. They bickered about the location of the page, which Woollcott hoped would run before "Talk of the Town," but Ross was dead set against that. "He loves to show off at the theater, and the Algonquin, and his apartment, and everywhere else," Ross said, "but he's not going to show off around here." Their next battle was over Rea Irvin's decoration to go with the title. Rea had to do dozens before he got one both men agreed on—the comic mask on one side, the tragic on the other. It was easy to get drawings in those days, but prose did not exactly flow in, and the Woollcott page made a good backlog when copy ran short.

Upon Katharine White and later Wolcott Gibbs fell the heavy burden of "handling Woollcott." Katharine managed to coax him into making changes, over the telephone most of the time, but once in a while he asked her to call at his apartment and discuss some problem of grammar, taste, Ross, or make-up. I saw him in the office only once in my life. The two inimical friends communicated by note, and the exchanges were usually sharp or bitter. Woollcott liked to stab Ross, in prose or speech, with a stiletto, and could not forgive him for using a ball bat or a bung starter, as in a saloon brawl. Sometimes Woollcott picked up and threw whatever was handiest, never realizing that Ross enjoyed nothing better.

If Woollcott had the emotions of a fish, Ross had the hide of a hippo. I remember the day, at the office elevators, when he read aloud to several of us a letter from old Vitriol and Violets that ended, "I think of you as dead. Hoping I shall soon be the same . . . ."

Ross got a kick out of provoking stinging letters from his

old AEF buddy and, in the case of one real blisterer, had twenty copies of it made and sent them to various friends of his and Woollcott's. "I wanted the goddam thing to pop up everywhere he went," Ross explained to me. The editor of the *New Yorker* knew nothing about such celebrated literary feuds as those between Henry James and H. G. Wells, Dickens and Thackeray, Stevenson and Henley, and it didn't seem to occur to him that Woollcott did not at all mind having his written philippics perpetuated, that he must even have hoped some of them might attain the stature of deathless literary epistles. All of the letters, and even the shortest notes, bore signs of the sweat of rewrite. Labored expressions like "Your urchin defense mechanism" were lost on Ross, but they are preserved here and there in books in the libraries of friends.

The thing that widened the breach between the two men beyond closing was the three-part profile Gibbs wrote on Woollcott in 1939. The fuss raised about it after the third part had appeared became one of the most memorable crises in the history of Ross's weekly. I'll let Gibbs himself say something about that strange interlude.

"Woollcott did O.K. the galleys, with only minor protests. Actually, he didn't seem to realize that there was anything particularly unkind about the pieces until Beatrice Kaufman, Edna Ferber, Neysa McMein, and a bunch of those girls started needling him. I mention these because they were the only ones who reproached me personally.

"I think what Woollcott's friends really resented was that I implied he was a bonehead whose conception of genius could hardly be taken seriously.

"When I first started on the Profile, Woollcott wanted me to come up to Lake Bomoseen and spend a month with him, getting the flavor of his personality, I guess. It was March, but he had a great big fireplace. It was very hard for him to imagine anybody turning down a chance like that.

"Ross was very odd about the Profile. He supplied most of the really damaging stories—like the one about Woollcott's dearest friend who turned out to be a forger—and then seemed terribly alarmed when he saw them on paper. He took the buck for them, though.

" 'Shouts and Murmurs' was about the strangest copy I ever edited. You could take every other sentence out without changing the sense a particle. Whole department, in fact, often had no more substance than a Talk anecdote. I guess he was one of the most dreadful writers who ever existed."

The loyalty of Woollcott's friends and the loyalty of Ross's friends were among the strongest anybody ever heard of. ("I hope they deserved it, few mortals do," said a man who remained neutral throughout the final years of the war between Ross and Woollcott.) I was, to be sure, a Ross man, but I have never been able to get wrought up by attacks on him. When Woollcott sliced up Ross for a full half hour the time I called on him, I did not jump to my feet, or double my fists, or do anything but listen. I guess I always saw H. W. Ross, and still do, as something one has the right to criticize, like a show, or a pageant, or a monument, or a movement. I openly disagreed with Woollcott several times on points of fact, but let his opinions ride. He loved to make everybody mad, and used insults the way other people use simple declarative sentences.

It is reported, in the Samuel Hopkins Adams biography of Woollcott, that Alfred Lunt and Lynn Fontanne would not read the *New Yorker* again after the profile, and I experienced myself the chill that fell upon the once fairly warm friendship between Ross and Noel Coward. In 1936 Ross and I had given a party for Coward at Ross's apartment, and many of his friends were there. Later I saw Coward several times, on a friendly basis, but then there came a post-profile night at the theater when he turned a nervous and self-conscious fixed grin upon the two of us, but said nothing.

From Bill Levick, who called Woollcott "Foolish," to John Mosher, who said, "You must admit the old horror is competent," the put-upon Aleck was beset on all sides at the *New Yorker*. Some of us, though, were simply outside the battle and the cat-scratching. The point at issue was not, at bottom, Woollcott's ability as a writer, but his importance as a friend, companion, and counselor. Woollcott himself used to brag that he was the best writer in America, but had nothing to say.

It was about 1940 that Alexander Woollcott, sensing that his years left on earth were not many, retreated to his famous island place at Lake Bomoseen, "to set his house in order." He decided to make up with his old friend Harold Ross, but began feeling better and told other friends he was certainly not going to make up with Ross if he was not going to die. When his end was again clearly in view, he told several of his intimates that he was no longer able to deceive himself about the nature of his relationship to the editor of the *New Yorker*. "If I made up with him now," he said, "it would be a hypocritical and insincere gesture." He never changed his mind about that.

I was listening to a radio discussion panel one night in January, 1943, and heard Woollcott, one of the participants, say something flat and sharp that took in Germany, Hitler, Chicago, and the Chicago *Tribune*. I was convinced that the old boy was going to give 'em hell from then on, but ten minutes went by and his voice was not heard again. It was to be heard no more over the air on this planet, except in transcriptions. He had suddenly held up for Rex Stout, Marcia Davenport, and others on the program to see, a piece of paper on which he had scribbled, "I am sick." He was helped quietly out of the room, showing up to the end the courage for which he was known to both friend and enemy. He died in the hospital at midnight, while extra operators at CBS were trying to handle the thousands of anxious calls that kept coming in to the studio.

In January, 1951, eight years almost to the day after the

death of Aleck Woollcott, I found Ross sitting dejectedly in his office and asked him if he was all right. He ran his big right hand slowly over his face, wiping away the invisible web of regrets and sorrows, in a gesture long familiar to me, and said, "All of my friends are dead." He didn't mean that literally, for he had many loyal friends left on earth, but I knew the ones he was thinking about. He was thinking about Bob Benchley, Heywood Broun, Ed MacNamara, Ring Lardner, and a dozen others, but the name uppermost in his mind and heart that day, although he didn't say so, was Alexander Woollcott.

"What is it ends with friends?" wrote William Ernest Henley, the original of Long John Silver, and the friendship he must have had in mind was his own with Robert Louis Stevenson. There is a curious memorial, by no means poetic, to the broken friendship of Harold Wallace Ross and Alexander Woollcott. Everybody who knew the two men well, or anything about the history of the *New Yorker,* seems to remember it, and it is continually bobbing up, not only in conversation, but in actual reproduction. It is a parody of the memorable *New Yorker* anniversary cover, but the face of the nineteenth-century dandy is the scowling face of Harold Ross, and the butterfly he is examining contemptuously through his monocle is the winged Aleck Woollcott. The parody cover was used on a privately printed burlesque of the *New Yorker* on the occasion of the first anniversary of the magazine. It is an odd and inalienable part of the American success story of H. W. Ross, the boy from Colorado with the urchin defense mechanism.

16

The Last Years

Every time I go back to the letters, and there are dozens of them, that Harold Ross wrote me during the last three years of his life, I realize, and marvel, that they formed only a small corner of the correspondence he kept up with scores of writers, urging them on, praising their work, cheering them up, ironing out snarls and misunderstandings, patiently explaining, vigorously denying, running the whole range of emotions, and all that time he was far from the peak of health. Only one or two of the letters even touch on his many visits to the Lahey Clinic in Boston for checkups and treatments. "My trouble is mainly acidity, I guess," he wrote in one note, "but the X-ray of the stomach ulcer scar shows it was a beauty." Then he would set about answering some complaint of mine, straightening something out for me.

Our exchange of letters in 1949 when, I now know, the onset of a hyperthyroid condition made me irritable and often unreasonable, shows that he was far less the snarler than I was. His letters are filled with commendation, even of my most minor pieces, and with solicitude, too. "I admonish you not to show up at the office for the next few days. Painters are at work in several offices and the halls look like a secondhand store.

You'd kill yourself." I had once bumped into a ladder in a corridor, and that had worried him almost as much as the chair placed at the top of a newly painted flight of stairs with a sign on it reading "Danger." Somebody had yelled at me as I was about to walk into it and break my neck.

Picking up at random a clump of his correspondence, in 1949 and 1950, I found this brief memo about the opening of the Nugent-Thurber play in London: "Jim: Hot review of 'Male Animal,' London pleased. R." Actually, the reviews could scarcely have been described as hot, nor was there really enough, in a brief casual I did at the time, to call forth this: "I got back from two weeks away, and the pleasantest thing I found was your piece, 'The Comparable Max,' which, I think, is very fine and funny. . . . It is unquestionably a very high-grade light piece." This kind of Rossian reassurance came frequently in his last two years, 1950 and 1951, the dark heyday of McCarthy, during which humor fell off at the *New Yorker* and throughout the nation, and Ross kept urging White and Perelman and Sullivan and Gibbs and me to write something funny. I kept hearing from him all the time I was in Bermuda in the spring of 1950, and he pulled out all the stops: "I'm proud of your production down there. I may see Truax about a medal for you."

That June he went out West "to fish and to show Colorado to my daughter." He had gone up to get her at her school in New England, and also to receive the honorary degree of Doctor of Humane Letters at Dartmouth. "I'm so sheepish I won't discuss that," he wrote, "beyond saying that it is not for letters and that the magazine has been called Red so much that it may be a good idea to get a bit of conservative recognition. Some guy told me that he was in Ohio and attended some gathering that numbered ten. There was an argument as to whether or not the *New Yorker* is got out by Communists and the split was five to five, for Christ's sake." When a columnist spread the report that the *New Yorker* was "Red from top to bottom," I wrote Ross that it wasn't even read from cover to cover, but we shared a serious concern and a deep anger about the reckless charges of subversion that then threatened to make a chaos of the republic.

One so-called patriotic publication, devoted to denigration and innuendo about many writers and artists, often followed an attack on some author by saying in parentheses, "Also writes for the *New Yorker*." This both saddened and infuriated Ross, editor of a magazine that had been attacked at least once by Moscow, an editor not only conservative in such politics as he embraced, but an anti-revolutionary in everything. There may have been a Communist or pro-Communist here and there who had occasional pieces printed in the *New Yorker*, but their writing was neither subversive nor political. To the end, Ross never let the general fear and hysteria get him down, although it did depress him and send him off on occasional streams of good old American profanity.

Late in May, 1950, after Lillian Ross's widely talked-about running interview with Ernest Hemingway had appeared in the *New Yorker*, I wrote Ross from Bermuda in praise of the piece as a refreshing new kind of profile form by a writer who showed evidence of being able to do anything from a Talk story to a three-act play. Ross replied that Lillian had got great acclaim for her piece and that at least a dozen letters of applause had come to him. "A funny thing," he added. "I just answered one letter that wasn't applause, from Milton Mac-Kaye, who is outraged and violent; says Hemingway was 'pilloried,' continues: 'Is this modern reporting? If everything is privileged, I quit.' He is writing under the assumption that the story was one of a drunken man, of a man on a bender, and hence an arrant invasion of privacy, which it would be if Hemingway had been drunk, which he wasn't. I saw him then. He's one of the best drinkers I know."

I was glad that, during much of Ross's last year, when he had his suite at the Algonquin, my wife and I were also there. We had lunch with him often, and I remember my last dinner alone with him. He said he hadn't yet read a certain casual of mine that had appeared the week before, but he added, as he always did, some exaggerated quotes about it from others. It was characteristic of Ross that he had ended his letter to me about the Hemingway profile this way: "By God, I'm glad to know you are starting in on some casuals again. . . . Perelman says he is starting up, too. That 'Cocktail Party' story of yours was a big sensation and, so far as the magazine was concerned, lasted until L. Ross's Hemingway piece came along. Since then they've been talking about *it*."

I set this all down, not only to preserve in type some cherished signs of that warming touch of his, but to show his deep concern about the decline of humor in his magazine. He knew that the writers of the time, under the gloomy threat of world annihilation, were departing from Euphoria to live in Jeopardy, and it was a continuous and major worry. His old dread, that the once carefree *New Yorker*, going nowhere blithely, like a wandering minstrel, was likely to become rigidly "grim," afflicted his waking hours and his dreams. He tried, by cajolery, and even fulsome praise, to whip his dwindling stable of aging humorists into action. As long ago as 1933 Ring Lardner had died, at forty-eight; then came the death of John Mosher, at fifty, and Bob Benchley, at fifty-six, and Helen Hokinson. The humorists were going fast, and Ross kept at those who were left with spur and laurel.

In his last three years he wrote five letters to John McNulty, one of his special favorites, and here are quotes from them. "That was a fine piece, John. I heard about it all around." "You have what it takes to write a story." "Your best story in behalf of the humanities was that one about the old horse player. . . ." "I enjoyed your last piece, the episode in your wife's girlhood. I enjoy all your pieces." "I've just read the Irish story, which I found highly interesting, entertaining, amusing, and touching."

For his old and intimate friend Frank Sullivan, who was

in a fallow period, he got out the spur. He had introduced Frank, about that time, to his pal Mayor O'Dwyer by saying, "This is Frank Sullivan, Mare. He sulks in his tent." He kept sending Sullivan ideas for pieces, some of which I had thought up, and he told him, "Get to those things, and give my love to your sister, Kate." Later he wrote him, "You have been a hell of a disappointment to me. You didn't even get up that football series. Maybe it isn't too late yet, for one or two, if you are so disposed. Oh hell."

I think it was in April, 1951, that a routine checkup Ross underwent following a low-grade temperature revealed the presence of a minimal bronchial malignancy. Regular periods of treatment at the Lahey Clinic reduced this primary lesion, but his fatal infection could not be contained, for metastasis set in. I was unable, happily, to see the growing parchment tone and tightness of his facial skin, but I detected his decline in vitality by the tone of his voice and his increasing difficulty in breathing. One day, during one of the many times we crossed the street together, from the office to the Algonquin or back, he said suddenly, "Oh, well, you can always write for the theater." It has taken me seven years to figure out what he meant by that. The other day I turned up a letter I wrote him in 1948 saying that I intended to write a play about him and the *New Yorker*, in which he would appear as the central character, one Walter Bruce. His reply was self-conscious and evasive, but he said he would mull it over and tell me what he thought about it later. And now I know he did tell me about it later in that one sentence, "Oh, well, you can always write for the theater."

On another day, halfway across the street, he said, "I've given up smoking. I'm grown-up now," and there was profound dejection in his voice. It came out that one doctor, he didn't say who, had told him to go ahead and smoke now and then, and I think, and hope, he did. I told him that one of my doctors had said, "The way a doctor gives up smoking is to cut down on it." Ross had not had a drink of hard liquor for years, his bland ulcer diet bored him, and giving up cigarettes was almost too much. As in the case of most American males who live in tension at the corner of work and worry, smoking had been his great relaxation. He had only a few others, playing backgammon or cribbage or gin rummy with his cronies, and reading *True Detective* and similar magazines, and once in a while he had gone to a baseball game with Grantland Rice. He got nothing whatever out of music, or poetry, or the philosophers, and gay parties were a thing of the past. He went to one or two, at long intervals, but never lost himself in them.

In the office, in the final weeks, he was abstracted, to use Shawn's word for it, and couldn't do much work. For eight months, as November came along, the task of selection, editing manuscripts, and querying proofs had been shifted to the overburdened Shawn and his associates. But there is in my hands his final opinion sheet on a Talk visit piece, and it is pure Ross at his perfect best. A reporter I shall call Higgins had gone to some kind of garden exhibition indoors and had described, in his copy, a man-made waterfall there. This was just the kind of thing Ross loved to get his fangs into, and demonstrate his knowledge, or intuitive sense, of what the hell was wrong with the description of it. His physical strength was going fast, but his mental alertness could still stand on tiptoe. Here is H. W. Ross's final "Talk of the Town" outburst, dated November 8, practically an epitaph for that diminishing department he had once so greatly loved:

"1. Now, for Christ's sake, this cannot have been a pile of some rocks. For one thing, if the pile was high enough to make water fall, more than *some* rocks required—tons and tons. But a base of rocks wouldn't possibly make a waterfall possible. The water would all run down through the chinks in the rocks, internally. What the hell Higgins saw, I don't know, but it wasn't this. Real facts should go in.

It's some kind of structure faced with rocks, I should say, at guess.

"2. Please get the God damned book and check to see if the quote is correct. *I will do fixing on this story if not used A-issue.*"

"You can see him walking up and down, you can hear him talking," someone at the *New Yorker* said about those notes, written a month before he died and two days after his fifty-ninth birthday. My wife had bought him a handsome two-tone scarf, and after he got it he telephoned our suite from his and I answered. "Thanks for the muffler, old fellow, and thank Helen, too," he said. "Goddam it, I knew when Forster called up this morning from the office and told me it was my birthday I'd be hearing from *you*." On an earlier birthday, in a happier time, I had once sent him a dozen red roses at the office, and one of the girls had put them in a vase, and there they were on his desk, exchanging blushes with him when he got to work. "Don't send me red roses, Thurber," he had said later. "It's goddam embarrassing. Men don't send each other red roses, for God's sake." I told him I would get one of the girl secretaries to substitute a card for mine, reading, "In everlasting memory of those Riviera nights." He said, "Nuts," and grinned, and shambled away.

My mother, when she heard about the gift of roses, didn't think it was very funny. "You should give him a sweater or a scarf," she told me. "You see, he's Scorpio, and with his moon where it is, his weak spot will always be his chest." She told him that, too, and cautioned him to bundle up well when he went out in the winter weather. My mother and Harold Ross were fond of each other, and besides having me in common to worry about, they shared a deep interest in *True Detective,* and discussed it one day in his office—my mother was absorbed in a story about a warden's wife who was in love with a condemned man in the death block. Ross thought my mother was wonderful, and never lost interest in my stories about her and her pranks. Sometimes, in his mother hen phase, he reminded me of her. After I had scared him by coming down with a ruptured appendix in Virginia, that time, he wrote Helen a letter during my convalescence, objecting to my being brought back to New York too early, in a wheelchair, and said, "Wheeling him through town might have a permanent effect on him. Also he might get cold and wet."

On the day we gave him the scarf we met him in the Algonquin lobby later and he growled, "Well, I'm wearing it." I am sure he had put it on carelessly, the way that made every woman want to give his tie, or muffler, or jacket a couple of smart tugs and a tidy pat, and say, "There." He was pleased that we had remembered his birthday. I could translate that old growl of his.

We didn't see him much after that. He sat with me one evening in the Algonquin Bar while I had a drink, and he said he thought he might go up to Boston and have something drastic done about the goddam cancer. This was the first time he had used the word to me. "It's a long story," he said, "and it doesn't go well with drinks." He was, of course, not drinking or smoking, but it was the slowing down of his ability to work that dejected him most and made him decide finally on an operation. When he left for Boston, early in December, he slipped away without fuss or formal farewells.

The last old-timer on the *New Yorker* staff to see him on the nineteenth floor was Rogers Whitaker, who had been on the magazine when I got there in 1927, and has long been one of its stalwarts, a man who has ably handled make-up and proofs, and edited copy. "Ross rarely edited me," Clifton Fadiman told me. "For some reason he felt I was engaged in something mysterious that didn't respond to the normal editing process. Rogers Whitaker was my copy editor, and I have never known a better one." Fifteen years ago, when Ross had written a hasty letter to the governor of Connecticut, complaining about people from the Bronx trespassing on his property and littering it, Ralph Ingersoll's *PM* had attacked Ross, and there was a flurry about it in the press that died out after Stanley Walker wrote an editorial in defense of Ross in the *Herald Tribune*. During the flurry Ross had said to me, "I should have let Whitaker see the letter. He wouldn't have let me send it." Ross's farewell to Whitaker was typical. He met him at the elevator and said, "I'm going up to the clinic. I don't know what will happen up there. All of you will have to carry on for me. God bless you."

None of us will ever forget that characteristic good-by of Ross's. This is the way Andy White ended his, and the *New Yorker*'s, farewell to H. W. Ross in the issue of December 15, 1951: "When you took leave of Ross after a calm or stormy meeting, he always ended with the phrase that has become as much a part of the office as the paint on the walls. He would wave his limp hand, gesturing you away. 'All right,' he would say. 'God bless you.' Considering Ross's temperament and habits, this was a rather odd expression. He usually took God's name in vain if he took it at all. But when he sent you away with this benediction, which he uttered briskly and affectionately, and in which he and God seemed all scrambled together, it carried a warmth and sincerity that never failed to carry over. The words are so familiar to his helpers and friends here that they provide the only possible way to conclude this hasty notice and to take our leave. We cannot convey his manner. But with much love in our heart, we say, for everybody, 'All right, Ross, God bless you!' "

Ross told Sam Behrman that he wanted to spend one night at the Ritz in Boston before going into the hospital, but he hadn't made a reservation. He said there weren't any chairs in the Ritz lobby—he had once had to stand around and wait, the very kind of trivial annoyance that always kept popping up in his mind to override, momentarily, his major worries. Behrman promptly got Ed Wyner, owner of the Ritz, on the phone from Ross's room in the Algonquin, and introduced the two men that way. A special easy chair was put in the Ritz lobby just for Ross, and this small attention was the kind of thing that meant more to him than a scroll or an honorary degree. Mr. Wyner was a gracious and attentive host during Ross's last night at the Ritz, and the editor went into the hospital in a good mood. He had always been a pet patient at the Lahey Clinic, and he regarded many of the staff as friends. One of these was Dr. Sara M. Jordan, who had written, at Ross's urging and in collaboration with the *New Yorker*'s Sheila Hibben, a book called *Good Food for Bad Stomachs*, to which Ross had contributed a foreword. In any hospital he ever entered, Ross was always the star patient. Years before, when he had spent two weeks at a sanitarium, a woman in the ninth month of hysterical pregnancy had been the doctors' and nurses' pet until, as the legend has it, "A man showed up who thought he was editor of the *New Yorker*."

Ross got, and put in, a great many phone calls while he was in bed. Dave Chasen called him from Hollywood, but Ross told him not to fly East because "I won't really be out of the anesthetic for a couple of days." At his side, practically all the time, was his old friend and one of his chief lieutenants at the *New Yorker,* R. Hawley Truax. They talked, and played cribbage, and Ross gave him some brief final notes and instructions he had written in case anything happened. If anything should, one note said, "My friends at the *New Yorker* will take care of things." Another expressed the wish that his daughter, then only sixteen, should scatter his ashes over the mountains near Aspen, Colorado, when she became twenty-one, but he left it completely up to her. I have not pried into Patricia's feelings about that and, as the father of a daughter, I would have argued him out of the idea. I don't think it actually mattered; he was just making notes. I do not believe he had a premonition of death, I think he had a hope of restored vigor.

Those of us who know about it will always be glad that

Hawley Truax was on hand at the end. He had not only shared with the Rosses their cooperative house in West 47th Street for most of the twenties, but Hawley had been, and still is, the main balance wheel of the *New Yorker,* the only man as close to Ross as he was to Raoul Fleischmann, and the great keeper of peace, or at least truce, between the editorial and the business departments. Praise of him shines out in many letters I got from Ross. We were also glad that, by chance, Ross's close friend George S. Kaufman was in Boston that last week.

I have a letter from Kaufman about Ross, one of the most prized of the numerous documents I have been lucky enough to collect in support of my own pieces. It goes in part like this: "Ross, as I recall, was a complete misfit when I first encountered him. He was slightly drunk and shooting craps on a blanket in my apartment at 200 West 58th Street, along about 1919. I think Jane Grant brought him around. The blanket had been ripped off a bed for the purpose because Ross had used a blanket for crap shooting when he was in the Army. If I had any thoughts about him then, they were to the effect that he didn't belong in the Army or in civilian life either. I would have said he had a good chance of starving to death, and when he came along with the *New Yorker* idea, about '23 or '24, it didn't improve him. On type he was completely miscast as an editor—nobody, not Broun or Woollcott or any of us— thought it would get started. He carried a dummy of the magazine for two years, everywhere, and I'm afraid he was rather a bore with it.

"As the years passed I can only say that I got to love him, if the word may be used between men. Then, on the day he died, I was in Boston with a show, and at one o'clock in the afternoon he phoned me. 'I'm up here to end this thing, and it may end me, too. But that's better than going on this way. God bless you. I'm half under the anesthetic now.' I suppose I was the last of the old gang to talk to him. I could not reach Hawley until after the show at night, and Hawley said, 'He died at a quarter of six.' I had to have it repeated. I said, 'What happened at a quarter of six?'. . . . And that was that."

Helen and I learned about Ross's death on the operating table two hours after it happened, when Louis Forster, who now occupies one of the two rooms into which the editor's old office has been divided, called us at the Algonquin. Helen went into the bedroom to answer the phone, and I heard her say, "No, no," and knew what it was. The rest of that evening is dim for both of us. I remember telephoning Gibbs and White, and I think Helen and I went over to Tim Costello's for drinks, and to see people who knew Ross, but not to eat much dinner. Faye Emerson was there later, one of hundreds of persons who, by midnight, had heard the news and were shocked and grieved, and didn't want to be alone. There were tears all over town, and some of those who wept were men, and one of them was Sam Behrman, who had seen a great deal of Ross in his final days. The last meetings of the two friends had been good for Ross, partly because Behrman had dug up, too late for his series of profiles, some new and valuable anecdotes about Duveen. How to get these into the magazine gave Ross something to take his mind off himself. He figured they could be run in a "Department of Amplification" in the back of the book. He didn't like to lose anything good, and when the chance of time and circumstance frustrated him, it gave him something to goddam about, and pace up and down, and try to solve.

On the night of Thursday, December 6, Andy White began the sad task of writing the memorial to Ross that took up the Comment page the following week. Gibbs and I stood by, in case we might be able to help. The magazine, for all its crises, had never faced anything like this. Several of the top men of the staff had gathered at William Shawn's apartment after Hawley Truax telephoned from Boston to say, "It's all over." Shawn and the others began notifying the rest of "my friends at the New Yorker." The magazine, with Ross dead, was suddenly without an editor-in-chief. Ross had made it clear to some of us that he wanted Bill Shawn to succeed him, but the appointment of his successor was up to Raoul Fleischmann. The night, in 1948, when I had sat around with Ross and Mencken and Nathan, the editor kept talking so much about Shawn that Nathan said, "Who is Shawn? Who is Shawn?" I explained that Shawn was a quiet, retiring, tremendously efficient and hard-working man, who had begun as a Talk reporter and risen to the position of fact editor. His great desire is to be anonymous, a word he frequently uses, a word no one ever applied to Harold Ross. But when Ross died, so unexpectedly, Shawn, as fact editor, and Gus Lobrano, as fiction editor, were next in line.

Things were "taken care of" smoothly enough, but in the wrong direction, it seemed to some of us. The clergyman was a good and distinguished man, but he had not known Ross or a great deal about him. Ross's friends at the *New Yorker* could have meant twenty or a hundred, and there was no space, and no time, to bring them all together in a conference about funeral arrangements. For Ross's services the chapel was, of course, crowded, with as distinguished an array of celebrities of literature and the theater and the arts generally as has ever gathered there. A couple of years later I got a letter from a writer who said, "The last time we met was at Ross's funeral when we were captives of that man of God." The reverend gentleman had dealt as tenderly and well with Harold Wallace Ross as could have been expected under the circumstances, speaking of the everlasting mountains of Colorado, where Ross had been born, and mentioning a tear on the monocle of the dandy of the *New Yorker*'s anniversary cover, but he rolled the *r*'s of the name Harold Ross in a way that would have abashed the editor when he was alive. What should have been done, it has always seemed to me, either did not come up at the prefuneral conferences, or came up and was rejected. As in the case of the funeral of Robert Sherwood, a few years later, when that playwright's friend and colleague, Maxwell Anderson, supplemented the formal religious services with words written for the occasion, some friend of Ross's, associated with him through the years, and used to appearing on a rostrum, would have been a happy choice to say the few relevant sentences of eulogy that we all so greatly missed that day. The chapel was literally filled with such persons.

After the ceremony a number of people met at Sam Behrman's apartment to discuss an impulsive project that was, fortunately, abandoned. They included Gibbs, Robert Sherwood, Frank Sullivan, Marc Connelly, Lillian Ross, and others. Ross's daughter Patricia and her mother were also there. The project in hand was a plan to take a full page in the *New York Times* to denounce Walter Winchell for something he had printed in his Sunday *Mirror* column just before Ross died. In the column Winchell contended that Ross was not really sick, but malingering, hiding out in Boston from certain responsibilities. Almost everybody present at Behrman's place had a hand in preparing tentative copy for the ad. "Gibbs wrote the best copy, the least enraged and the most dignified," Behrman says, "The whole thing was squashed by Bob Sherwood, who said that a full-page ad in the *Times,* with all those signatures, would please Winchell no end!" Winchell had never forgiven Ross for the six-part profile that McKelway had written about the columnist in the *New Yorker* in 1940, and had continued through the years that followed to snipe at Ross in the *Mirror,* sometimes brutally. I never discussed the Winchell profile with Ross, but years after it appeared he ran into McKelway, who had been gone for a long time, and greeted him with "Hi, Mac. That stuff on Winchell was too long."

Shawn became editor of the *New Yorker,* as its founder had so devoutly hoped he would. People still speak of "Ross's *New Yorker,*" and his name is heard in conversations and seen on printed pages. At least half a hundred people in the past seven years have said, or written, to me, "I never knew Ross, but when he died I felt I had lost a dear friend." One man, a literary agent who gets around town, told me, "You could feel the sorrow all over the city the day after Ross died. I don't think I have ever experienced such a sense of communal grief about a man most people I met had never even seen." We were all asked, a hundred times, "What will happen to the *New Yorker* now that Ross is dead?" We had our separate answers to that, but Joe Liebling's is perhaps the one that will last: "The same thing that happened to analysis after Freud died."

Out of all my million memories of Ross, one keeps coming to mind more than any other. It was the day he came into my office, carrying a copy I had given him of a collection of my pieces and drawings, which I had dedicated to him. I hadn't told him about the dedication in advance, and he had come upon it unprepared: "To Harold Ross, with increasing admiration, wonder, and affection." In my office, with the book open at this flyleaf, he said, "Affection?" I imitated his mock growl. "Yes, affection," I said. "Do you want to make something out of it?" He stood there a moment, then began chortling, went to the door, turned, and said, with that old limp wave of his hand, "Thanks, old fellow. I appreciate it." Ross, I found out later, sent out dozens of copies of it to his special list of favorite people.

H. W. Ross had a world and wealth of warming and wonderful things to look back upon as he lay dying. He had been a great success, he had made hundreds of friends and thousands of admirers, he had contributed something that had not happened before in his country, or anywhere else, to literature, comedy, and journalism, and he was leaving behind him an imposing monument. He had got his frail weekly off the rocky shoals of 1925 and piloted it into safe harbor through Depression and Recession, World War II, and the even greater perils of the McCarthy era. His good ship stood up all the way. He sometimes threatened to quit, and he was at least twice threatened with being fired, but he kept on going like a bullet-torn battle flag, and nobody captured his colors and nobody silenced his drums.

A hundred editorials, after his death, acclaimed the genius of the Colorado urchin who had reached the High Place the hard way. The back files of the magazine in his years shine with triumphs that time cannot darken. Scores of admiring, and envious, editors attested to his brilliant command of a staff of wartime writers whose coverage of all theaters of the conflict forms one of the outstanding accomplishments of American journalism, good writing, and excellent editing. Many eulogies of him ended with the identical words: "He was a great editor." He made, as I have said, a lot of friends and lost a few; he made the right enemies and kept them all. Some of the things he touched were smudged, but most of them were stained with a special and lasting light, as hard to describe as the light in a painting.

On the morning of December 7, 1951, Hobart Weekes took some pictures of Ross's office. One of them clearly brings out, on the west wall, a photograph of William O'Dwyer, a list of the names of *New Yorker* artists, one framed sentence of an editorial in the Lynchburg, Virginia, *Advance,* and four of the drawings I made for Ross poking fun at the goings on of the art meetings. My drawings were given to Patricia Ross, who isn't sure where she put them, just as my own daughter isn't sure where she put the drawings I have given her. I hope that the quotation from the Lynchburg *Advance* still hangs on that wall, where it belongs, but I have been reluctant to ask, or to feel around for it, in the fear that it might have been lost. Of the thousands of appreciations of the *New Yorker* that have been written, this must have been the one of which H. W. Ross was proudest, and I shall end my long fond view of him, and his life, and his work by reprinting it here. "It is a supposedly 'funny' magazine doing one of the most intelligent, honest, public-spirited jobs, a service to civilization, that has ever been rendered by any one publication."